Sermons On The Second Readings

Series II

Cycle C

John T. Ball
Richard Gribble, CSC
John B. Jamison
Clayton A. Lord, Jr.
Donna Schaper

CSS Publishing Company, Inc., Lima, Ohio

Copyright © 2006 by
CSS Publishing Company, Inc.
Lima, Ohio

Some scripture quotations are from the New Revised Standard Version of the Bible, copyright 1989 by the Division of Christian Education of the National Council of the Churches of Christ in the USA. Used by permission.

Library of Congress Cataloging-in-Publication Data

Sermons on the second readings. Series II, Cycle C / John T. Ball ... [et. al.].
    p. cm.
  ISBN 0-7880-2398-5 (perfect bound : alk. paper)
  1. Bible. N.T.—Homiletical use. 2. Church year sermons. 3. Lectionary preaching. I. Ball, John T., 1933- II. Title.

BS2341.55.S472 2006
252'.6—dc22

                                                            2006001005

For more information about CSS Publishing Company resources, visit our website at www.csspub.com or e-mail us at custserv@csspub.com or call (800) 241-4056.

Cover design by Barbara Spencer
ISBN 0-7880-2398-5   PRINTED IN U.S.A.

Table Of Contents

Sermons For Sundays
In Advent, Christmas, And Epiphany
The Good News Of Christ
by John T. Ball

**Sermons For Sundays
After Pentecost (First Third)
God's Grammar
by John B. Jamison**

Sermons For Sundays
After Pentecost (Middle Third)
God Is Rock Solid
by Clayton A. Lord, Jr.

Sermons On The Second Readings

For Sundays In Advent, Christmas, And Epiphany

The Good News Of Christ

John T. Ball

Advent:
The Call To Holiness

Anytime we center on First Thessalonians in our devotional reading or in a study group or read a passage from it in worship or hear a sermon preached on it, we're dealing with the earliest of all the New Testament's witness. First Thessalonians, written by Paul in the early 50s C.E. to this congregation in Macedonia, of which he was the founder, pre-dates all the rest of the New Testament writings. It may be the reason that such a text has been chosen by our Common Lectionary for the first Sunday of Advent. The primacy of Thessalonians matches well with our worship today. Thessalonians stands alone at the beginning of the New Testament's take on the gospel; likewise we come together today at the beginning of a new worship year.

We know that Paul gathered his converts into congregations mostly in the urban centers of the Roman world — Philippi, Corinth, and Rome. Only his letter to the Galations was sent to several churches in that region, and if Ephesians and Colossians are also authentic letters of Paul, then these cities may be added to the places to which he sent his correspondence. It may be worth a passing thought that our faith originated in first-century urban settings, not in rural areas. In those cities, especially in the parts we would call slums, Christianity began its life and history. Today, when we are so tempted to run away from the violence and oppression of our cities, preferring the suburbs or countryside, we need to remember this. We do not show the courage and guts (just below love, said Francis Allshorn) that was the new faith's edge, attracting a multitude of have-nots, and a few of the haves. Most of our hymnals include Frank Mason North's hymn, about Christ calling us to join him in mission to the city which few of our modern congregations can sing without dropping a veil of disconnect over the plain meaning and challenge of its lyrics:

Where cross the crowded ways of life,
Where sound the cries of race and clan,
Above the noise of selfish strife,
We hear your voice, Son of Man.

We just don't like to think about our cities as a call from Christ as we zip into the office by car or train, and back out in the evening. Of course, our urban troubles are almost beyond opening to any serious solution. But we are far from our Christian forebears. Without denying the need for spiritual consolations for the many pains and tragedies of life — even those of us in insulated suburbia — it could be that we have too often been singing "softly and tenderly Jesus is calling." We like, and occasionally need, the Jesus who comes to us as a gentle shepherd, becoming the balm from Gilead. Yet we so easily forget that our Jesus faith also calls us out into danger, risk, controversy, and standing for causes and truths that may not have their fulfillment in our lifetime.

So what's today's compelling word in our passage from First Thessalonians? Well, such a choice is up to any who choose to preach from this selection. But here is one pastor's choice, almost hidden in the wonderful benediction, closing the third chapter: "And may he (the Lord) so strengthen your hearts in holiness that you may be blameless before our God and Father at the coming of our Lord Jesus with all his saints" (3:13). This sermon is aimed at that hope that we may become holy so that when Jesus comes — in whatever theological style we prefer — he will say, "I know you!"

Advent, taking our cue from this text, can be a call to holiness in all its wide and deep meanings. Now modern Christians are often a bit wary of any talk about personal holiness. This is in spite of the so-called holiness and the Pentecostal movements of the nineteenth and twentieth centuries. In various ways, these movements have taken seriously the issue of holiness. While many modern traditions were veering away from speaking in any fashion about

16

holiness, the Holiness and Pentecostal folks were preaching and teaching personal holiness as a fundamental ingredient of the Christian life. They have had the courage as well as the spiritual insight to sense that a concern for holiness is not some accessory that we may or may not prefer to deal with.

Of course, any call to seek the blessing of holiness comes with dangers and distortions. The downside of Christian holiness is the reason that it has been discarded or disregarded by much modern Christian teaching, preaching, and personal devotion. These unholy things that sometimes cling to our experience of what may be termed "spurious Christian holiness" are separation from the public world and its struggles, a sense of spiritual superiority, and the lack of an understanding that holiness is gifted, not the result of personal achievement. These distortions give any call to a life of Christian holiness a bad name.

Holiness that cuts us off from the sufferings in our world tells others that we do not believe that God is found in the world and in our pains to make it more godly. Holiness that creates an elite cadre of holy gents and gentesses should make us remember George Orwell's *Animal Farm*, where "all pigs are equal but some pigs are more equal than others." This doesn't sell well in the church anymore than it sells in politics. Finally, holiness misses the point when it forgets that holiness is more like humble thanksgiving than a cause for bragging.

Our sense of holiness today must be worldly, as Bishop John A. T. Robinson said in his little book, *Honest to God*. Modern holiness must be free of any spiritual prerogatives, and profoundly aware that it has little to do with our modern spirit of frantic striving after our self-generated goals. So what would valid holiness look like for today's Christians — progressive, evangelical, or fundamentalist? The late Albert Outler offers some comments on Christian holiness from his study of the writings of John Wesley. Outler says that Christian holiness is linked to the gifts of the Spirit enumerated in Paul's later letter to the churches in Ephesus.

But there is a crucial distinction between what extraordinary gifts holiness brings to some Christians — healing, tongues, prophecy, discernment of spirits and teaching; and the ordinary gifts of

17

holiness that may be given to all Christians — love, joy, peace, patience, kindness, goodness, fidelity, gentleness, and self-control. All this means is that those who think they have been given the extraordinary gifts of spiritual holiness are not exempt from the common gifts of spiritual holiness. Furthermore, they can be called before the church for not exhibiting these common holiness gifts, no matter how impressive their extraordinary gifts are.

So where is all this leading us — this Advent call to open ourselves to Christ's life of holiness? We have already suggested one way. First, there is a holiness that grasps our personal lives as well as the public life all around us. There's an old saying that says, "When a person becomes a Christian, his dog ought to be the better for it." Sometimes business executives or government officials are criticized for abusing their colleagues and underlings. Christians, in our homes, our work, in the church, and in the world, exhibit holiness when we display the common gifts of holiness. We must love those close to us in these relationships. We must relish life's joys, certainly having a sense of humor and the ability to laugh at ourselves. We must be patient and kind, we are to be good to a fault; we must keep vows and promises; we are to be gentle — no blustering about; and we must have self-control over our relationships, especially those troublesome ones. Part of holiness would be any and all of these.

Secondly, holiness is also our vital involvement in the public world from which we can never be separated. A pastor brought some realism to a family grieving over the death of their teenage child, by linking his fatal, contagious disease to the possibility that the child contracted the disease by hanging onto the straps in the New York City subway. On his way home to the city's suburbs, their son may have grabbed the strap that had been touched by a child from the slums where this disease was rampant. We may fault the pastor for his timing and insensitivity to the family's grief, but he was dead right that we cannot insulate ourselves from the terrible conditions under which so many in our world are condemned to live. And, the conditions that force them to live in such misery can spill over into the lives of those who think they are well insulated from their oppression, as it did with the son of this affluent family. Modern holiness also entails getting entangled in the problems and possibilities of public issues. Jesus will judge us severely for trying to escape through feel-good private religion; through being continually entertained by the media; in political affiliations that encourage selfishness at the expense of the poor and powerless; and in our pleading that we don't know what to do.

This final comment drives to the heart of the Christian experience in all things: we open ourselves to be grasped by the power of God enabling us to live an authentic holiness. So much of our contemporary Christianity falls into two distorted emphases. One is to see our faith only as giving us forgiveness and the peace of God beyond life's anxieties. Certainly, we are grateful for the grace of God that restores the presence of God in our lives, helping us to manage those personal threats of sin, fate, and death. Evangelical and Fundamentalist Christianity usually fall into this distortion. Here, faith in Christ is highly personal and few such Christians see the wider picture of the call to discipleship as imbedded in Jesus' announcement of God's earthly kingdom. Mel Gibson's movie, *The Passion Of The Christ*, is largely in this style. It gathers everything of the faith into that last week in Jesus' life, implying that the forgiveness and mercy of God are available only through the passion, suffering, and death of Jesus. But there is more to the faith than this, important as forgiveness, mercy, and the courage to live beyond our anxieties. Biblical holiness leaves us dissatisfied with this narrow sort of holiness.

A second type of holiness that demands our rejection is the worldly holiness that sets out single-handedly to refashion the world without realizing that our zeal can be corrupted by our sin and our frantic pace so that we take little time to listen to God. An old hymn of the church imploring us to "Take Time To Be Holy," demands a hearing for those of the mainstream and liberal congregations. However, this hymn has little to drive us to think about public issues and their need for change. Contrast for example, stanza 2 in another hymn, "Love Divine All Loves Excelling":

> *Take away our bent to sinning;*
> *Alpha and Omega be;*

19

End of faith as its beginning,
Set our hearts as liberty.

We who are inclined to practice our holiness, find that our hustle and intense activity can make us guilty of insensitivity and arrogance. We label any who object to our plans and conclusions about improving everything as uneducated Christians whose distress at our activity must not be taken seriously. We are not inclined to deal with them at any level as Christian brothers and sisters. Certainly in the challenge to long-standing moral convictions such as gay rights, we tend to shout rather than talk, dismiss rather than listen, and demonize rather than see them as under God and Christ just like ourselves.

Something called "Progressive Radio" attempts to make a voice for the progressives and liberals on the issues of the day. It brings some light and truth to the complicated reality of modern life. However, progressive radio also evidences much of the narrow and distorted broadcasting voiced by the Rush Limbaughs of the rightist radio. It, too, can defame its challengers, and lace its broadcasts with ridicule and outright lack of courtesy and decency. Progressives in the church, like the radical right can easily contribute to unnecessary social and political divisiveness, requiring lengthy periods of cooling down so that the important issues may be addressed. Holiness does mandate serious worldly action. Nothing denies this.

Holiness does call us to discern and nourish the kingdom of God in the world. Yet real biblical holiness means allowing God's Spirit to change us at the core of our being. We find ourselves invited to a point of radical trust in God's mercy, along with the gift of courage. This deeper holiness delivers us from arrogantly thinking that we are privy to the major and minor plans of God ordaining us to crusade against all that are not part of our entourage. Advent is a great time to remember how high and how deep our call is to biblical holiness. In some rather contemporary language, biblical holiness is not messing around with the type of holiness disconnected from the world, nor is it taking over from God the management of the world. It is a call to listen to God, be continually converted, and to bring light to God's world where there now is darkness.

Advent:
A Wider Context

The congregation at the Macedonian city of Philippi was the first church established by Paul in Europe. Like all our "firsts" it had a special place of affection. We remember fondly our first car, our first job, the first home and community in which we lived, and our first romance. We still can recall our first excitement with hearing the first song or rock band that gained our attention, and those first moments when Christ became both a frightening challenge, as well as an abiding consolation.

Sometimes we get a bit restless with those who are always reciting the time when Christ took saving control of their lives. We wish they would tell us about the progress they have made in the Christian life. But we cannot deny that, with some exceptions, there is something in us that holds many of our firsts in grateful memory. A best-selling autobiography, *Angela's Ashes*, tells of the grim life the author endured growing up in poverty-stricken Ireland. It is a testimony to our wishing to preserve with some gratitude of our first life experiences, even under such terrible circumstances.

A church organist, in the midst of the sexual revolution of the '60s and '70s, told a wedding soloist she would not accompany her in the popular song, "The First Time I Ever Saw Your Face." She objected to the line, "The first time I ever lay with you." This offended her and it was certainly not something to be remembered in the music sung before Lohengrin and the grand processional. Whatever ethical violations this song remembered with fondness, it touched a realistic part of all of us — our firsts are warmly remembered. The pastor overrode the organist's objections, thinking that our so-called "hot sins" may not be so central to the faith as uncaring, selfishness, hopelessness, and social injustice. At any rate, we have had too much focus on serious, adult consensual sex, with or without the approval of the church or state, and too little attention to these other sins.

The upshot is that the image of Christianity is fixed at the level of sexual behavior, for teens and young adults, allowing them to come to the conclusion that the faith's wisdom is not for them, because it is all about sex, the intense biological drive of their lives. It is certainly better for us to bind our sexual loyalties to the consent of our religious communities and of the public affirmation of the state. But any narrowness here can bring about other sins and sinful structures that Christ would condemn.

Paul tells the Philippian congregation that he is thankful for the monetary gifts and for their steadfastness in the gospel. They have been struggling with intra-congregational disruptions. Some in the Philippian church are cliquish and unwilling to fellowship with others in the congregation. Much of this behavior then and in present congregations is mild. But sometimes it is deadly. One contemporary church decided that an excessively tattooed youth did not fit into their definition of a Christian person. He left the church under their condemnation. A couple of years later, the youth pastor was asked by the police to come and identify him at the morgue — he had blown off his head with a shotgun. And we fuss about tattoos? Yet, even less forms of divisiveness poisons the spirit of the church. This is tied to the second concern of Paul at Philippi. Apparently some of the members of the church were professing they had become perfect in all spiritual matters. There are always two problems here: One is that personal perfection confessions create divisions in the church; and second, it is obvious to others that the self-acclaimed perfect Christian is not so perfect after all. Such a person is living out a lie.

> *It is right for me to think this way about all of you, because you hold me in your heart, for all of you share in God's grace with me, both in my imprisonment and in the defense and confirmation of the gospel.... And this*

is my prayer, that your love may overflow more and
more with knowledge and full insight....
— Philippians 1:7, 9

But something more is noticed in this lection and the whole of Philippians. Some commentators describe it as setting the difficulties "in a wider framework." Most of our life issues can be better managed and overcome when we acquire "a wider framework!"

Peter Storey is a retired Methodist bishop in South Africa, active during the struggles to overcome his country's segregation laws. For many years, he and Anglican bishop, Desmond Tutu, joined the forces of resistance to the Apartheid system of separating the whites from the blacks and the browns. After the 2004 American presidential election, he wrote an open letter to American Christians who were dismayed at the election's outcome. Acknowledging the sadness of many American Christians because the election seemed to endorse violence, war, the affluent, racism, narrow religious and political mindsets, and the enthronement of economic success at the expense of precious human and public values, Storey wrote:

> *In South Africa too, we were up against a "Christian"*
> *government, acting in the name of Christ, supported by*
> *significant numbers of members of our churches. It be-*
> *came crucial to expose the false gospels of national-*
> *ism, militarism, racism and security right within the*
> *church ... It means re-evangelizing the church in Jesus'*
> *way of enemy-love, inclusion, of not fearing Caesar, of*
> *standing for the most marginalized. It took a long time,*
> *but it helped bring transformation.*

Then Bishop Storey encourages us, who are both angry and depressed, to take a wider view and "get on with the tough business of witnessing!"

Bishop Storey's letter makes two points that would be welcomed by Paul. His advice is also applicable to both personal and social issues. One is the necessity of a continuous evangelism in

23

the church. Reinhold Niebuhr once said something like this: "It is not tragic that the church has to face a godless and secular world; it is tragic that we have a godless and secular church with which to face a godless and secular world."

This sermon will close with the wider view and our personal pains and sufferings. But it is certainly with a note or two to say that an undue dose of personal religion has afflicted our mainstream churches. We can go from church to church on Sunday morning and find very few notices of Christ confronting the many public issues, sermonic or otherwise. The frantic drive for membership growth, huge facilities with even higher mortgages attached, the pastor's concern to be popular and not unsettle his or her base of financial and numerical support — all push our churches toward a personal gospel, avoiding any public or social controversy. The image of "evangelism" in almost all our churches is exclusively joined to personal religion. Evangelism on a wider view is desperately needed in the church.

Storey's second suggestion is to remind ourselves that God doesn't work exclusively with Christians. A silly, but terribly sad tale hitting the networks, tells of a North Carolina pastor who expelled from his congregation, members who did not support President Bush, and who would not come to his office, confess their political sins, and ask for reinstatement. The pastor is certainly a fool, but not for obvious reasons. Grant his conviction that President Bush was doing God's will. His foolishness, however, is believing that God has no chance for doing godly things other than through Bush Republicans; no non-Bush Republicans nor any Democrats could be counted on to be on God's side.

There are several biblical witnesses that God has the power to get things done through non-Israelites. The Persian king, Cyrus, is called Messiah since he fulfilled God's promise to free the people from captivity. Jesus once told his narrow-minded disciples that anyone doing the good works he was doing was God's disciple, even though he didn't belong to Jesus' entourage. And that wonderful Pope John XXIII directed his cyclical on world peace, *Pacem et Terris*, "to all persons of goodwill." If the human race is going to make it through we must sense that God is working far beyond our own religious tradition. Muslims, Buddhists, Hindus, secularists, and humanists are our allies despite the differences in our traditions, or even the lack of any religious tradition.

And, in the great numerical gains of Islam in our day, we must not throw up a wall of resistance insisting that our tradition is the "God-approved" faith compared to all the rest. There is plenty of work to do for all our religious traditions, and if our own is judged to have a better sense of God and life than all the others, it will be known only by its results in our lives, not by our wordy arguments and scriptural concoctions. God's work and reality are not so limited as we Christians are often encouraged to believe. Here is a wider view clamoring to be heard.

Finally, a wider view with our personal sorrows, given limitations and loads of guilt and spiritual depression — our Advent season can help steady us. Advent is a season of hope, and human creatures must always be open to the hope that God wills us to have, in this life and the next. Trust in God does not exempt us from sorrow, nor will it heal our minds and bodies beyond what medical science can do. Trust in God does not blot out our guilt so that we never recall its reality, nor treat it trivially. Trust in God does not break up our depression over our own life situation, or our distress at the state of affairs in the world.

But, trust in God does call us to believe that we can be given the power to manage our grief, our ailments, our guilt, and our low spirits. This is the image of Jesus in our New Testament. He knew all these troublesome moments, perhaps even guilt as when he was a bit short with his mother and family, when he read out his adversaries, or when he allowed despair to momentarily overcome him on the cross. Yet he trusted that God could empower him to handle all these troubles and put them into the wider context of what God was doing with humanity, with history, with nature, and with the entire cosmos.

John Haught, a Roman Catholic lay theologian, often speaks of God and our "unfinished universe." He argues that God is not done with things as they are — neither the world, nor human individuals. God cannot perfect either instantaneously, but God is luring all things and all people toward an earthly and heavenly perfection. This wider view enables us not only to endure suffering and disappointments; it enables us to fit them into God's never ending "love divine, all loves excelling," as that great hymn puts it. Or as Paul says in the wider view, "All things work together for those who love God" (Romans 8:28).

Advent:
An Irrational Sense Of Peace

We are always touched by newspaper or media stories of people who have come through some terrible experience and yet seem unhinged by it all. Some people find their health slipping away, yet exhibit courage and trust in both the provisional and ultimate goodness of life. Others witness the death of a child, or spouse, or partner, and do not give in to the despair that invites them into its darkness. We hear of people who live through one of nature's raging storms, inflicting great damage to their homes and surrounding areas, but after a brief period of grief, set about to rebuild their homes and neighborhoods. Many discover the betrayal of friends or loved ones, their character and reputation sullied, yet, like many of the psalmists, remain faithful and composed.

Our scripture this morning gives witness to this God-given human capacity. Paul tells the Philippian congregation, "Do not worry about anything" (4:6a). We know that Paul's life as a witness to the gospel in Jesus Christ gave him a lot to worry about. He was badgered constantly by those who wanted to keep the new faith a matter of rules. Then he had to deal with those who preached that detachment from the world was the way to go. He was physically beaten and stoned, and in one of his writings he spoke of experiencing hunger and thirst. Perhaps Paul won more converts by his trusting demeanor than by his preaching or teaching.

At any rate, Paul says that if we pray and give God thanks, speaking to God of our honest needs, then we will know "the peace of God, which passes all understanding (guarding our) hearts and minds in Christ Jesus" (4:7).

The inner peace to which Paul attests does not pass the "reason test." This test comes in three forms. The first: Does our peace seem appropriate in the face of some great personal tribulation? Isn't a deep pessimism a more realistic response to our life's shattering? To cease believing in any goodness, provisionally or ultimately, often feels more reasonable. Paul's articulation of peace in spite of all sufferings and troubles fails this first reason test — it comes on as quite abnormal and strange.

The biographers of Mark Twain point this out. They tell us this folksy humorist hid a deep sense of the unreasonableness of human existence in his writing. This rejection of any present or final peace was fed by continual financial troubles, then the death of his daughter, and finally by the death of his wife. We must not lightly judge Twain, for in similar circumstances all of us would discover the almost insurmountable temptation to give in to despair. All of this makes Paul's offering a hope that is unattainable and likely an unreasonable possibility.

The second reason test looming up in the face of Paul's "the peace of God, which passes all understanding," holds that seeking or testifying to this peace is a form of escape from life's troubles and sufferings. Some people are burdened by terrible panic attacks. They become unable to function on their job or in the normal run of their lives. Some of them progress until they cannot leave their home or those places where they feel safe and free from their paralyzing panic. We know that much of their panic is caused by a malfunction of the chemistry in the brain. Most of them cannot free themselves from their panic by trying harder. Wise medication from a doctor or specialist, along with some helpful therapy, enables them to resume a more normal life.

But these panic-ridden folks, while not deserving any of our moral judgment for their escapist life responses, do depict some of our chosen escapisms seemingly tied to the detachment Paul offers. Some religiously inspired detachment from living a normal life, by ministering to the sufferings of others, and accepting our share of making the world a less harmful place, also fails reason's insistence that we cannot and should not withdraw from life.

When Buddha found the same "peace that passes all understanding" as Paul, he insisted one could not enjoy this peace while others suffered. Instead of stepping over into the ultimate peace of Nirvana, Buddha gave himself to teaching others how to reach this peaceful goal. Christians in the season of Lent focus on Jesus who did not stay out of harm's way by remaining in the peace and safety of Galilee. Rather, he headed up to Jerusalem, plunging himself into the middle of the personal and public sufferings of others.

A recent best-seller, *How the Irish Saved Civilization*, tells how Irish monks tenderly preserved much of the classic literature of Greece and Rome during a time when the educational lights had died out in Europe. Wonderfully, the book argues that these Irish monks were not satisfied with keeping these classic treasures for themselves. Instead they set out to leave their safe island, taking this lost learning to schools, which they created on the continent. They saved, says the author, civilized literature and philosophy for civilization then and now. So any temptations for our inward peace, pushing us to detach from a worldly life fails this second form of the test of reason. Therefore, it must be rejected.

The third reason test of Paul's "the peace of God that passes all understanding" is that this peace is finally at the mercy of personal and cosmic oblivion. A young college student in a philosophy course was studying the works of Immanuel Kant, an eighteenth-century German philosopher. Thinking that Kant's detailed reasoning would nail down some important philosophical matters, the student was distressed to learn that Kant said that philosophically all the great issues could be argued both ways — for and against. Reason gives no firm conclusion. The student wondered if we were all adrift in a meaninglessness sea.

Following Kant, reason can say that Paul's insistence upon an inward peace beyond our sufferings and despair is unreliable. Reason can argue powerfully that this so-called inner peace is an illusion, often self-created to shield us from present troubles, and from the conclusion that life — the cosmos and ours — is doomed. Atheists, scientific materialists, and many types of humanists all reason this way. The classic statement of this is found in Sigmund Freud's, *The Future of an Illusion*. From the title of this book we instantly know that he finds religion an unreasonable commitment, illusionary but helpful to many who cannot face their troubles and the everlasting death that awaits all creation and us.

Christians must take this third objection of reason seriously. We do not want to live with a basic illusion. Later Kant offered a place for faith beyond any of reason's questions, saying that God, freedom, and immortality, while not affirmed by reason could be held beyond reason. Kant's lean faith was not sufficient for any full explication of the gospel, or of Paul's testimony to the "peace that passes all understanding." Yet, he made room for us, along with Paul, to trust in the basic goodness of life, despite all the hurts, disappointments, and suffering we face along the way.

Sometimes this trust formed by our inward peace pushes us into risky and courageous actions. An elderly and "straight" retired pastor was distressed by his denomination's refusal to accept and bless marital unions and ordain gay and lesbian people. Of course, as for heterosexuals, he held gay and lesbian people to the basic Christian standards of commited and faithful relationships. But in his deep concern, he surrendered his ordinational credentials and all his pension and health benefits as a form of protest. Now he functions as a lay person in another denomination. His sacrifice will not create changes in the denomination that he served for so many years. However, he becomes a small part in creating the tension that will someday honor his convictions.

For most of us, our discovery in the reality of Paul's "peace that passes all understanding" will not take such drastic form. As someone once said, "We are not to die on all the crosses; and certainly not all of us are to die on any cross. But in exuding a calm, trusting faith in life's basic goodness we make an important witness that others can hardly miss noting." In one of William Faulkner's novels, he tells of Dilsey, the domestic who was the single person in Faulkner's fictitious, yet believable southern family, who was stable. Summing up Dilsey, Faulkner said, "She endured."

Well, endurance is certainly a Christian virtue. One pastor says he found himself telling troubled people coming to him for strength, "Hang in there!" This wasn't said glibly or as taking lightly the pains and sufferings of those looking to him for help. It was said with the unspoken belief that in our resolve to endure, we discover a strength and ability beyond ourselves. Our peace is grounded in God's love, not something we manufacture. To suggest that we must come up with this strength all by ourselves would be cruel. We cannot create it, but we can open ourselves to receiving it into our lives. When this happens, nothing outward may be changed. We still suffer the same hurts and tragedies as anyone else. The world continues to be a place disappointing our hopes for peace, justice, and well being for the lowly. But inwardly, we are freed from the despair that keeps us running away from life and for concluding that life adds up to absurdity. Instead, we have the "peace that passes all understanding" so that we can live with dignity, peace, and rejoicing in the present blessings and provisional goodness that are finally caught up in God's everlasting life.

Advent:
Jesus, The Suffering Savior

This is our final Sunday in Advent. When we next gather, we will be filled with the sights, sounds, and scriptures of Christmas Eve. That will be a celebrative occasion because we will center in on the joyous news of the birth of a Savior delivering us from our sins, from the fate of human existence, and from the grief and hopelessness of death.

No wonder people who are not baptized or active members of any church will join us on Christmas Eve. No wonder, either, that those who have no faith in God or in some ultimate meaning of things will show up, too. While Christmas Eve for serious Christians proclaims the love of God that in George Matheson's hymn, "will not let us go," those for whom the church claims no central place will yet rejoice in good news. Those who see no need for regular involvement in the life and work of the church, or who feel somewhat alienated from the church, will find themselves caught up in the optimism of Christ's birth. Even those of fierce doubt who come to our Christmas Eve service will be warmed by the Christmas message, even though they finally judge it to be illusionary. So, there are great moments just ahead of us.

But this morning we still have serious worship work to do before we can fully open ourselves to "the great glad tidings" of Christmas Eve. A friend tells of Dr. Jack Evans, the director of the famous all-brass Ohio State University Marching Band, self-proclaimed as TBDBITL, "the best damned band in the land!" Obviously the band has a humility problem.

The band members lived for Saturday afternoons. They would burst down the ramp at the curved end of that horseshoe-shaped stadium onto the stadium floor, the drum major thrusting his baton toward the opposite end zone with the band playing "The Buckeye Battle Cry," in front of 75,000 screaming fans. No drug could deliver the high that such moments created. But Jack Evans, in his stern and compelling way, always had words for the band about this frenzy in the weekday rehearsals. He told the band that unless they did the work of memorizing the music, something the band prided itself on in contrast to other bands, and learned the various formations for the band show, the band's Saturday afternoon performance would be embarrassing. Both the band members and the director would be unhappy. Great moments come only after hard work, some pain, and sacrifice.

Advent is something like this. Before we can fully come into the saving joy of Christmas, we must give ourselves over to hard work, pain, and sacrifice. Today's text reminds us of this so we will not glide into Christmas Eve without the strengthening struggles that develop into a faith which endures and fulfills. The Hebrews author says, "And it is by God's will that we have been sanctified through the offering of the body of Jesus Christ for all." The gospel has a tough, realistic nature about it, separating it from all the spurious gospels that tell us "we can have it all," without any serious suffering. The Christmas Eve Jesus saves us because he lived out his life in strenuous effort, pain, and sacrifice.

This has two consequences for us. The first is that any saving religious tradition saves because its founding figure's life, with little self-concern, was turned over for the desperate needs of others, thinking little of their own concerns. Certainly, this is true of the three major figures in the religions coming from the story of Abraham and Sarah.

Judaism's Moses led a life of suffering for the people of Israel. While the biblical reflections on Moses' deliverance of the Israelites from Egypt tell of this becoming the transmitter of the law of faithful life, they also tell of his occasional complaint about his role. Yet his arguments with God and of the personal hardships of his leadership make him all the more attractive. Because

34

he ultimately accepted the suffering God's call put upon him, he became a saving figure. Without this he has no power to evoke faith in us.

The second major figure grounded in the narratives of Abraham and Sarah is Mohammed, the founder of Islam. In the Koran, the Islamic scriptures, Mohammed is a person of great pain and suffering. He suffered because the cultic religions of his early life were insufficient for his restless godly spirit. When God, Allah, confronted him and called him to proclaim a tough and serious faith, he suffered at the hands of those who preferred the soft, old ways. Mohammed gave the world one of its most profound religious traditions because it came out of a troubled spirit, and much turmoil generated by his hearing the will of God. Again, without this, he would have no power to evoke faith in us.

Jesus is our third religious figure for whom suffering has become saving for us. Our text makes this clear: "We have been sanctified through the offering of the body of Jesus Christ once for all." Christianity hardly allows us to miss this. The gospel centers on the cross of Jesus as the place where his meaning all comes together. Because Jesus suffered there, and all throughout his lifetime, he has become the saving significance and power for us. Without his suffering, as the cross insists, he has no ability to evoke faith in us.

However, beyond the traditions developing out of the Abraham and Sarah story, non-biblical traditions make the same point. Certainly this is the case in the person of Gatauma Buddha, the founder of Buddhism. In his early adult life, he broke from the sheltered existence of his privileged place in the palace. For the first time he saw raw, human suffering. The resulting outcome was his giving his life to minister to human suffering. His suffering over the misery of the people of his time became a new religious tradition that cut the nerve of misery. Yet when he was about to select this option of freedom from suffering for himself, he refused this exemption for himself and chose to become a sufferer on behalf of the sufferers. His example has inspired a religious tradition of widespread caring for others and it is called Buddhism.

The suffering of others for us, unmerited and given without condition, becomes a saving moment coming from so many of our religious founders. Their suffering on our behalf becomes an authentication of their message. A glad, happy, carefree religious figure would have no power to get at the depth of our own pains — those pains that come simply with being alive as well as those self-created pains. Isn't this the reason the Apostle Paul said he would come among the Corinthians; only with a message of Christ crucified?

A second response to this tough-minded Advent lection is its call to emulate our Savior and live out lives of suffering and caring for others. How this note falls on deaf ears in our time, even in the church. In so many ways, we fall for a gospel of success wrapped in a feel-good package. Seldom in the church are we reminded that Luther said we have only a gospel of the cross — Jesus' cross and the call for us to join Jesus there. The great American theologian of America, Reinhold Niebuhr, said so many times that the perfection of human and cosmic existence lies beyond history not within it. We have no earthly gospel of glory, only a gospel of suffering love.

But in our choosing the life of suffering love, inspired by Jesus and others, our lives become saving places for the suffering of those near and far. The play, *Sunrise at Campobello*, is the story of the young Franklin Delano Roosevelt. This wealthy, ambitious politician became stricken with polio so that he could never walk again. This seemed to end any political career. He had the means to live out a life as an invalid on the family estate at Hyde Park. Instead, he chose politics with a new sense of the troubles and sufferings of others. Becoming president at the depths of the Great Depression in 1932, he pushed, shoved, and inspired the federal government to deal with the suffering of those terrible years. We need not endorse all his political achievements or defeats on behalf of the sick, unemployed, and desperate. Yet, we can hardly miss that this pampered, privileged man turned his own suffering into ways that alleviated the suffering of others in those days.

Advent calls us to this sturdy message, not some soft and undemanding cooing over the baby Jesus arriving on Christmas Eve. How many people has the church lost because we cover over this "cross gospel" with a veneer of successful, painless living that is disconnected with the troubles and miseries of humanity? A chirpy, *all is well* message may suit the majority of people in the church. But the sum total of human suffering is hardly reduced by this gospel. Wouldn't it be good news to some of the hard-headed, no nonsense people in or out of our pews to say that with the African-American spiritual, "I see trouble in the air." Some refreshing honesty in the church might connect with the unbelievers in and out of the church, calling them to an honest blik on human existence and calling them to join ranks with any who dare to suffer with and for others.

In the popular "Jesus died for my sins" gospel, it seldom moves beyond dwelling on that note of the unmerited love of God in Christ. What Advent's hard realism announces is that the only response to the saving love of the suffering Christ, is to commit ourselves to a similar sort of life. In the opening chapter of the book of Acts, Jesus ascends into heaven and while this is happening, two men in white robes confront the disciples who are looking heavenward, awed by the moment. These two mysterious figures then say, "Men of Galilee, why do you stand looking up toward heaven?" In other words, "Quit standing around and doing a lot of religious talk — like speaking over and over again about the awesomeness of God. Get your eyes fixed on the raw needs of your sisters and brothers everywhere, in Judea, Samaria, and the ends of the earth, and get on with it." Advent struggles to save us from a mushy and irrelevant Christmas, offering instead a suffering life that will save the lives of others and in the process, save us, too.

Christmas Eve/Day
In A Minor Key

One of the best things in the modern church is the creation of our Common Lectionary. For most of our mainstream churches, including Roman Catholic churches, we have settled on a common reading from the Hebrew Bible, the gospels, the New Testament letters, and the psalms, for each Sunday of the church year. In all our diverse congregations we centered our preaching on the readings from the letters: Thessalonians, Philippians, and Hebrews. We found rich and stirring words in these readings, and we discovered a unity beyond our honest differences.

Tonight, on Christmas Eve/Day, we have a reading from the book of Titus. Unlike most of the other readings that change on a three-year cycle, Titus remains the reading for Christmas Eve/Day each of the three years. I must tell you, those of us who have determined to preach from the letters during this season of the church year find it somewhat difficult to put together an inspiring Christmas Eve/Day sermon from Titus. Titus has no stirring words or rhythmic cadences like other possible selections from the New Testament Letters. Certainly those who created our Common Lection could have chosen a more spiritually challenging reading from one of Paul's letters, or from other letters written in his name, or in Hebrews.

Yet here tonight/today we have Titus, a plodding and subdued voice, and quite a contrast with what might have been our text this evening/today. Titus has no "Hallelujah Chorus" stuck within its lines, lifting us out of our spiritual doldrums. Titus is a bit like

Seinfeld, the television sitcom. Nothing extraordinary or meaningful ever happens. It just goes along episode after episode after episode. The committee that selected Titus for Christmas Eve/Day must have been in a Psalm 131 mood.

O Lord, my heart is not lifted up, my eyes are not raised too high; I do not occupy myself with things too great and marvelous for me....   — Psalm 131:1

Titus is like a piece of music written in the minor key, not raising our eyes too high. It is nothing like great music that lifts us out of our pew.

Great Music In A Minor Key

In music class in elementary school we learned that the scale used to create music could be in either a major or minor key. A major key would go: do, ra, mi, fa, so, la, ti and end with do. A major key sounds cheerful and optimistic. Most music, popular or classical, is written in a major key. But then there is a minor key. Being a bit simplistic, the difference between a major and minor key is how we treat "mi," the third note in the scale. To produce a minor key all we do is flatten the mi, playing it a half step down. So music written and sung in a minor key has a much different sound than music in a major key. Minor-key music has a brooding quality, as if there is some hidden pathos or sadness mixed in the music. It is even emphasized in how a major and a minor key are listed. Major keys are noted with a capital letter, but minor keys are designated with a small letter: F Major or F minor.

Sometimes it seems that some of the great music is written in a minor key, not a major one. Many of us are familiar with Beethoven's Fifth Symphony, written in the minor key of C. At the beginning of the first movement we hear what is called the musical equivalent of the Morse Code for the letter "V" — dot-dot-dot — dash. Beethoven pounds out this little phrase over and again, all in a tense minor key. Some musical commentators say this recurring theme is Beethoven's musical way of lamenting his

40

growing deafness, something devastating for a musician. If true, no wonder this symphony is written in a minor key. Take the nineteenth-century Russian composer, Peter Tchaikovsky. Tchaikovsky was a gay man in a world where this sexual drive and preference could not be openly admitted. Hence, in much of his music he poured out his inner pathos, in fact, his Sixth Symphony in B minor is often called "The Pathetic Symphony." Did his inner secret and its suffering spill over into the rich minor tones of that symphony?

So if Titus seems a bit minor rather than major, even on a "high holiday" such as Christmas Eve/Day, we might ask if there is something profound in this reading that our more celebrative Christmas Eve/Day readings suggest. While we prefer major-key music, the minor-key reading of Titus could be a wholesome corrective to our overdosing on the major-key offerings.

Christmas Eve/Day In A Minor-Key World

The late Louis "Sachmo" Armstrong sang in his inimitably gravelly voice, "What A Wonderful World." The song touched something within us. Yet our ability to sing such an affirmative song comes from recognizing that our Savior was born into a terribly violent, cruel, and far from a wonderful world. No sooner do we rightly rejoice at Bethlehem's stable, than the family rushes in the night to Egypt, escaping the murderous terror of King Herod.

The subdued "I do not occupy myself with things/too great and marvelous for me ..." mood of our Christmas Eve/Day reading from Titus may be in a minor key. It has no stirring major-key music about itself. But as it doesn't imitate Luke's shepherds in "rushing over to Bethlehem to see this thing that has happened." Titus knows that there can be moments "when the cheering stops."

President Wilson experienced this when he went to Europe to arrange the Peace Treaty in 1919, ending the slaughter of World War I. The popular crowds hailed him as the savior of Europe in city after city. But when the task of hammering out a just and fair treaty began, the cheering stopped. Europe's political leaders wanted no just and fair arrangements. They wanted revenge and the destruction of Germany as a major power. Even today the glad hopes of world peace and justice are sung against the minor key of national insecurity, selfishness, and an unwillingness to sacrifice for such dreams. Titus reminds us that the great hopes are still with us, but they are cast in a somber and frightening minor key. In short, Titus may be the most realistic reading we can muster this or any Christmas Eve/Day. In Bruce Caton's trilogy on the Civil War, he writes that one battalion from Massachusetts furled their flags and banners before they went into battle. They knew that war is killing and awful violence, not glory and flag waving. Says Caton, "They knew there was no poetry in a fight."

Christmas Eve/Day In Our Minor-Key Lives

In some of the modern and revised liturgies for the Sunday morning service in many mainstream churches, a congregational prayer of confession has become optional. The older worship liturgies have seemed out of place for those of us who want upbeat lives. We are desperate to think highly of ourselves. We are encouraged to "stuff" any recognition that there are serious moral and spiritual dislocations in our lives. Famous preachers and congregations have made a point of celebrating the gospel only in a major key. Self-esteem, even to the point of blatant dishonesty about how we stand with God is the rule. No wonder we don't want to impede this quest by interrupting our major-key spiritual mentality.

Along comes our Titus reading and it seems to be saying, "Now wait a minute. There is a darkness about ourselves with which we must come to terms. Otherwise, we will fall victim to our unwillingness to tell it like it is." A great American theologian often said that we are redeemed in principle, but not in fact. What he meant is that our sins no longer lodge themselves between God and ourselves, thus we are redeemed in principle. In fact, we are still sinners easily resisting the love of God and our call to love our neighbor.

In our terribly "immediate and now" world we are often under the curse of thinking that only the present holds any saving truth for us. Hence, we have jettisoned centuries of Christian thought and understanding because they are not current and supposedly up-to-date. We are under the spell of the now and we are paying a huge price for abandoning this spiritual treasure. Cutting loose from some of our traditional Christian reflections that call into question our shallow and current modernisms, we doom ourselves to despair when we finally own up to the minor-key elements in our personal lives.

We would do well to listen again to one from the fifth century C.E., Saint Augustine, the Bishop of Hippo. There is little in his exposition of the Christian faith that is shallow and spiritually mushy. Augustine tells us something not frequently heard in many modern Christian circles, that the love of God and neighbor is not something we can will. We cannot roll up our emotional sleeve and really love that pesky neighbor, or a God who presides over a world full of violence and tragedy. Love cannot be commanded. It must come from the Spirit beyond us. This is certainly a minor-key theme, putting a damper upon our self-deceit, claiming that we are really an admirable loving sort of gal or guy.

Hence, Titus as a Christmas Eve/Day reading is much more realistic and saving than many of our celebrations of the birth of Jesus. Titus says quite straightforwardly, "For the grace of God has appeared, bringing salvation to all" (2:11). Then, with no apology to our "we must have this now" spirituality he says, "We wait for the blessed hope and the manifestation of the glory of our great God and Savior, Jesus Christ" (2:13).

Would a minor-key Christmas Eve/Day halt the flow of people from the congregation after Christmas Eve/Day? The sentimental warmth of much of our celebrations of this great event does not last. Not only do these emotions fade — the shallow presentations of our Christmas Eve/Day falter against the darkness of world and our inability to manage a life of love against our sins. Could neglected Titus be the locus of an evangelistic renewal of the church?

Our Christmas Gift

Since the 1600s, in a historical period called the "Enlighten-ment," scholars have been studying the scriptures in a new way. They have rejected the older theory that the scriptures were in-spired, word for word by God, and therefore were infallible and without error. Instead they approached the scriptures as a human document, meaning that it could be studied with all the tools of literary and historical scholarship. Yet they did not deny that the scriptures, studied in this new way, could bring us into the pres-ence of God.

Some of their major conclusions have been with us for some time now: Moses did not write the first five books of the Hebrew Bible, Genesis through Deuteronomy. The psalms are attributed to David, but he did not write all of them. Isaiah seems to come from at least two authors, 1-39 and 40-66. Matthew, Mark, and Luke's words are nearer to the historical Jesus than the Gospel of John. Some of Paul's passages such as the subordination of women to men are likely insertions into his writings.

Of course, some have resisted this way of studying scripture. They feel that it takes away the authority and the uniqueness of the Bible. They hold that the scriptures are from God and are free from all errors — historical, ethical, scientific, and religious. We may admire these folks for their sturdy faith grounded in scriptures. They have an attractive fix on faith with all questions and doubts settled by an uncritical understanding of the Bible. We, in contrast, are not so certain of our faith and are always struggling to grasp the mercy of God in Jesus Christ. But, for some reason, we cannot stand with the uncritical Christians. We may admire them deeply, but we must come to faith by understanding the Bible as a human document, inviting the best of our critical study and understanding. We cannot go back to an earlier time and way of approaching the Bible. Something — the enlightenment of the 1600s — has happened and we cannot live and have faith as if it had not occurred.

This brings us to our text for the morning. Colossians 3:12-17 is a wonderful passage on living the Christian life. It urges us to have compassion, kindness, humility, meekness, and patience. It tells us that we must forgive others because the Lord has forgiven us. We must always love each other and be open to that peacefulness which Christ brings us. It says we are called to a ministry of teaching and worship, doing all this in the name of Jesus.

This calls us to a life far beyond looking out for ourselves. Looking out for "Old Number One" is the life to which the world calls us, but this is a call to a life of death and despair. Christ calls us through today's text to a life that pours itself out to the needs of others and discovers rich joy and peace. One modern scholar called Jesus "the man for others." We are to emulate Jesus and live, not for ourselves, but for others. So a passage like this from Colossians is an inspiring challenge to our Christians lives. It is a fitting text for this first Sunday after Christmas.

However, the authorship of this passage and the entire letter of Paul to the Colossians is under question. Many think that Paul has not written Colossians. They tell us that some of Paul's typical phrases are missing from Colossians. They say that some of the theological expressions of Colossians are not as Paul would put them, and some of the issues to which Colossians is speaking are not those with which Paul concerned himself. In short, Colossians seems to have been written by someone else and attributed to Paul.

This is how reverent, modern, scriptural scholarship explains and rationalizes the scriptures. It works just like any critical scholarship. Some years ago, there appeared *The Secret Diaries of Adolf Hitler*. The discoverer of this supposed work claimed its authenticity and basked in the attention of modern historians. But it soon appeared this diary was not as advertised. Great parts of it did not seem to be from the late Nazi leader, nor did it square with certain times, dates, and happenings. The conclusion of most was that it was a hoax perpetrated by the discoverer. Solid human study and reasoning saved us from a work that would deceive us.

Questioning Paul's authorship of Colossians is not so crucial. In Colossians we may not be getting the real Paul, but we are given an impressive call to the Christian life. Apparently, as in the ancient world, writings were purported to be those of some great figure, and in that person's spirit. We might think that if Paul had seen the letter to the Colossians, he might have said, "Well, now there's a great statement of what it means to be a Christian. I'm proud that someone has honored my Lord and me by attributing it to me." Even if we felt that at certain places he might have put it differently, it is thinkable that Paul would have rejoiced in Colossians, and would have given it his endorsement. On this Sunday after Christmas we, too, may rejoice in the richness of our text and find inspiration and encouragement in our Christian lives.

1. "Clothe yourselves with compassion." Compassion is simply to feel with another. Some of the most despicable profanity is, "What do I care?" Martin Noemiller, pastor of a prestigious congregation in Berlin during the rise of Hitler in the 1930s, confessed a classic indictment of not having compassion. He said when the Gestapo came for the criminals, he said nothing. When they came for the mentally retarded, he said nothing. When they came for the Communists, he said nothing. When they came for the homosexuals, he said nothing. When they came for the Jews, he said nothing. "Then one day," he said, "they came for me." In our nation today we need more than just personal compassion. The political powers seem to have little compassion for the poor, the inner cities, the broken educational system, the sexually different, the mentally ill or mentally handicapped, and non-Christian religions. Christmas is a good time to think about this.

2. We are urged to have kindness. The opposite of a life of kindness is one of judgment. How often our lives are filled with the judgmental spirit. We berate others and ourselves sometimes, for not living up to expectations. Often we hold up these expectations for others, but excuse ourselves for falling below our standard. When one or both people in a marriage or partnership

becomes overly judgmental, then that marriage or partnership is doomed. We cannot live under a constant fear of failing, for it saps us of our physical and spiritual energies. We could make the case that the appeal of Christ in his lifetime and beyond has been that our lives in him are marked by mercy even after he has laid the most severe judgment on us. Again, Christmas is a good time to consider this.

3. The author of Colossians calls us to have humility. Something distressing has come into sports — professional and all the way down to the amateur level. This is the volume of self-congratulation that occurs. Let's take football, professional down to the peewee level, allowing that what follows applies to all other sports. Joey or Rakeem scores a touchdown and in the end zone, dances and boogies as if to call attention to his prowess. One longs for the days when a back or receiver crosses into the end zone, drops the ball or hands it to the official, and returns to the huddle with no showy behavior. It's as if athletes cannot let the crowd reaction, or the media attention be sufficient for recognizing their exploits.

However, Christians are not beyond a lack of humility, too. Some Christians are so focused on their decision for Christ that they constantly talk about "being saved." It almost seems as if they are saying they have done God a great favor. They will inject their take on their salvation into all conversations, church meetings, and conversations at home. They will eye all the unsaved as their personal project, and make themselves a nuisance in the process. A little humility about our relationship to Christ is in order. After all, salvation comes in many styles, and not just in the highly personal and otherworldly style of some. We would wish them humility and the same for ourselves, particularly where we have accomplished some worthy thing. Colossians prompts us to ponder humility on this Sunday after Christmas. We might even wonder at so much of the so-called gospel and praise music for its singular focus on one's individual relationship to God and Christ with little attention to salvation to gear ourselves up for gutsy service to our brothers and sisters in a painful world.

48

4. We are advised to have meekness. Now meekness seems a bit like humility. Yet, meekness may be understood as not having to be right in all situations. Years ago, there was a local television newscaster, before local television news had given itself over to murders, bank robberies, a load of weather, and ugly divorces, who always had a moment of commentary at the evening broadcast. He always began by saying, "I may be wrong, but...." It is refreshing to be in the company of those who can say, "I may be wrong, but...." The Christian does not always have to assert his correctness. Of course, in serious matters, Christians must speak up, and speak up loudly at times, but we are most unattractive if we think we have all the answers and it is our duty to correct and admonish all others. We might think about this on a Sunday after Christmas.

5. Colossians calls for patience. We live in a world where patience is difficult to come by. Everything must happen instantly. Our modern technologies make travel, long-distance communication, and scientific progress come faster than any previous generation, but the summons to Christian patience has little to do with any of these wonderful speeds. Many a pastor reads from Isaiah 40 to those they visit in the hospital:

> *But those who wait for the Lord, shall renew their*
> *strength, they shall mount up with wings like eagles,*
> *they shall run and not be weary, they shall walk and*
> *not faint.* — Isaiah 40:31

When we are ill, patience is often the key ingredient. Convalescence is hindered when we insist that we must regain our health instantly. Years ago, Bishop Hazen G. Werner, wrote a book of sermons titled, *No Saints Suddenly.* The title sermon centered on the letter a little girl wrote to a Christian counselor about her disturbing anger at her little brother. She wanted to overcome her fault and wondered if she could be cured by Christmas! Wisely, the bishop reminded us that there are no saints suddenly.

The maturing of our Christian character and of the redemption of the world must come about slowly and patiently. If Darwin's truth holds, it suggests that God is patiently calling the world and all creation into God's own self over the long haul of eons and eons. For individuals, our redemption must be beyond this life and history out into the eternity of God, as we grow to become the people God would have us be. Colossians, on this Sunday after Christmas, wants us to think on all of us, too.

Our Colossians passage wants us to gather up all these Christian virtues in worship — not entertaining or escapist worship — but worship that implants these things in to our individual and public lives. Marva Dawn has written that our worship could be *A Royal Waste of Time*, but if we keep these things from Colossians — compassion, kindness, humility, meekness, and patience — our celebration for the first Sunday after Christmas can be a rich and wonderful time of this season, a great gift from God.

The Epiphany Of Our Lord
Ephesians 3:1-12

Two For The Price Of One

Today is an important day in the life of the world and the life of the church. In the northern hemisphere this is the first day of the New Year. Last night many of us celebrated the eve of this New Year — noisily or somberly. Noisy types went out to dinner and danced until our feet grew weary. We counted down the last seconds of the old year, and wildly greeted one another with shouts, drinks, hugs, kisses, and fireworks. Then we sang the traditional lines of Robert Burn's poem, "Auld Lang Syne," and went home. A few of us remember a time when we were part of that great crowd in Times Square in New York City, and watched the ball descend as it announced the year's end and a year's beginning.

Others of us closed out the old year and the beginning of the new a bit more quietly. We went to small gatherings in each other's homes for food, games, conversation, and listened to Dick Clark do his broadcast from Times Square. Drinking was minimal or not at all; but we did have the shouts, hugs, and kisses as January 1 appeared. In addition, some of us gathered in our places of worship where we offered prayers of thanksgiving and hope, closing with some hymns of praise. Of course, a few just went to bed at their usual times and woke up to a New Year.

The Importance Of The New Year
Most human cultures have thought it important to dissect the flow of time into yearly segments, and not all of them have chosen January first to indicate a New Year. But ours has done this. The reason seems to be that in our northern hemisphere, the sunlight in

51

the days of autumn and late December grows shorter. Prehistoric people — whose habits and customs have often been incorporated into our own historical understandings — became anxious that the sunlight might wink out altogether. Then the cold would be a prelude to the frost and freezing of all things and all life.

However, our forebears were more intelligent than we give them credit. Somehow, in the few days after December 21, the winter solstice, they perceived that the length of the day's sun was getting longer by just a few minutes. This meant that warmer times were in the offering, and crops could be planted and wild game would again become plentiful. For us, as for our pre-historic ancestors, it became appropriate to celebrate the return of the warmth of the sun, in the few days on, before, or after January 1.

Celebrating the new year, aside from the frivolities or the "no nonsense" styles in which we mark this moment, really means that we are thankful for the recurring renewal of nature. Even with a nod to quantum physics' disallowance of a rigid, regularity of nature, there is enough dependability in the flow of nature to enable us to extend to it our trust. The return of the sun dissolves our anxieties that the future might be so radically different that it would threaten all of life. January first is really an appreciation of the stability of the natural world, which gives us our life.

Going deeper, the regularities giving us the New Year, raise the question about the origin about these dependable regularities. One of Robert Frost's poems, "Accidentally on Purpose," seems to be asking this question: "Do these cyclic regularities of nature imply a Regulator, or did they just happen out of the long flow of natural evolution?" For the believer, one of the exasperating things about such theological questions is that they can be argued either way — for or against. For believers, it does seem to strongly suggest a God who providentially arranges the universe so that nature proceeds on a regular and dependable course.

The conviction about the cyclic renewing of life allows two things. One comes from prehistoric sources effecting both our pagan and biblical traditions, enabling us to create the ability to think and explore reality scientifically. Science does not rise out of traditions holding that all is finally chaotic. Science begins with the belief that reality is patterned and regular. The ancient January experience is a position of science.

The second conviction comes from ancient and Christian sensing that the return of the sun and life is theological. It caused our prehistoric ancestors to think that darkness and death were not final. Prehistoric persons were terribly concerned about the meaninglessness of death. Archaeological discoveries tell us that they wished for something better than to give their loved ones and themselves over to an everlasting death. For them, and within our modern souls, the slow renewal of life as the minutes of light lengthen in our winter days, is more than a meteorological calculation given on the evening television news. Deep within it speaks for a vital human hope that life conquers the unhinging despair of death.

The Co-celebration Of Epiphany Sunday

In Matthew's Gospel, and in his gospel only, we are given a story of Wise Men from the East coming to the Bethlehem to give reverence to the baby Jesus. The church celebrates this event twelve days after Christmas, or January 6. Occasionally, January 6 falls on a Sunday, but in most years it comes somewhere in midweek. The busyness of modern life has crowded out most midweek celebrations. So the church honors these occasions not always falling on a Sunday by celebrating them on the nearest Sunday — before or after.

This year (2007), Epiphany, or January 6, is next Friday, and we are taking note of it today. Epiphany, then, is our co-celebration: Wise Men from the East bringing their gifts of gold, frankincense, and myrrh to the Christ Child. We have little knowledge of why Matthew created or preserved this tradition in his gospel. Perhaps he wanted to affirm that the many non-Christians gave deference to Christ and Christianity. This note of the superiority and uniqueness of Christ has been the dominant theme of the church's spirituality across the centuries.

In the book of Acts, Peter proclaims, "There is salvation in no one else, for there is no other name under heaven given among mortals by which we must be saved" (4:12). The Wise Men as Matthew presents them, certainly make the same point — Christ and Christianity are the only truth by which salvation comes to humanity, but the mood is changing in our world today. Many, but not all Christians, are sensing that God's saving truth is not limited to Christ. Our time is one when some traditional ways of understanding are being transformed into new and different ways of thinking. In the seventh and eighth centuries before Jesus, such a moment happened in biblical and non-biblical religions. This time is called "the axial age" because human understanding took a major turn away from previous understanding. It was in such a time that the biblical prophets rose — Amos, Hosea, Isaiah, Jeremiah, and Ezekiel. All of them presented the human situation before God in challenging, yet disturbing ways. In Greece, this time saw the tragic playwrights and the philosophy of Plato and Aristotle. In the Far East, this axial age gave us Vedic Hindu reformation as well as the teachings of Buddha.

If history can tell us about past eras when major changes came in our human understandings, perhaps we can sense that we live in such a time today. Modern science has become less confident that we live in a blind and purposeless universe, one that is going on its rigid law-abiding way, heedless of our human hopes and needs. This is a major change; one that the new physics has brought us. In religion, a major change that has been with us for many years, reaching back to the prophets of the Hebrew Bible, is the insistence that religion cannot be divorced from public needs — especially the plight of the poor and the oppressed. No longer can we think of salvation as restricted to be something that kicks in at our death, and is restricted to those who mumble a few words about allegiance to Jesus.

It is also possible for us to sense we are living in another religious axial age where all religions are seen as human responses to the merciful and loving God. No religion has any monopoly on salvation in this life or the next. For Christians who ponder the spirituality of Wise Men from the East, we might begin to think of the term "Christ" as meaning much more than the historical Jesus. Christ can be the saving grace that was present in Bethlehem and in all his life, but it is not limited to him. Christ can be the saving mercy of God reaching out to all humanity and reflected in many different ways, and many different traditions.

Modern communication and modern transportation conspire to break down our religious isolation in today's world. When we are confronted with the many other religious traditions we can react in two ways. One is to intensify our insistence that Christ, known in Jesus, is the only true religion and the only true way to earthly and heavenly salvation. This approach appeals to many simply because moving out of an old way of thinking and believing and into a new way of thinking and believing can provoke a deep anxiety within us. Some think that the success of the Christian fundamentalist, evangelical religion is forced by this tremendous anxiety, what Paul Tillich once called, "The Shaking of the Foundation."

But borrowing a line from Paul, "but to us who are being saved" (1 Corinthians 1:16b), our time is exhilarating and exciting. We sense some of the fears and anxieties of leaving the old and launching out into new and uncharted territory, as that experience by those early explorers or the American northwest, Lewis and Clark. Yet like them, we also know something of the awesomeness of what is confronting us. We feel the freeing experience of leaving behind old, binding ways and traditions.

Hence, our co-celebration this New Year's Day enables us to ponder the godly regularity of nature and the conviction that life conquers death. And in the Epiphany part of today's worship, we can rejoice in the new and more expansive nature of the meaning of salvation, exhibited by the Christ Child, but not confined to him. This is truly a spiritual rich and wonderful day. Today we are getting two for the price of one.

The Baptism Of Our Lord
Epiphany 1
Ordinary Time 1
Acts 8:14-17

Getting The Complete
Understanding And Experience

Many times we settle for lives and experiences that are limited and incomplete. The late Albert Outler said that the American frontier circuit riders, disdaining the whole range of tradition and learning, "already knew what they didn't need to know." We can hardly blame those courageous young men who took the faith to our nation's westward expansion. They understood that deep theological thinking and religious reasoning were not prime requirements on the rough and primitive frontier. Yet, as the years passed and these areas of our nation became settled communities, the need for religious thought in touch with the historical tradition of the faith became important. In the book of Hebrews, the author calls his hearers to leave elementary understandings and experiences of the gospel and "go on to maturity" (6:1), a maturity that assures a more complete experience of the good news of Jesus Christ.

All this is said because today in the first Sunday after the celebration of Epiphany Sunday when we focus on and celebrate the baptism of Jesus. However, the lection pushes beyond Jesus' baptism and suggests a more complete baptism — the baptism of the Holy Spirit. All this is suggested in Acts 8:14-17. The apostles in Jerusalem heard that some Samaritans had responded to the Word of God and were baptized in the name of Jesus; but the apostles were concerned that the Samaritans had not yet experienced the completing experience of the baptism of the Holy Spirit. So Peter and John were sent by the Jerusalem church to pray with the Samaritans, lay their hands on them, and allow them to receive the Holy Spirit. It is important to consider that the Jerusalem church was not content to let these Samaritans believers miss the enriching understanding and experience of baptism in the Holy Spirit. So what might all of this mean for us?

I

So often we understand the Holy Spirit as some overwhelming emotional experience in our lives. Our culture encourages us, infecting our religious understandings. The loud-volume-shrieking-singing complete with bodily gyrations and flashing lights in some contemporary music helps us to think any serious experience must have this shattering element in it. Mistakenly, we go out seeking some similar high volume, emotional moment as evidence that we have received the Holy Spirit. The difficulty looms because nothing or anyone can deliver this moment to us; so we go away disappointed and vow to limit our expectations and our hopes.

In Psalm 131 there is such a mood. The author has hit a low place in his or her life. We have no clue about what has happened to put them into such a dark moment. Nonetheless, it is unmistakable that some experiences can cause a serious withdrawal from any bright affirmation about the invigorating presence of God or of any significant dreams for ourselves or our times. Listen to these words:

> *O Lord, my heart is not lifted up,*
> *My eyes are not raised too high;*
> *I do not occupy myself with things*
> *too great and too marvelous for me.*
> *But I have calmed and quieted my soul,*
> *like a weaned child with its mother;*
> *my soul is like the weaned child that is with me.*

It's possible that a later editor could not allow these somber words to stand alone, so they added a closing verse,

> *O Israel, hope in the Lord*
> *From this time on and forevermore.*

Now two things need to be offered here. One, we can understand that life — personal or a time in which we live — can beat down our hopes in the future, and cast away great joy within. This drives us, like this psalmist, to clip and trim what we expect from God and life. We have suffered so much that we have no spiritual energy to think great thoughts, to dream great dreams, or to focus on much that is beyond just living out our days until death claims us. From our grief studies, we know that the experience of losing a loved one plunges us into such a mood. We must trust that this mood gives way in time, and with wise management, to a renewal of life's meaning and joy. But in the interim, we are almost paralyzed, bodily and emotionally. Hopefully, a brazen and insensitive, chirpy optimism has not taken residence within us, so that we cruelly lecture the grief-bound person with our hollow-sounding bright tidings rather than listening to such a one and bearing their sorrow with them.

The second thing to say is as noted, that we don't have to feel the hopefulness of the Holy Spirit for it to be operative in our lives. Many are touched by the little story of one, crushed by life walking along the beach with Jesus beside them. For a time, there were the tracks of both in the sand, Jesus' and our burdened soul's. Then there came a time when there was only one set of tracks. When the person later asked Jesus why he had abandoned him in his time of crisis, Jesus replied, "The single tracks were mine when I carried you after you were no longer able to walk." The Holy Spirit, like Jesus in this story, is with us even when we are unable to sense it.

None of this would authorize us to shut down our hopes and dreams and attempt to remain content with the small pleasures and meanings of life. Just because we cannot point to some great moment of its baptism, we must come to understand that the Holy Spirit is a continual part of our lives, even at those times when we feel most bereft of its consolations and energies.

II

Another understanding of the Holy Spirit is more secular than a typically religious experience. Solid Christian and biblical teaching has always said that God and God's concerns are always worldly

59

as well as spiritual. God is in the world as well as beyond the world. God is often known through worldly experiences and worldly knowledge. Many scientists are driven to consider the godly mystery of the world and the cosmos through their work and study. They challenge their fellow scientists who proclaim a fundamentalist materialism, telling us that reality is nothing but blind matter and energy in action. These scientists, impressed by the mystery of life, call for a reading of reality at deeper levels than the "nothing but" position.

All this means that God and God's Holy Spirit are not limited to some religious interior place where we think we might keep the faith safe from the assaults of the ungodly. No, the whole world, the whole of life, and the whole cosmos are filled with the signs of the presence of the Holy Spirit. Don't our scriptures begin with a description of creation in Genesis 1 where it is implied that God may be discovered?

When we feel impelled to take upon ourselves some worldly task, it could be a valid experience of the Holy Spirit. Do we forget that this is the point made in Matthew 25:31-46, as Jesus speaks about what will happen when the Son of Man comes and establishes the day of judgment? The Son of Man welcomes those who fed the hungry, and filled the thirsty, visited the lonely, clothed the naked, and took care of the sick, and visited those who were in prison. These deeds are part of the kingdom. But those who did none of these worldly ministries are banished from the blessedness of the kingdom. As a caution, Paul in 1 Corinthians 13 warns that not all worldly caring for others is prompted by the Holy Spirit, as it may be done for recognition or self-satisfaction. Yet much of our caring for others is legitimately an expression of the Holy Spirit working in our lives, often at great personal cost.

One of our great American heroes whose birthday is celebrated at this time of year is that of Martin Luther King, Jr., the great hero of civil rights for all. Martin Luther King, Jr., was primarily an intellectual. He really wanted to be the dean of a theological seminary after receiving his Ph.D. from Boston University. Going to Birmingham, Alabama, he waited for some opportunities in the academic field, and became a local pastor in the interim. But in

1955, Rosa Parks refused to give up her front seat on the bus and move to the rear seats, so she was arrested. Immediately, a boycott of the Birmingham city buses was announced.

The black pastors called on Martin Luther King, Jr., to organize and lead the boycott which entailed helping blacks to walk or carpool their way to work for almost a year. King said that he was uncomfortable with the position, feeling, like Moses, that he was not really suited for doing something like this. We are grateful that he finally agreed to lead the bus boycott, not just for its success, but that he soon became one of the great leaders who helped change the ugly practice of segregation in our country. But King did this task at great personal cost, for he never was able to settle into the academic life for which he yearned, and of course it cost him the ultimate sacrifice — his life! Worldly caring for others may be part of the richness of the Holy Spirit in our lives, though it always comes with a price.

III

Let's close by suggesting that the understanding and experience of the Holy Spirit also may be found in art — visual, musical, and literary. It is sad that our Puritan forebears were so negligent of these manifestations of the Holy Spirit. They preached against all the forms of human artistic endeavor with a heavy hand. Not only did they restrict artistic freedom in their community at large; they also stripped their places of worship and their liturgies of any artistic richness. Plain, unadorned, and simplistic were the norms for these folks. At Thanksgiving, while we can remember their courage and tenacity of the Plymouth Pilgrims and their neighbors in the Massachusetts Bay Colony, we do not have to applaud their cramped understanding of the place of artistic achievement in the celebration of life before God.

Today we wonder at some of our modern megachurches who seem to have fallen once again for impoverishing plainness in their sanctuaries. Gone are the cross, candles, icons, vestments, and the heroes and heroines of the faith caught up in rich stained glass, the organ, sturdy hymns, and choral music. Instead, there are potted plants, a preaching stand, and a drop-down screen. Of course, we can argue that this plainness may help win those without any church artistic experience, but some of might wonder if all this is as effective in winning converts as it is touted, and whether or not we are settling for a plainness that dooms us to the artistic welfare rolls.

Let's not settle for anything but the fullness of God's blessing of the Holy Spirit. This blessing does call us to serious discipleship, but it also fills us with a richness of faith, joy, and hope that makes it well worth the venture. Let's keep the spirit of the Apostolic Jerusalem Church that was not content to let anyone be without the wider and more complete blessing of the Holy Spirit.

You Can't Whistle The Finale
From Beethoven's Fifth Symphony!

Halford Luccock, onetime professor of homiletics at Yale Divinity School, told of going to a children's musical recital when a program announcement caught his attention. The announcer said, "And now Daisy Smith is going to whistle The Finale from Beethoven's Fifth Symphony." In horror, Luccock muttered under his breath, "No she isn't. It can't be whistled!" Luccock had it right. It takes a full orchestra of strings, brass, woodwinds, and percussion along with an able conductor. The Finale from Beethoven's Fifth is no solo job!

I'm quite certain that our text from 1 Corinthians 12:1-11 would have been one of Luccock's favorites. Paul is writing about the gift of the Holy Spirit and how it endows Christians with diverse gifts — teaching, preaching, healing, and others. Then, just to make certain that no one thinks the gift of the Holy Spirit is for one's own personal, private edification, Paul says that the Spirit is given only for the common good of the church. There is no receiving the Holy Spirit for one's personal enjoyment or edification — it's no solo thing. Luccock must have loved this passage.

One of the biggest dangers to our secular or sacred lives is to think that we can live to ourselves, in our own private, little world. In response to some concerns about the future solvency of the Social Security System, it has been proposed that we allow a certain privatization of future individual accounts. Essentially, this means withdrawing monies that would be normally deposited into the system by all Americans. Many are alarmed at this proposal, for it moves toward an individualism that favors the well-to-do, and favors those of means at the expense of the less favored. Spiritually, it creates a pervasive climate where people are encouraged to think that they can manage their economic future apart from all others. Privatization does not reflect the best in American values or those of our major religious traditions. Even when there is no Revolution at stake, Benjamin Franklin's comment rings true, "If we don't hang together, we'll all hang together." Hanging together is not very high on the list of many Americans today, and certainly not on the agenda of many political types today.

Unfortunately, the church has a long history of "Daisy Smithism," concentrating on personal, individual salvation without any concern for others, or the salvation of nature and the cosmos. The Protestant evangelistic tradition has traveled along this unbecoming fault line, blind to contrary traditions like we have from Paul today. Protestants have allowed Christians to speak of "personal salvation in Christ" while having no developed sense that salvation means involvement in the church, and involvement in ministering to the personal and public needs of the world. Talk to many Christians in the Protestant evangelical tradition and they will speak glowingly about having accepted Jesus Christ as their personal savior, with the only obligation seeming to be bringing others to this glowing, private moment.

One of the grandest exceptions to all of this was John Wesley, the founder of the Methodist tradition. Wesley was no slouch on the matter of personal evangelism. But he didn't stop there. He knew it wasn't sufficient, he got off a famous saying that went, "There is no religion but social religion, and no holiness, but social holiness." Wesley, like Luccock knew that the things that really count are corporate, not private and individualistic. And, both of them were aware that any private and individualistic achievements came out of corporate backgrounds.

We may be pleased that many churches that have largely presented an individual gospel are getting involved in social needs around them. Most of them have become involved in world and national hunger. While they do not touch the "not button" issues like tax structures, affirmative action, homosexuality, global warming, or the care of the environment, their newly found sense is that salvation is linked to something larger. They know it isn't just hustling down to the altar and mumbling a few words about accepting Jesus while the organ plays, "Just As I Am," and this is refreshing. Not only the conservative churches but also the mainstream churches, caught in their frantic plunge into frantic efforts at church growth, have often muted their social concern and settled for a comfortable, individualistic faith. A recent news comment in *The Christian Century* makes the same point, in responding to some remarks by Sally Morgenthaler in *Theology, News & Notes*, Spring. She says:

> *The preferred form of worship in many congregations consists of a welcome twenty minutes of singing contemporary music, then a special musical performance and a sermon ... Whatever else happens in contemporary worship is secondary to "disseminating information people need in order to gain more control over their lives" and to ensure that they achieve "individual happiness. (Never mind that control is an illusion and happiness is transitory. See Ecclesiastes.)"*

Let us list four places where our salvation can be whistled more effectively. The first is within the local congregation. Perhaps this is already clear from what has been said. The local church is a place where we join with other Christians on a journey toward a personal Christlikeness, and a personal reality that will ultimately have an effect on the whole world. We must always remember that the Apostle Paul placed his converts into those tiny churches he found or founded in the cities wherever he went. Paul certainly knew the shortcomings of those churches, just as you and I know the shortcomings in the churches to which we belong, but we also ought to know that without the church, any church, our lives in Christ will wither and die. The church is the first place where the fullness of salvation in Christ is recognized.

The second place where our salvation can be more effectively whistled is in contact with other Christian traditions. These are

Christians from styles of doctrine, worship and actions that often are quite different from our own. At first they will seem strange to us. Sometimes they will seem frightening or even threatening to our faith, but in time these encounters can enrich our own faith and witness. We will learn that there is a Christian diversity that fits Jesus' comment, "Other sheep I have, that are not of this fold" (John 10:16). Another scripture that would ground this experience is Paul's classic word, "In Christ there is no Greek nor Jew, no slave nor free, no male nor female, for you are all one in Christ Jesus" (Galatians 3:28). Bridging over into our Christian traditions is the second place where a more full Christian salvation may be experienced.

The third place where our salvation may be more effectively whistled is opening ourselves to the many non-Christian religious traditions. To shield ourselves from these non-Christian traditions is becoming more difficult each day. A friend says he went out one morning to pick up the paper. As he looked up he saw a man dressed in a business suit and tie, with a turban wound around his head, coming around the corner in his Volkswagen. My friend said that one, single moment informed him that he lived in a much different world than the one in which he had grown up. He would have to grow into this new world.

Our salvation in Christ may mean discovering how the revelation of God's love in Christ fits in with the other revealings of God's love and truth in the other religious traditions. For many of us, at least initially, this may be very difficult. To do this may seem to give up too much of our own faith. It may not be something that we can do at first. Yet gradually, perhaps by the power of what we call the Holy Spirit, we find it within ourselves to join in this effort — we want to discover where God has been sharing God's own love apart from our own biblical tradition. In doing so, we will not cease to be Christians, nor will we cease giving our witness to Christ, but we will find enrichment in knowing the wider mercy and love of God to all humanity. So, immersing ourselves in the traditions and scriptures and worship of non-Christian religions may be a third place for us to discover the fullness of salvation in Christ.

The fourth place where our salvation may be more effectively whistled is the company of right-minded unbelievers. It has often been noted that Pope John XXIII began his encyclical on world peace, *Pacem en Terris*, by addressing it "To All Men of Good Will." He wrote before our consciousness about politically correct language, yet we can think that had he propagated his encyclical some years later, his church Latin would have been translated, "To All Persons of Good Will." Either way, his was a radical statement. He was insisting that the issue of world peace was not just a matter for Roman Catholics to concern themselves. Nor did he seem to think that the larger Christian community was up to bringing about a peaceful world. Strikingly, he called upon all people of "good will," believers and nonbelievers alike, to give themselves to the task of making a safe and peaceful world.

John XIII, perhaps unknowingly, has set a precedent for modern-day Christians wanting to work out their salvation. There are these great issues threatening humankind in today's world. Pope John got hold of one: world peace. We might also name a few more — hunger, AIDS, terrorism, global warming, disappearance of the South American rainforests, illegal drugs, crime, street violence, underfunding of public needs, and shortage of medical care. You may have a list of your own. The point is this — our lists mean that we are all convinced that Christ calls us as much to these great public needs as to the private evangelistic moment. Furthermore, we are all at risk and there is no secure shelter from the consequences of not trying to solve some of these problems.

If Christians are going to join the effort to battle some of the problems that plague humankind we will soon discover that the effort will need more than just dedicated Christians. We will need those Pope John called "persons of good will." These will often be people of no faith. They do not belong to the church and if we begin to take church to them they will refuse to listen to us. If they were part of the church at one time in their lives, they have parted from it and have no intention of going back. Yet, they are as deeply concerned about these issues as are Christians. They will give of themselves as sacrificially to these causes as Christians, and sometimes more so. They may have a deaf ear for Christian doctrine and any talk about salvation in Christ, but for many of them they live lives of loving concern that can put us to shame. We need not fear that being with, and working with, these nonbeliving "persons of good will" will shatter our faith, or even lessen it slightly. Interestingly, it will increase our faith in Christ, for we will discover the miracle that Christ's love can come to us through those who profess nonbelief in him. The fullness of Christ overcoming the falseness of an individualistic understanding comes to us as we give ourselves in great tasks alongside the good-willed non-believers.

No, Daisy Smith can't whistle The Finale from Beethoven's Fifth Symphony, but she can play it if she finds someone beyond her solitary self. Might I suggest she drop down into the second violin section, or the cellos, or violas? Perhaps Daisy would prefer the clarinets or the oboes or English horns. If Daisy is the noisier type, we might go over to the trumpet or trombone or tuba section, and if she likes variety, she could join the percussion section, for they play all those wonderful instruments from drums to cymbals to chimes to marimbas. And, if she joins the orchestra in the Beethoven Fifth, then it will really be played with all the passion and wonder that such music has to bless us.

Epiphany 3
Ordinary Time 3
1 Corinthians 12:12-31a

Who's Going To Play Second Horn?

I know someone who achieved a modest excellence in playing
the French horn in his high school days. He mastered the first movement of the Strauss Horn Concerto in F, and received a superior
rating in a music educator's contest. Then he entered the school of
music at the state university thinking that surely he would become
the first horn immediately, but this didn't happen. At the university
there were other fine horn players, one in particular. It became obvious to our friend that he would never sit in the first chair. The
best he ever could do was play second or assistant first horn.

This is the way it is in life, isn't it? We are not going to play
first horn on the SAT list, at the office, as a pastor or a layperson in
the church, as a public servant, or as an author or literary figure.
Recently, a sportscaster was describing a player who parlayed his
mediocre talents into a starting berth on the Major League All-Star
Team. "He's a bit slow, and he doesn't have a good arm," the sportscaster said, "and he doesn't bat for a high average. But here he is
tonight, starting at second base." This player accepted his "second
horn" status and has become an inspiration to all the rest of us
"second horn" people.

Our lection for today deals with a lot of Corinthian folks in the
church who thought they ought to be playing first horn. Since there
were only a few leadership positions available, many were going
to have to settle for "second horn" spots. Of course, Paul puts all of
this in terms of the various gifts of the Holy Spirit. In last week's
lection, he describes how the Spirit offers a variety of gifts for the
common good of the church. Today, he is continuing this theme

69

that the Spirit allows no superiority among Christians in the church, for all are one and all gifts of the Spirit are one — the gifts of the first horn, as well as the gifts of the second horn.

Most Churches Need To Learn To Play Second Horn

Someone needs to voice a bit of realism to the churches of our day — most are going to be fated to playing second horn. They will not double or triple their size by using the right church growth program, nor will they fantastically increase their membership by having some winsome, razzmatazz pastor in the pulpit. Unusual growth isn't going to happen. They may experience no growth at all. They certainly aren't going to become one of those mega-churches, so perhaps a lot of us can quit spending our money on church growth books and attending church growth seminars. We can cease going to our judicatory and pleading for a pastor who will win a whole bunch of new members to our congregation. Even if we have been a first horn church in the past, it is not likely that we will recover that status. We must settle, graciously, to being a second horn church. And still further in sober realism, some of our churches will die despite all our efforts and prayers.

The church growth movement in today's church is often a cruel deception. Driven by the social sciences, meaning it is more guess and hunch than solid science, it programs, charts, categorizes, and details how a church can grow. Church leaders from the highest levels of the judicatories down to pastors and members in the local churches have been caught up in the slick frenzy of church growth. A lot of time and money has been spent on church growth projects. Expectations have been high. Yet there is little proof that most of the programs work. The statistics have come forth that tell us that we cannot manage the Holy Spirit in such a way as to get new folks into the pews on Sunday morning.

The cruelty in all of this is that pastors and congregations sense they are failures because having tried these church growth programs, held prayer meetings to petition for growth, and slipped in a bit of contemporary music into the morning service, they still have not seen any growth. Is it possible in God's wisdom that most churches will not ever grow, that growth in members is not one of the measurements of the witness of the church? I know this is difficult in modern America where almost everything important is measured in numbers, bigness, and size.

The late Norman Cousins, editor of *The Saturday Review*, said that he didn't think that the world would end as T. S. Eliot said, "with a bang and a whimper." Cousins said the world would end with some CPA shouting, "cost benefit ratio." We prize everything that can be measured and the largest measurement receives the greatest honor. First horn is always more honored than second horn. A 3,000-member church is always more honored than a 300-member church. Church denominational leaders and leaders in the local congregation, pastors and lay leaders, could do much for the rampant false measurement of success in the life of the medium- and small-size churches, by insisting that growth is pretty far down the list of things that count, if it counts at all. We all know that there are some churches that are dying and soon will cease to exist. Yet, they can be successful right up to the day they close their doors — something the church growth folks' doctrines fail to consider.

Churches Can Help Their Pastors Play Second Horn

Sometimes it is overlooked that churches can have a role in ministering to their pastor. Today in our topic, I am suggesting that congregations can help their pastor to play second horn. Most pastors, particularly young pastors, are full of ambition. They are impressed with their own abilities and think, like our culture encourages, that pastoring a large church would honor their talents and skills. Once in a while, this happens; a young pastor is called or appointed to a large congregation. But most pastors begin in small congregations and hope to move up to larger and larger congregations until they reach that large church that matches their estimate of success.

Most pastors, however, stay at the medium and small congregation level. It is not that their skills and talents are less than those who move on to larger congregations, it is because of supply and demand. Today, there are many more pastors than there are congregations. Much of this is because of the entrance of able and fine women into ordained ministry creating an excess of pastors. This means that some men and women go without a call or an appointment. Judicatories have difficulty finding congregations to which to send these folks. This means that pastors just entering the local church pastorate, as well as those already there, will find the sluggish mobility from small to larger congregations a burden on their spirits. This is in contrast to the '50s and '60s when a shortage of pastors meant a more rapid upward mobility. In the late '60s, a national denomination merger played out in one judicatory that the smaller partner to the merger brought 200 congregations and only about ten of those being sizeable. All this meant a huge loss of upward mobility for the larger partner of the merger and a gain of upward mobility for the smaller partner in the merger. This has not changed to this date.

Now pastors are not angels or saints. Try as they might, they cannot completely stuff their culturally fed feelings that success is pastoring a large church. Listen in on any group of pastors talking about the churches they pastor and you'll hear something like this:

Pastor A: Hello, Pastor B, how's it going over at your church?

Pastor B: Oh, we're getting along. How is it with you?

Pastor A: Great! We took in 200 new members this year and we're now up to 1,550 members and almost 800 in Sunday morning worship. Our budget is now $2,000,000. *(puffed with pride he comments)* You didn't tell me much about your church.

Pastor B: Well, we've no great story like yours. We confirmed five new adults, and four teens this year. But for some reason attendance at morning worship is dropping. We get only about 140, and our budget may not cover our missionary concerns next. I feel pretty depressed about it all.

72

As you can see in this conversation, Pastor A has little sense that he/she is the right person in the right place at the right time. His or her success probably has little to do with his or her abilities. They are in circumstances where the church is destined to grow, like the '50s and '60s when it was said that if a church was built almost anywhere and opened the front doors, people would flock in, regardless of the competence of the pastor. Pastor A seems to be in that situation.

Pastor B is caught in the cruel circumstance of our cultural assumption that a larger bottom line is indicative of more success than a lesser. He/she judges himself/herself by growth of the congregation, the budget, and the size of the congregation at Sunday morning worship. He/she has been told by the church growth movement, that there is no reason that his/her congregation should not be growing. So Pastor B considers himself/herself a failure.

A local congregation can minister to Pastor B by helping himself/herself to see that pastoral success is not a matter of bean counting at all. Pastoral success is measured by how effective the pastor has been in enlarging the congregation's vision of what the church can be in their community wherever they are. The pastor's success can be measured by how skilled the pastor has been in creating the reality of the church over the comfortable but restrictive congregations of which we so often are a part. One woman from the deep south found herself in a small northern, suburban congregation undergoing racial integration. When leaving the congregation as her husband was being transferred she said, "I don't know that I always liked being here, but it really made me think." The pastor along with his laypeople had successfully been the church, in this woman's discomfort, but in a way not reported on some judicatory report.

A congregation can help Pastor B to be successful when it affirms his/her right to preach the scriptures and doctrines in new and modern interpretations no matter how distressing they are to some of the members of the congregation. The congregation will understand that there is no win-win place in this matter. Either way fundamentalists or modernists will be upset. A choice must be made, and if the church looks to the future and to those who will come to

Christ and to the Bible and the teachings of the church, it makes sense to present them in a modern style. A congregation that affirms their pastor's right to preach and teach freely from his/her pulpit is helping their pastor to feel successful no matter if he or she is playing second horn.

When They Are Gathered At The Chancel

We have all witnessed this scene: the bride and groom are standing at the altar of the church surrounded by the members of the wedding party, their families, and the congregants. The pastor has opened the ceremony with scripture and prayer, and has sought the blessing of both sets of parents to the marriage. Then the members of the wedding party sit on the front pews and the bride and groom are seated in the chancel facing the congregation. The pastor prepares to read some scripture before offering a brief homily to the couple and to the congregation. Often, the pastor reads the entire thirteenth chapter of Paul's first letter to the Corinthians.

What a privilege we have today to ponder this great New Testament writing, one which can be affirmed by all religious traditions and faiths. It is a universal statement of the sort of inner transformation out of which we may live to make the world a more decent place for others and for ourselves. Without force, it falls into three sections that we will take up in order.

The Centrality Of Love (vv. 1-3)

In these opening verses, Paul says that if I have a real, staggering God-charged moment, so that my tongue rattles on in strange sounds, but have not love, I am just a lot of empty pop cans on their way to the recycling center. If I have a ton of smarts and can predict the drift of the political scene, and if I can really understand quantum physics, and if my faith impresses all my friends and acquaintances, but do not have any love, I am not on God's short list.

If I play a lot of rock concerts and turn all the proceeds over to feed the poor, I may only be a grandstander. And if I fast in my comfortable apartment on behalf of the dying children of Africa, I may only be calling attention to myself, not doing any love stuff.

Paul is calling attention to the truth found in all the religious traditions that the inner motive must be pure or else the outward deed is suspect. It is this inward transformation that is the personal goal of the faithful devotee. There is the story of an old-timer who said he believed in life beyond death "because he was just getting fit to live with!" There have been some parts of our Christian traditions claiming an instantaneous conversion from an ungodly will into a perfectly loving godly will and emotional bearing. We can admire the high standards and aspirations of such folks, but most of us think that our old-timer was more correct: It takes a long, long time for us to grow into the inward love described by Paul.

Christian religious scholars have long noticed that the New Testament scriptures follow the Hebrew Scriptures in being "eschatological." This is a word that sounds strange to many of us sitting in the pew. However, it is just a Greek word used when the New Testament was compiled in Greek. Eschatology or eschatological simply means "the end." One meaning of eschatology points to what will happen at the end of the physical universe or the cosmos some billions and billions of years in the future. For today's text, it means something a bit different — that we must think that the transformation of our hearts into a fully loving reality is eschatological — it can only come at the end. We will always be aware how even our best outward displays of love to others, and to ourselves, are not unmixed. Often our actions are only for our own self-satisfaction or to fill our need for recognition and the approval of others. In such painful awareness we will confess our lack of love and pray for strength to have more love for tomorrow, hoping that there will be some margin of increase as we go toward the end.

What This Love Looks Like (vv. 4-7)

So now Paul gives us some clues as to how we may observe love working in others and in ourselves:

Patience
Kindness
Not envious
Not boastful
Not arrogant
Not rude
Does not insist on its own way
Is not irritable or resentful
Does not rejoice in wrongdoing
Rejoices in the truth
Bears all things
Believes all thing
Hopes all things
Endures all things

In these fourteen virtues, seven are positive and seven are negative. I doubt that Paul was counting how many positive and how many negative illustrations of love he was listing. My bet is that it just came out that way. The case hardly needs to be made for the positive things in life. The late Mr. Rogers, of television, has taught us how dangerous the negative is to children and adults. Part of the terrible violence of our day comes from people made to feel that they are worthless and of no importance. Every day we all need to sing one rousing chorus of the old '40s pop song, "Accentuate The Positive, Eliminate The Negative." But once in a while we might pay attention to the negative, for if properly handled it has some important stuff for us to consider, too.

Paul gets off four negative unloving traits in a row: Don't go around hanging your tongue out over that fancy car your neighbor has (envy). Don't tell everyone at the office how big a raise the boss gave you at your annual review (boastfulness). Don't snub your old high school football buddy at the class reunion who's had lots of bad luck while you've done pretty well (arrogance). Don't mistreat the clerk at the airline counter when she can't find the reservation you made six months ago (rudeness). Don't throw your cards down on the table and leave the Friday night social gathering if they don't want to play your particular brand of gin rummy (insisting on your own way). Don't always remember how Uncle Charlie talked incessantly while you wanted to watch the Super Bowl (irritability and being resentful). And don't refuse to offer your elderly neighbor a ride to the polls because you know he will vote differently than you for the school levy (rejoicing in wrongdoing).

Of course, something needs to be said for those seven wonderful, positive love virtues: patience, kindness, rejoicing in the truth, bearing all things, believing all things, hoping for all things, endurings all things. Couldn't we run a little comment on each of these, too?

> Patience — being in life and commitments for the long run
> Kindness — remembering we all need a large dose of forgiveness
> Rejoicing in the truth — welcoming the truth, even at our expense
> Bearing all things — trusting that nothing is beyond God
> Believing all things — God will reveal the right things to believe
> Hoping for all things — hope will never cease
> Enduring all things — knowing that the end will make it all worthwhile

Pastors know that the brides and grooms hearing these words at their weddings are not really hearing them. Nor are the members of the wedding party hearing them, either. The mother of the bride is wondering if the caterers showed up. The father of the groom is wondering if the band will play some of those danceable, old, Guy Lombardi tunes. And the grandparents of both the bride and the groom are hoping they can gracefully leave the reception at an early hour in order to get home for a good night's sleep. But a few in the congregation might be listening.

Chapter thirteen of First Corinthians is not specifically about marriage at all. It is working over a larger field — that of loving Christian discipleship, but there is no harm in reading it. It certainly is considerably better than those mushy, murky, and placid alternatives like Kahlil Gibran and others. After all, your text at a wedding or anywhere else has a starchy realism about it that, even errs on something like a football coach's pre-game locker room talk. It plays better in our world where Pollyanna does not reign supreme. A marriage or two might be renewed with such works as these positive virtues and they will continue to be read.

Real Love Is Like Super Glue (vv. 8-13)

Most of us have had a traumatic experience with Super Glue, that bonding agent in a tiny little tube, that sooner or later glues our fingers together. Then comes a cry and a dash for our wife's finger-nail polish remover. Well, real love of any sort is like Super Glue — it is permanent. The only difference is that for real love there isn't any solvent to break the bonds of love.

Paul says our predictive ability is seriously limited and our great spiritual experiences can stop suddenly, as will our ability to penetrate the knowledge of existence. We are doomed to know only just a bit of the truth. All our vaunted ways are like the ways of little children and we will know the full truth only at the end. He says it's like seeing in a dim mirror and then coming face-to-face with the whole truth of things. Right now, we know only a fraction of things, heading toward a day when we will know completely, just as God has always fully known us. It's true that faith, hope, and love are part of us now, but it is Super Glue love — always permanent and something we can count on — God working within us and in our world.

Epiphany 5
Ordinary Time 5
1 Corinthians 15:1-11

The Good News Of Christ

Now I would remind you, brothers and sisters, of the
good news....   — 1 Corinthians 15:1a

Some years ago, there was that gentle stage musical, *The Fantasticks*. It must have struck something about our human condition because it established a record-breaking run and still is produced in many university and amateur theaters. The centerpiece song was titled, "Try To Remember," a waltz-like song that urges us to remember back to the mellowness of September life when the cold chills of December have descended upon us.

Our biblical religions — Judaism, Islam, and Christianity, are religions of the future. We sense that God is always calling us out into tomorrow, even in the midst of our distresses, both publicly and privately. The Hebrew Psalms make this point again and again. There is something joyful and hopeful in September's life. However, there may also be December moments, when the presence of God seems closed off either in our private lives or in our historical future. In one of the of the German prison camps during World War II, where some Jews were imprisoned, they knew they were doomed to die by the gas chamber or by starvation, a few of them gathered daily to celebrate the Torah and the prayers of the faith. Even in such terrible circumstances they could remember the September lives they previously led before God, who held them in whatever future awaited them.

The crucial issue is when we come to our December moments. Some of these might be heartbreaking disappointments, a

81

devastating illness, the death of a spouse or partner, the betrayal of a friend, or the loss of a job. It could also include the narrowing of our congregation's or denomination's theology and teaching, the outsourcing of our jobs, or the prejudice against an ethnic son-in-law or daughter-in-law.

At this point, if we have no warm September to remember, we will be in wretched shape. It was the genius of the biblical religions that they had rich September resources to remember, going all the way back to Abraham and Sarah. In the seventh century B.C.E., while in captivity in Babylon, they developed a metahistory that included the whole humanity and creation. They concluded that God was really doing something with creation and with the human race that even their suffering and death could not deter. Paul called this the "good news" which Christ had so wonderfully acted out in his life, death, and resurrection. All this would take them through their Decembers, whether they lived or died, whether they became successful or failed, whether they overcame their illnesses or not, or whether the public life improved or not.

Last of all, as to one untimely born, he appeared also
to me.   — 1 Corinthians 15:8

Some of us have always been part of, or have become part of, denominations that elect their denominational leaders. I suppose the majority of us do it this way. America has democratized the church in many, many ways. However, there is a lingering undemocratic pretense that prevails in many judicatory elections. It holds that anyone panting to be elected to a denominational high office must pretend not to be interested any such office. Even more uncouth is to openly solicit votes.

Well, it was certainly not this way in the early New Testament church. People had to struggle for recognition of their skills and abilities to leaders, pastors, administrators, teachers, apostles, and evangelists. Paul was among those folks who needed to make their case to be among the higher level, early church leadership. How did he do it?

One way was to claim that the resurrected Jesus had appeared to him, too. Those who had witnessed the empty tomb, had seen Jesus and touched his resurrected body and wounds, had talked with him on the Emmaus Road, and had stood with him just before his ascension — all these were authorized by this experience to be leaders of the church. The catch is that Paul was not there for all of this. He was still a young rabbi and not yet a Christian. The genius of Paul was to insist that the Jesus who spoke to him on the Damascus Road was the same resurrected Jesus who appeared to those earlier witnesses of the resurrection experience. Therefore, his later resurrection experience made him just as much a top-drawer disciple as anyone else. Apparently, he made his argument stick, for otherwise we would not have his ministry or his writings filling up most of our Christian testament. He interpreted his experience of Jesus on the Damascus Road as a resurrection experience equal to all the rest.

In many ways, we're also grateful that Paul's take on the resurrection gives us a way of understanding it that better fits our modernity. Many of the older, traditional Christian testament resurrection accounts of the empty tomb, of touching the resurrected Jesus, of talking with him on the Emmaus Road, are profound accounts of the effect of the resurrected Jesus on the lives of the early Christians and those of the early church. But to many moderns they seem to be dubious history and when they are studied or preached as actual history, we feel the best part of these stories is left out. These older accounts are personal statements of faith. If we insist on them as history, some of us are eliminated.

Paul's resurrection experience was a moment when his faith was radically changed and his life-direction reoriented. Something real did happen to Paul that could best be described as a real, historical event. It made him turn from evil to good, from Satan to Christ, and this is resurrection, no matter the vehicle that delivers its truth and power.

... and so you have come to believe.
— 1 Corinthians 15:11b

There are two sets or groups who have made us what we are. One set is our immediate and larger family. We are all immigrants to this land, even the Native Americans, whom Will Rogers said met the arriving boats filled with New England Puritans. In many ways, these new arrivals paid little attention to their native heritage and culture. The lure of a new beginning in a new land was so strong that second generation immigrants made serious attempts to free themselves from their forebears.

Now we are quite interested in our forebears. We search out our families back through the generations as far as we can. The genealogical records comprised by the Mormons in Salt Lake City attract thousands of people who are searching for information about their past families. Most modern families have someone who is looking into their family history. My pastor friend has a first cousin doing this for his family. She reported that he and all the family are distantly related to both Theodore and Franklin Roosevelt.

The humor in all of this is that his uncle and her father would have gone ballistic at this information, for they considered FDR to be the ruin of America! But the drive behind all of this family information of generations gone by is to gain a sense of reverence and appreciation for their gifts of character, faith, and courage to us. Even when we sort out what we now call "dysfunction families" or even "abusive families" there are usually strong and stable families that have blessed our lives, even people that live only in memories to present generations as the Hebrews line, "by so great a cloud of witnesses" (12:1). Early television newscaster, Edward R. Murrow, said all that he was, he owed to his handicapped college speech teacher, Clara Anderson. For the rest of us, the person who makes us who we are is generally found in our families — immediate or somewhere in the past. "And so you have come to believe" (v. 11).

This same truth applies to our religious life. Others have been the conduits through which the currents of the shocking news of the gospel comes to us, declaring that "God is light and in God is no darkness at all" (1 John 1:5). Others have shared with us that God loves us no matter what — that there is nothing that can separate us from the love of God. Some have dared to call us to believe, as does William Barclay, the translator and commentator of the New Testament for the average reader, a scandalous version of the love of God. Barclay says that the love of God is never conditional. It continues after death for all — even for the lowest of the low.

Heaven, for the saints and average Christians, may be a delightful place with only a few remedial classes on godliness required. Heaven for the pervasive ungodly may seem awful — like hell — and they will seek out the nonexistent exits. But in time, the ungodly will find their resistance being penetrated by the persistent love of God and by the loving godliness of their companions in heaven. They will slip into one of the remedial classes on godliness, slouching in one of the chairs in the last row. Bit by bit, they will discover that they were created for godliness, not for the old life of selfishness and security on their own terms. This may take a long, long, time. However, salvation is on its way and none will be left behind.

It is this wonderful gospel, this good news, that we have been taught by other Christians, not good news up to a point then bad news thereafter. We are deeply indebted to them. They have not taught a faith that requires anything but acceptance, and the opportunity for accepting God's offer in Christ never expires. This really is good news. This is certain good news that the people of world are urgently seeking.

You Can't Undo Appomattox —
So Let's Get On With It!

There are some things that once begun, cannot be undone. One of these is the surrender of the Confederate army under the command of General Robert E. Lee at Appomattox. Within a few days all the other Confederate armies in the field surrendered and the violent, bloody American Civil War was over. One of the major outcomes of our Civil War was the freeing of the slaves on the plantations, small farms, cities, and villages, mostly in the South. The cessation of hostilities at Appomattox inaugurated a dramatic social and economic change. No longer could anyone be kept in servitude to another without pay; nor could anyone or anyone's family be separated and sold as property at auction to the highest bidder.

Slavery was a cruel system and destructive to our civic, social, and religious values. While there were many who defended slavery on biblical, political, and economic grounds, many who owned slaves and understood its cancerous grasp on America's present and future felt helpless in freeing our nation from its destruction. One can sense this anguish in many of the founding fathers, especially those from the South who held slaves. We see this as they gave themselves to working out the Declaration of Independence in 1776 and later the Constitution of the United States in 1787.

To the North, Appomattox meant they had suppressed a political rebellion and freed the slaves in the process. To the South, Appomattox meant the humiliation of military defeat and the abolition of their distinctive way of life. To the slaves, Appomattox meant they were free from the bitter, inhumane, and crushing system of slavery. That for which they had hoped for over two centuries in America was a reality. Appomattox could not be undone. Freedom was real, not just a hope.

I

In our scripture for today, Paul says, "If for in this life only we have hoped in Christ, we are of all people most to be pitied" (v. 19). Like Appomattox, which can't be undone, Paul is saying that Christ's resurrection can't be undone. It is not just some fond hope; it is a hard reality giving us faith and strength for the living of this life. We may fully agree with Paul but still reserve our sense that hope is a prime commodity in the life of faith. Much of the time we have no solid, concrete, undeniable reality on which to lean. Of course, we would prefer otherwise. Yet, there are many times when the only thing we have is hope. Paul would say that a good dose of hope is better than none at all.

We must always remember that a balancing dose of realism must always be taken alongside a dose of hope. We sometimes hear that an attitude of optimism and hope in seriously ill patients almost guarantees their survival. We would certainly like to think that a positive attitude translates itself into a curative effect upon the body and its diseases. However, studies do not show that this is true. Patients who are hopeful and optimistic die from their disease at about the same rate as those who are not hopeful that they will survive. This could help our so-called faith healers to back off a bit when they suggest that faith and hopefulness will prolong their lives and overcome their illness. On the other hand, it could suggest that creating a hopefulness and optimism grounded in the determinism to live as well and happily as one can under the circumstances of one's illness, rather than succumbing to bitterness, futility, and hopelessness is to be preferred. Somewhere along the line, such people learn to sing a song, like, "We Shall Overcome" to express their hard-pressed hope.

Many slaves before Appomattox must have had only faith to keep them going. They hoped that one day they would be free — maybe themselves, perhaps their children, or their grandchildren, or their great-grandchildren. They hoped they might find their wives, children, and grandchildren who were sold to some far-off plantation in another state and resume some sort of family life. Even if they didn't see any real earthly possibility of this, they projected their hopes heavenward. All their hopes would come to pass in the great king's palace in heaven where all hurts and sadness would find solace. Paul would not deny them this and he certainly overwrote when he said, "If for this life only we have hoped in Christ we are of all people most to be pitied" (15:19).

II

But the slaves knew that after Appomattox their freedom from slavery could not be undone. It was a reality, hard and strong, with several protecting amendments soon to be written into the Constitution. Even then, this undeniable reality met with those who would attempt to undo it or blunt its force. Fairly soon the practice of racial segregation arose in both North and South. Laws denied African Americans the full exercise of their Appomattox freedoms. They could not associate with whites in public places, theaters, or stores. Restrooms and drinking fountains had separate facilities for whites and blacks. In many places, African Americans were denied the vote by ingenious means of exclusion and were restricted to the balconies of the churches or to creating their own separate churches.

Racial intermarriage was prohibited, and the public schools from the elementary grades up through the universities were also segregated. It was not until 1954 that the Supreme Court ordered the integration of the public schools, which proceeded in to some places at the point of the bayonet of the National Guard. President Lyndon Johnson and the Democratic Congress eliminated other segregation laws in the middle 1960s. Finally, much of the reality of Appomattox became clear to America and most of America realized, however reluctantly, that we were not going back.

Similarly, Paul is arguing that the resurrection of Christ is not some fond hope but has really happened. God has acted to raise him to a renewed ministry of love and justice for the lowest of the low. God has brought Christ out of the powers of death and made him even more effective as a spiritual leader than he was in life. His followers were beginning to ascribe all sorts of wonderful titles to him, trying to say something of their experience of how he had changed and renewed their own lives and called them into God's earthly and heavenly kingdom/realm.

We need not pick apart all these titles and descriptions that have been given to Christ as if they are tight, technical terms that can be judged as "good," "better," best," or even "unacceptable." They are all ways that Christians, in an earlier time, have attempted to talk about the risen Christ who became an escapable part of their personal and social world. This is why Paul writes in this nineteenth verse, "If for this life only we have hoped in Christ we are of all people most to be pitied." But we need no pity, do we?

III

Some years ago there was a book that was published by the title, *Stop Pussyfooting Through a Revolution: Some Churches That Did!* I don't know how many churches adopted the message of that book — perhaps very few. After all, most churches are places of great timidity, both conservative and mainstream churches. New ideas and new ways of thinking are not congenial to most congregations. Trying a new hymn or a new liturgy is almost always out of the question. In ways it is fitting to say of the church,

> *Our forebears have been members here,*
> *A hundred years or so,*
> *And to every new proposal*
> *They have always answered "no"!*

A similar line about the church's typical pussyfooting around serious proposals of the day is, "Well, if we've done it before, we'll try it."

The risen Christ who cannot be overcome by any of the forces of evil should embolden the church and its members to lose their timidity. Somehow, the conservative church has lost its focus on the evils that are destroying our lives in this world and instead is concentrating on getting us into a sin-free and evil-free heaven, just for mumbling a few words about Jesus, a rather minimal requirement, wouldn't you say? In all this concentration on getting ourselves and all the rest that we can to heaven, we are able to avoid the messy problems of hunger, political corruption, racism, family breakdown, drugs, war, terrorism, injustice, poverty, and the like. In the liberal church, the focus is on organ concerts, seminars on contemporary theology, church growth crusades, spiritual retreats, successful living preaching, and the correct liturgical colors for the church year. Again there is little engagement of such churches with the hurting world for which Christ died. But the risen Christ should force us out into these issues with Christians being in the avant-garde, not in the safety of the ranks in the rear. Perhaps our timidity of the pussyfooting type is why many non-church people have no good words for the church. They see the church as more interested in preserving or deflecting the world and seeking its own safety and comfort, than in wrestling with the tough issues of the day.

The film, *The Royal Hunt of the Sea*, has a telling moment. The Portuguese conqueror of the new world is moving through Peru's mountainous region until he comes to a place between two gigantic peaks. Only a flimsy rope bridge stretches between the peak where they are camped and the opposite peak where they must go. All are frightened at the thought of such a crossing. Inspecting his trembling force he discovers the clergy, immobilized by fear and apprehension, huddled at the rear of his column. Then he calls out in a loud voice, "The church goes first!" Could these words be something like the hard and uncompromising words of scripture from those of us who know the risen Christ? So why are we so timid?

> *The strife is o'er, the battle done;*
> *The victory of life is won;*
> *The song of triumph has begun;*
> *Alleluia!*

When Arlington National Cemetery Is Full

The honored dead from our fighting in Afghanistan and Iraq have created a problem for Arlington National Cemetery in Washington, D.C. So many have rightly claimed burial in Arlington National Cemetery that the cemetery is running out of space. Rightful burials may soon have to be denied because there is no place for them.

Some civilian cemeteries also face the same issue. They find their space locked in by developments or recreational layouts. They have a future of limited burial ground available for those who wish to bury their family and loved ones where they have buried family and friends for generations. When so much of our nation was unsettled and land was cheap this was not a problem. But with a growing population and industrial development there has become a scarcity of land for many things, including the burial of the dead. All this may force us to review our traditional ways of burying our dead. Land restricted only for the burial of the dead may no longer be an option for us.

A pastor I know was ministering to a young sportswriter who was dying from a dreaded disease. He told his pastor, "What I really want is to be cremated and have my ashes scattered from a plane over Yankee stadium!" Yankee stadium may not be the choice for all of us. We could be Cardinal fans, or we might prefer one of those modern stadiums named for orange juice or some predatory bank. Furthermore, this may not be legal, but it does suggest that we could begin to think of creative ways of handling our loved ones and ourselves at death.

I

Something of this whole issue comes out in our passage from 1 Corinthians today. Paul is working in Gentile territory but the gospel is coming from Hebrew culture. Gentiles are having great difficulty with any talk from the Hebrews about the resurrection of the body. While for the Hebrews, to speak and believe in the resurrection of the body poses no great intellectual or spiritual concern.

How often we have seen this in the long history of our faith. As the gospel has moved from one cultural and intellectual setting into another, there has often been great stress and conflict. Already Paul has been at the center of the kosher food law controversy — Hebrews versus Gentiles. The Hebrews wanted strict cooking and eating food laws while the Gentiles would have none of it. In the early 1500s when Europeans discovered they could think for themselves in human and religious matters, there came the great disruption of the church, focused in the person of Martin Luther.

Something of a continuation of this has pressed on into the twentieth and twenty-first centuries when Christians have felt no irreverence in testing doctrinal and biblical truth by what United Methodists often call "the quadrilateral." Sounding like a fancy football play, this is a statement about the four issues by which humans make judgments about theological truth, since we have no absolute, revealed, and final religious truth in this life. These four things are:

1. **scripture** — as studied and interpreted by persons;
2. **religious experience** — as informed by the church and the heritage of the church;
3. **tradition** — as the long history of individual and corporate experience of Christian life and living; and
4. **reason** — as the ability of critical thinking to sort out truth from competing alternatives.

Now this does not mean that all Christians of the twentieth or twenty-first century have adopted this style of Christian understanding. Many of them have wanted their faith to be sturdier — an inarguable absolute that will give all the truth about everything.

They want to eliminate the risky venture of faith to which the Bible really calls us. They want to know all the answers ahead of time. This is the Hebrew/Gentile disruption of the church in our time: absolution versus risky faith.

The Reverend Dr. Richard Wing of First Community Church in Columbus, Ohio, says there are really only two sorts of churches: "Answer Churches" and "Journey Churches." "Answer Churches" pass out the answers from the pulpit or in Sunday school each Sunday morning to eager folks in the pews, Bibles open, with pads and pens promptly scribbling all the wisdom down. Then there are the "Journey Churches" where the pastor and teacher challenge themselves to set out on, or continue on, the life of faith without knowing just how things will come out — save that God will be with them. The congregation and pastor are not given any guarantee their faith will bring them health, success, long life, or any of their dearest desires. Faith is no protection against the hurts, tragedies, and pains of life, but it does promise us something better, something that the folks who pant after clear and inarguable answers do not understand — God will be with us to help us make it through and help us grow in strength in the process. Perhaps this is something Paul had in mind when he wrote that phrase in the eighth chapter of Romans, "Nothing shall separate us from the love of Christ." This is all we really need.

II

Yet, there is this lingering issue of the resurrection of the body across the centuries. There seems to be a large portion of what we have already called the "Answer Church" taking its cue from some of the New Testament images of the return of Jesus that would resist any disposal of the body except burial in the ground. They reason from the scripture that when Jesus returns, the dead will rise from their graves in bodily form to meet Jesus and share with him in his kingdom. Certainly they would resist removal of bodies from cemeteries to make the land suitable for housing, industrial, or recreational development. Along with their distress at such a removal and relocation, they would also feel a certain irreverence about the whole process itself. Burial of the body in the earth has a strong hold on many in the church in our time.

Most of the folks in the "Journey Churches" would say that what we do with the body at death has only one concern: Can it be disposed in a reverent way? Some of these ways could be donating the body's organs for transplants or donating the body to a medical school for study. After this the body would be cremated and the ashes appropriately scattered or closeted. There would be no need for special land for burial of the body, making land space more available as our population increases.

Paul, in our Corinthian passage, argues for a reverent disposal of the body other than burial in the ground:

> *What I am saying, brothers and sisters, is this: flesh and blood cannot inherit the kingdom of God, nor does the perishable inherit the imperishable.*
> — 1 Corinthians 15:50

The kingdom of God is a reality that is experienced in this life and comes to us in its fullness at death. We have a strong taste of this realm through so many of our experiences of life. The Greeks named them Goodness, Beauty, and Truth, even though they were not thinking in biblical terms at this point. In the Bible, the kingdom is said to come to us when we pause to wonder at creation or nature. We sense the kingdom when we care for the poor and the disadvantaged. We are close to the kingdom when we hold out for righteousness even if it costs us much. We have already stepped into the kingdom when we have walked across the artificial boundaries of race, class, gender, sexuality, and nation. The kingdom is this all-encompassing coming together that God wishes for creation and humanity, a togetherness that is completely fulfilled on the other side of death.

It doesn't really matter much what we do with our deceased outside of three things:

1. We reverence their bodies and, in death, honorably dispose of their bodies.

2. We consider cremation as a reverential way of disposing of the body since Paul has suggested that it is not needed in the kingdom beyond death.
3. We might consider allowing the body to be used for organ donation or given to a medical school for study.

All of this could help alleviate the practical problem of space limitations for bodily burial in our nation's cemeteries from the impressive Arlington Cemetery on down to the cemeteries in the small towns and villages all across America.

When Truth Comes
Via An Invalid Argument

Sometimes truth comes to us by way of an invalid argument or perspective. Christopher Columbus sailed west over the Atlantic thinking that China was out there somewhere. But the truth of his search was clouded by his ignorance of the North and South American continents lying between China and himself. In France of the '30s and '40s there was the general concern, which proved true, that Germany would make a military move toward them. But this truth was embedded in a false premise that the Germans would make a frontal attack. Instead, they came down through the Netherlands and Belgium, as in 1914, and France fell easily.

In the Bible, the people of God caught the truth that God cared for their safety and well-being. Therefore, they argued, that they ought to destroy all their enemies: men, women, children, and all their livestock, when they defeated them in battle. The truth is sound — God does care for them, but the conclusion is abominable. God's care does not condone the abolition of our enemies. Then there are the biblical miracles. Their truth is sound. They speak to us about life as we live it in Christ today — not some 2,000 years ago. Many give up the faith because they cannot accept the invalid arguments of this being historical fact.

Today's scripture is something like this. Paul's concern in this closing part of 1 Corinthians 15 is to affirm the truth of life beyond death. This is a hope and a belief which is part of any Christian life — except for a few Christians who limit the gospel to this life. Most of us will think them wrong for we have a larger view.

I

Today Paul's argument will obscure the truth he wants us to believe, for he ties it to a conviction about the near return of Jesus. Of course, Jesus did not return in Paul's time, nor has he since. Many moderns live in a world that is culturally conditioned by science and critical history. We ask questions about the convictions we are taught and the causes we are urged to adopt. We do not accept any of these uncritically just because it comes to us from some authoritative book, or religious figure, or wisdom teacher, or scholar, or church. Wisdom must pass the test of humans and inspection. This change in understanding has been part of our western world for the last 300 years and shows no sign of abating even though there are large segments who would not accept this change.

So Paul's argument if invalid, does not mean that the truth to which it points is also invalid. It simply means that we must find an argument that fits the truth and is accommodating to our time and age. We might think of a couple of modern arguments which, though modern, are quite as invalid as Paul's.

One is the psychics who pretend to bring messages back from the dead to the living, often grieving loved ones. The brilliant scholar and liberal leader of the Episcopal church, the late Bishop James A. Pike, was so overcome with grief at the death of his son, that he resorted to a psychic to hear some word from his son. For a time, a quick-tongued psychic had a network television show and worked the audience with his so-called abilities seeming to become a conduit with the dead. But many of us began to wonder why the messages were so trivial when it would seem that the dead would have more urgent things to pass on to the living. The psychics seem to be a limp argument for a modern person to argue for a life after death.

The near-death movement fits into this same category. The movement members and scholars tell us that they, or people they have known, have supposedly been clinically dead and have returned to life. When telling about their experiences of "death" most of them describe it similarly: a tunnel of light, a peaceful feeling, seeing long dead loved ones and friends, and returning to life with a new feeling of reverence and gratitude. Only a few describe the experience as frightening, terrifying, and having no positive influence after resuming their lives.

Even here we must be very careful; we can be happy for those for whom this is a pleasant and life-changing experience. But, further medical study may conclude that these experiences are simply the result of typical brain chemistry reactions. Knowing what modern psychiatry tells us about how brain chemistry affects our moods and behavior, these near-death experiences may be explained by this. We must seek another, more sturdy argument for our belief in life after death.

II

When are we going to get over our obsession with our search for certainty — for chasing after an argument that will prove, to us and others, our deepest convictions? The conservative Christians are berated for searching for absolute truth out of the scriptures by their liberal Christian counterparts. Then the liberal Christians are berated by the conservative Christians for searching for absolute truth from science and philosophy. Both are afflicted with the disease of "certainitus" — a condition that will snuff out all vitality and attractiveness, if untreated.

The treatment is this: Hold our arguments — conservative or liberal ones — quite tentatively, keeping our eye on that to which they point. If the argument seems a bit shaky, out of date, or not relevant to the times in which we live, stuff it and find another. In time, this new argument may also suffer from invalidity, too. This is how science works so well. When science has a theory that doesn't fit the facts anymore, they toss it in the trash can and find a somewhat better one. They know that this new theory will someday be headed for the trash can because the truth for which they are searching is bigger than any theory than they can put together. Again, the truth is still there — our arguments are always a bit short of the truth.

This means that the religious person, no less than the scientist, can never have certainty no matter how either may boastfully rant and rave how they have discovered the exact will of God, or the "general theory of everything." I'm not certain how Einstein dubbed this human limitation, but I think he spoke of it as "humility." Paul speaks of this as "justification by faith." Our godly truths are beyond any human arguments. They are all with some fault or they call out for verification that cannot be had in this life. Instead they ask for a risky commitment in either religion or science, and neither need presume to be dominant over the other. They are both in the same predicament — the lack of ultimate certainty.

III

When Martin Luther discovered justification by faith in teaching the letters of Paul to his students in the monastery, the church did something that it often does to any great teaching: It applied it to only one segment of life before God. In this case it was God's relationship to us and our relationship to God. Granted, that all this was good news to many of his day. Beyond this, justification by faith was used by many for expressing their distress with the Roman Catholic church, as well as to express their growing sense of identity as German, Swiss, Scandinavian, and Slavic people. But Luther refreshed the church with Paul's insistence that we are put right with God through our faith, and in some interpretations, a faith which is also a gift of God to us.

So we may insist that using Luther's doctrine as a way of being in the church without having to be under the authority of Rome, or of not needing to deny one's ethnic impulses, was a serious misuse of his teaching. However, then and since, there are many areas in human existence in which justification by faith is highly relevant.

1. God's love is bigger than the death of the cosmos. While estimates of this are billions of years away, and much can happen between now and then, many scientists predict that somewhere out in time the cosmos will cease to exist. Does this mean the death of everything or is God's love able to gather up a dead universe and all existing life and bring it into God's eternal life? The only argument is faith that justifies such a belief, but it is not a certainty.

102

2. God's love will save all people at death — even bad people. Christian or not, immoral persons or not, Adolf Hitler, sexual predators, Madelyn Murray, suicide bombers, all are or will be saved. Why? Because good or bad we are God's sons and daughters. God is our parent. No earthly parent hands a child over to everlasting death; a parent opts for life, even for a monstrously, wayward child. Is this a certainty? No. But an argument justified by a belief in God's love.

3. God's love will help human progress in this world. We can quit focusing on going to heaven, although this is an important belief, and concentrate on making the world a better place for all: education, justice, good government, sustainable environment, food for all, end of racism and feminism prejudice, and businesses that serve the customer, not just the bottom line. Is this possible? Tough job? Certainly. But this image is found in lots of places in the scriptures, especially with the Hebrew prophets. Will God's love help us? Maybe — but not certainly. We just have to take a chance. We argue, justified by our belief in God's love.

4. God's love will help us to grow in Christian grace and behavior. God will help us become more godly. However, we must remember what C. S. Lewis so wisely said. Not all Christians begin the Christian life from the same starting line. Some who come from good Christian homes and upbringings start way up front. Those from non-Christian or abusive homes start much further back. So in running around the Christian course of life, some have a distinct advantage and some have a lot to make up. Yet, wherever we start, God will help us toward the finish line of Christ-likeness. Again is this a certainty? No — but this is an argument of justification by our faith in God's love, and even if this is all we have, it is still an argument upon which we can heavily lean.

We began this sermon by noting that truth can come by an invalid argument. As we went along we noted that some arguments were quite invalid for our own time. Some seemed more valid than others. We were finally forced to conclude that all our arguments, religious as well as scientific, are invalid against the fullness of religious or scientific truth. All we really have are arguments based on our best conclusions from the facts, the experiences, the reasons we can muster, and the traditions which we follow. Some feel this leads to desperation. Yet for others, it leads to an exciting journey. I invite you to that journey today.

The Transfiguration Of Our Lord
(Last Sunday After The Epiphany)
2 Corinthians 3:12—4:3

We're On Our Way, Baby

Today is the Sunday when we celebrate the Transfiguration of Jesus, a moment in his ministry when up on a mountain with Peter, James, and John, he became "transfigured" before them. They saw him in a more profound way. Paul's use of transfiguration seems based on the Hebrew Bible's account of Jesus' Transfiguration in Matthew, Mark, and Luke as well as a similar experience of Moses and the people of God in the desert. Once observed, Transfiguration Sunday leads us into the following season of Lent, which prepares us for Easter.

Interestingly, our passage may really be part of Paul's "third letter" to the Corinthians. Many think he sent 1 Corinthians as his first letter to them. Then, hearing some disturbing news about their behavior and faithlessness, he wrote off a furious and scolding letter which we think are chapters 10-13 of 2 Corinthians. Then being told that the Corinthians had heeded his warnings and stern admonitions, he wrote them a gentle and encouraging letter, chapters 1-9 of 2 Corinthians, from which our passage comes today. We could call this Paul's "third letter to the Corinthians."

If you will pardon me from talking a bit like Dick Vitale, that noisy and excitable network basketball commentator, we could not say, "How'd he do that?" but, in our best Vitalese, "We're on our way, baby." There is a world of difference here.

I

Many churches think they must draw people to their services by having some celebrity say a few words in the morning service. A few more will come to hear the university head football coach, but it can be asked if their coming has been for genuine reasons, or if the cause of Christ has been advanced. The same can be said about Ferris wheels and carousels on the church parking lot, along with a pig roast and a rock band concert. It's all exciting, harmless fun, but it does little or nothing for Jesus. Sometimes, one longs for the quiet simplicity and the plainness of a small, country church on a hot summer morning.

Down through the Christian centuries we have wanted something spectacular as the focal point of our religion. Other churches have their own Christian brand of the spectacular: the Bach's Mass in B minor, Handel's *Messiah*, the awe of a medieval cathedral, or high mass on Christmas Eve in St. Patrick's' Cathedral in New York City. We may want the extraordinary preaching of James Forbes from Riverside Church near Columbia University and Union Theological Seminary or even the quiet, fatherly sermons of Billy Graham in a crusade in some football stadium.

Only a Christian fool would dismiss any of these just because they are not at the precise intersection of our own Christian witness. Of course their power is in "How they'd do that, baby?" We wonder how Michelangelo got those marvelous paintings on the ceiling of the Sistine Chapel. Or we wonder how Richard Forbes does his penetrating preaching week in and week out. We focus on the marvelous quality of the moment — and well we should. We should soak ourselves in the B minor Mass, or worship in some megachurch, or attend Christmas Eve mass at St. Patrick's Cathedral.

The issue is not that they are an impediment to the faith. The issue is that they are all subsidiary to real faith and discipleship. They are subtle temptations to settle down to this spectacular witness to the faith and refuse to go on. In the gospel story of Jesus' Transfiguration this is just what happened. The disciples wanted to make the mountainous place a religious shrine where Jesus was the centerpiece with side booths for Elijah and Moses. In short, they wanted a Jesus theme park. The price paid would be that their ministry to the poor and needy would come to a halt. And since the poor and needy couldn't afford to come up the mountain to this wonderful place, they wouldn't bother the well-off folks who could hire a donkey and guide and make the trip.

II

After we have enjoyed the B minor Mass or the rousing preaching of Richard Forbes, it is fair to ask ourselves, "Are we any better for it? Has this experience made us more forgiving or more caring? Have we become more aware of our own faults, and have we resolved to do something about them?" This is the real question coming out of the Transfiguration, "Are we on our way, baby?"

The test of a religiously spectacular experience ultimately is whether or not it drives us to a deeper Christian life, personally and publicly. People will come back to a church that offers a strong fare of entertainment, both high brow or low, a classic car show, or the organ works of Claude Widor. Again, there is nothing wrong with any of these on either end of the cultural measuring stick. Their danger comes when they entice us to think we are being religious when we enjoy these moments for the sake of enjoyment alone.

Again, a little more Dick Vitale language: "Biblical religion is one tough cookie, baby." And even if Psalm 23 says God "makes me to lie down in green pastures," it is only for a little while. Soon the shepherd pokes us with his crook and we are told that it's time to move on. Biblical religion is a "move on" religion.

Other religions might be ones that try to help us make the best of life until we die unto nothingness or into some eternity, but not biblical religion. Other religions might turn inward and forget the needs of others and the injustices of history, but not biblical religion. Other religions might think it proper to cozy up to the rich and famous so we can have our own share of fame and fortune, but not biblical religion. Biblical religion says its primary call is to the poor, the sick, and the needy. Biblical religion says that its call is to challenge the injustices of economics, of political arrangements, of cultural customs, and of ethnic, gender, and sexual discrimination. Why? Because this is what Jesus and the best of the biblical heroes and heroines modeled for us. Why? Because this is how God cares and what really counts with God. Biblical religion is a tough cookie challenging any move we might want to make toward limiting our religion to an emotionally exciting or self-pampering affair. This is why the gospel account of the Transfiguration says Jesus scolded the disciples for thinking that he would give his permission for a shrine on the mountain, for they had work to do among the needy down in the valley.

III

Let's enumerate a few unusual ways by which we might measure that "We are on our way, baby!"

The first comes from the patriarch of United Methodism, John Wesley. When Wesley conducted the annual conferences of his preachers, he asked reports from all of them — something that might frighten the alb or robe off any modern preacher. Inevitably Wesley got to the question, "Did anyone get saved under your ministry this year?" Sometimes the preachers had to answer, "No." Then Wesley would ask a question that may seem strange to us, "Well then, did you make anyone mad?" Isn't that priceless? The last thing most modern preachers or laypersons would think of doing is making anyone mad. Anger is off our Christian radar screen. Tom Mullins used to say that he wanted at least someone in the congregation to be "tickethed off!" in lieu of salvation.

Yet, has the church, its lay and ordained leaders, become so genteel and so tame that we cannot dare to think of making anyone mad in the name of Christ or the gospel? Over the years, a pastor made some parishioners mad enough to leave the church because he insisted on interpreting the Bible in the best of modern critical knowledge. He did this because he felt that many in his congregation were turning a deaf ear to the gospel, or leaving the church because the gospel had become so encased in a pre-critical style. Another anger-provoking witness could be directed toward many social issues within and outside the church. Certainly, the gay/lesbian controversy is one of these, as the church seems to be blinding itself to the data that declares that homosexuality is a given, not a choice. So it's like punishing people for being left-handed.

A second unusual pattern by which we might hunch that "We are on our way, baby," would be to challenge some of the fads that keep coming down the pike, presuming to save the church. We have seen many of these in our time: goal planning as derived from business management styles; more formal worship with split chancels and pastors with albs and stoles. Then there are the contemporary music and praise singers in front of electronic guitars and percussion, 36-week-long Bible study groups, and formal manuscript preaching from most pulpits that is a real sleep inducer for many.

One pastor's father back in a small midwestern town in the 1930s told of being cornered by his pastor one evening after a board meeting. The pastor, a likeable, university- and seminary-trained Ph.D. asked why the congregation wasn't responding to this ministry. The pastor's father said as gently as he could, "I think it's because you read your sermons. There's no life in them." Late in his ministry, John Wesley discovered the power and freedom of preaching without a manuscript. Many a mainstream manuscript preacher might ponder the effectiveness of many conservative preachers who forgo the smoothness of language and richness of illustration and speak to their congregation without a manuscript between them.

One of the most disturbing fads, the church growth movement, is insistent that every church can, must, and will grow if enough prayer, hard work, and study are done — turning out to be a huge lie for most congregations and pastors. This can lead to depression and a sense of failure. Christian discipleship must ask some hard questions about any movement proclaiming to renew and revitalize the church. We have had countless instances of them since 1775, most with self-created credentials, and almost all of them failing to live up to expectation. Could we not ask them to make more modest claims? This unusual Christian virtue of truthfulness and modesty is terribly needed in the life of our churches today.

A final Christian witness, fairly lacking today, would be to jump into the political arena and find candidates of either party whose agenda more nearly matches up with a Christian point of view than the opposing candidate. This means that we disabuse ourselves of thinking that we can find the squeaky-clean candidate. All candidates have a skeleton or two in the closet, but most of them have a voting record that will show how they will line up on the issues when they are elected to their offices. By our financial and other support we can help to keep them invulnerable from the lobbyists and other interests that would buy their votes in return for help in their reelections.

The Transfiguration teaches us that Christ wants more than "Wow!" He wants, "How can I help, Lord?" And when we have asked this question, we are on the deepest level of our Christian journey, "We are on our way, baby." Thanks, Dick. Your ordination papers are in the mail.

Sermons On The Second Readings

For Sundays In
Lent And Easter

Dying And Rising
In The Lord

Richard Gribble, CSC

The process of dying and rising in the Lord is one that not only encompasses the liturgical seasons of Lent and Easter; it is a daily process of transformation that each Christian must engage, in order to walk successfully in the path of Jesus. This book was written at a momentous time in history when one man demonstrated how to transform the hearts and minds of many through his own death. Karol Wojtyla, Pope John Paul II, served God's people faithfully on the Chair of Peter for 26 years. His Lent and Easter transformation was a daily event, which he taught others was a necessary part of life. It is appropriate that this book be dedicated to Pope John Paul II, as an example of a great Christian who understood well and lived daily his dying and rising in the Lord.

Introduction

One day, a young boy and his grandfather were in a boat on a small lake. They had been fishing and were not very successful. As the boat drifted slowly along the placid waters, the two spoke about all sorts of things. The little boy became somewhat restless and began to look over the side of the boat seeing if anything more interesting was happening. He observed a group of water beetles that were flitting about as if they were playing. Then, quite suddenly, one crawled up the wooden oar of the boat. It attached itself to the oar by digging its talons into the wood. Quite unceremoniously, the beetle died. The boy's curiosity prompted him to show this phenomenon to his grandfather. The two then went back to fishing.

About three hours later the boy looked down at the dead beetle. What he saw startled him greatly. He stood up, almost forcing the small skiff to capsize. The beetle had dried up and now its shell began to crack open. Both the boy and his grandfather were intrigued as they watched the scene before them. Something began to emerge from the an opening in the shell. At first, there were antennae, then a large head, and then wings, until a full dragonfly had emerged. As the pair watched in awe, the dragonfly began to move its wings, slowly at first. Then, in flight, it began to hover over the area where the other water beetles continued to flit about in a spirit of play. They did not even recognize that this was the same beetle that had been one of them only three hours earlier. The boy took his finger and nudged the dried-out shell of the beetle. It was like an empty tomb.

Nature manifests a periodic dying and rising, whether it be the transformation of a water beetle into a dragonfly, a caterpillar into a butterfly, or the barrenness of winter into springtime blossoms and flowers. This natural transformation of living things illustrates well the essential message of the church's annual journey through Lent and Easter. The new life of the dragonfly, butterfly, and flowers cannot be achieved except through the experience of death. There is a price to pay to achieve the new beauty which transformation or resurrection brings. Each person, like the insects and plants in the created world, must endure a personal death to find the new life we seek. This is not only true at the end of our days; it is manifestly true and possibly even more important that we seek this experience each and every day. Jesus, through his personal Lent, moving from his temptation at the hand of Satan in the desert, to his agony in the garden of Gethsemane, his feeling of loneliness at the denials of Peter and the desertion of his other close followers, to his ultimate crucifixion, has shown us the way that leads to life. Yes, all the portents of nature, as well as the example of the one whose name we bear, demonstrates the path we must follow. It is not an easy path, but it is the only one that leads to life eternal. Thus, we must confidently enter this path knowing that the goal we seek will be worth every difficulty, problem, and challenge we face.

The Second Lesson Readings during these special liturgical seasons call us to experience personal rejection or loss so as to be transformed into the new person that Christ seeks for all who faithfully follow his lead. We are called at the outset to overcome and persevere through various hurdles and obstacles so as to build God's kingdom in our world. Additionally, we are challenged to review the conduct of our lives, to help carry the burden of others, and to be reconciled with our brothers and sisters, as well as Jesus. Once we have accepted the need for challenge and endured the pain of transformation, then we are ready for the special glory that resurrection brings to our lives. Our Easter joy allows us feel the hope which only Christ can bring, to experience the new life that the Lord promises, and to know that Jesus, the light of the world, rewards those who have successfully negotiated the Lenten path to reach Easter glory. Then we are ready to care for others, as our common vocation of holiness mandates we do.

The dying and rising of Jesus as experienced in this Lenten and Easter journey is very much analogous to nature's periodic rebirth. Nature has no choice but to follow this path; God has this pattern well programed. Since we have been given the gift of free will, however, the decision to follow in the footsteps of Jesus is up to us. The question for us is, of course, "Are we up to the task?" A short, but appropriate, poem, "The Lenten Cocoon" presents us with the challenge and the reward:

> *May my purple Lenten days*
> *of prayer, charity and self-discipline*
> *weave around my heart a reforming womb,*
> *so that at Easter's sunrise I may emerge anew*
> *— reborn in heart and soul,*
> *enabled to love without limits*
> *energized to pray always,*
> *engaged in peace and justice —*
> *and so truly able to celebrate*
> *a freshly joyous Resurrection Day.*

— Richard Gribble, CSC

Triumphing Over Obstacles

Rabbi Moshe took a trip to a strange land. He took with him a donkey, a rooster, and a lamp. Since he was a Jew he was refused hospitality in the village inns, so he decided to sleep in the woods. One night he lit his lamp to study the holy books before going to sleep, but a fierce wind came up, knocking over the lamp and breaking it. The rabbi decided to go to sleep saying, "All that God does, he does well." During the night some wild animals came and drove away the rooster and thieves stole the donkey. Moshe woke up, saw the loss, but still proclaimed, "All that God does, he does well."

The rabbi then went back to the village where he was refused lodging, only to learn that enemy soldiers had invaded it during the night and killed all the inhabitants. He also learned that the soldiers had traveled through the same part of the woods where he had been sleeping. Had his lamp not been broken, he would have been discovered. Had the rooster not been chased away, it would have crowed, giving him away. Had the donkey not been stolen, it would have brayed. So once more Rabbi Moshe declared, "All that God does, he does well."

Rabbi Moshe was right, all that God does, he does well. God has done well in giving us this holy season of Lent, which we enter today. We sign ourselves with the cross, the sign of our salvation, and we hear a lesson from scripture that encourages us to overcome the obstacles of life and through perseverance in our actions to find God. It is certainly appropriate to start this season of grace in this way. Lent encourages us to review our lives, seek change and reconciliation, and find new ways to triumph over the obstacles of life.

Saul of Tarsus was a man who certainly experienced much adversity and understood the need to negotiate obstacles in order to carry out the mission he was given by Christ. He was born into a privileged caste and environment and was well educated at the knees of the great scholar, Gamaliel, but with God's help he was able to change direction in his life. As he journeyed toward Damascus to continue his virulent persecution of the "new way," Saul was temporarily blinded. He encountered the risen Christ who challenged him: "Saul, Saul, why do you persecute me?" (Acts 9:4b). Saul, who took the Christian name, Paul, was transformed from being a great persecutor of Christians to the new faith's first and greatest evangelist, who transformed the western world with his proclamation of the teaching of Jesus.

In his ministry as a traveling evangelist, Paul was forced to negotiate numerous hurdles. First, he had to overcome the obstacle of rejection; he was a man caught in the middle. On the one hand he was seen as a traitor by fervent Pharisaical Jews due to his preaching on behalf of Jesus, who had been rejected by the Jewish religious elite. On the other hand, followers of the "new way" feared Paul. They were mystified how one who had been so fervent in his persecution of Jesus' followers could now be even more zealous in the promotion of his message. Paul was also forced to endure many physical obstacles, including punishment and hardships of various kinds. He traveled the then-known western world, mostly by foot on three long, dangerous, and arduous journeys, preaching in synagogues and other places, and forming fledgling Christian communities wherever he went. In his corpus of letters and in the Acts of the Apostles, we learn how he persevered through many other hardships. In today's lesson, he states many of the afflictions he endured: incarceration, beatings, riots, significant labors, sleepless nights, and hunger. We also know he was shipwrecked and forced to flee from those who sought his life.

Paul somehow realized that suffering and adversity were part of his lot, and that in order to carry the gospel message to the Gentiles his task would necessitate much suffering. Even with this knowledge, Paul never wavered in his vocation, but courageously continued forward, preaching and teaching. He overcame the physical, psychological, and spiritual obstacles that came his way. He tells us today that all the apparent negatives, the challenges of life, have been transformed into positives. He calls the Corinthians to be in solidarity with him, to understand that his struggles and apparent negatives are shared by all, and must be overcome by all. He tells his readers that they are treated as impostors, but the reality is that they have the true message. Paul says that Christians are thought to be unknown but the truth is that they are well known. The Romans see the new way as dying, but in actuality it is very much alive. The Christian community may be punished, but it will not be vanquished; it may appear to be sorrowful under its circumstances, but it truly rejoices in the knowledge of God. Paul says his followers are seen as poor, as having nothing, but again the reality is that they are very rich and possess everything that they need. Saint Paul is telling the Corinthians that as he has overcome many obstacles in life, so, too, must this nascent community of faith. The apostle has used every manifestation of adversity as a tool to grow and gain greater strength, so as to continue toward the goal of building God's kingdom day-by-day in our world.

The season of Lent is a time when we use, as Paul also suggests today, the weapons of righteousness to fight God's battles in this world. Traditionally, the Christian community emphasizes three specific weapons during this season: prayer, fasting, and almsgiving. Lent is certainly a time to renew our prayer lives. Yet, there are many obstacles that seem to impede and frustrate our progress in this most important aspect of our lives. We are all busy people, a reality that seems only to grow greater with time. We never have less to do, only more. The busyness of our time is often a major barrier to progress in prayer. There are only 24 hours in the day; where will we find the time to pray? Attitudes or feelings of inadequacy are another hurdle we need to negotiate. People often say, "I don't know how to pray! I don't know what to say." Some feel unworthy to stand before God. We should not fear, however, for as Jesus says when the situation is most problematic, we will be given the words we need (Luke 21:14-15). Lent is the perfect time to renew our prayer lives, remove obstacles that hinder our progress, and stop making excuses for our failures to grow.

The basic necessity of prayer is followed by the related ideas of fasting and almsgiving. Members of many Christian traditions choose to give up something, such as a food or drink item, or refrain from some pleasurable activity during Lent. However, fasting is much more than not eating or choosing not to engage in some activity that brings joy; it is at its root an attitude. Here again, many obstacles stand in the way of our progress. Simplicity of life is not in vogue in our twenty-first-century American society. Yet, if we are to make this season of Lent one of progress in our spiritual lives, we must convert such attitudes that center on the individual to ones that center on the needs of the whole. As the popular expression goes, "Live simply so others may simply live."

Almsgiving to the poor and needy has been a staple of the Christian tradition from the outset. The comfortableness of our contemporary first-world society can be a significant barrier to giving, not simply from our excess but from our own need. We should recall how Jesus commended the woman who gave only two insignificant coins to the temple treasury, for she gave from her need (Luke 21:1-4). We can easily become complacent. Some even feel they have a right to all they have; people should reap the benefits of their efforts. Others still see the poverty of the world but do not understand their responsibility in alleviating the misery it causes. Amos, the prophet (6:4-8), warned people against such complacency, telling the Jewish ruling elite that such an attitude would lead to the community's destruction, a prophecy that was fulfilled seven centuries before Christ. While our visual acuity may be fine, we are, nonetheless, often spiritually blind to the reality of the world. Lent is the time to make every effort to remove these barriers that blind us to reality, so we can gain a much clearer vision.

Contemporary life is often hostile to Christians and their way of living. Thus, as Paul suggests in today's lesson (6:2c), "Now is the acceptable time; see, now is the day of salvation." Ash Wednesday is our annual wake up call — a time for us to get going again. It is a time to overcome obstacles; it is a time, as Paul rightly states, to (5:20c) "be reconciled with God." We must overcome the obstacles of today's world and its mixed up priorities that hinder us from pursuing prayer, fasting and almsgiving as vehicles to a greater union with God. This is not an easy task, especially when many voices in various forms seek to tell us of the emptiness and fallacy of our beliefs. But we must hold fast and continue, and as the Pauline author (2 Timothy 4:2) suggests, "Proclaim the message; be persistent whether the time is favorable or unfavorable; convince, rebuke, and encourage, with the utmost patience in teaching."

Lent is our annual opportunity to prepare for the church's celebration of the paschal mystery, but we cannot adequately carry out this mission without significant effort. We cannot think the obstacles will magically disappear. The reality of our need to act is illustrated in a book, *The Jungle's Neutral*, by Fred Spencer. During World War II, Spencer was forced to live in the jungle on the Malay peninsula for nine months in order to keep one step ahead of the Japanese who occupied the British colony of Singapore. Spencer had heard two conflicting stories about the jungle. Some told him the jungle was a horrible place to live, filled with snakes and insects, fruit so poisonous that one bite could kill a person, and brutal, wild animals. Thus, the jungle was seen as a place where one would die quickly. On the other hand, he had also heard that the jungle was a lush tropical paradise with plenty of fresh water and edible fruit. It was a place where one could live with relative ease. What Spencer discovered, however, was that the jungle was neutral; it was not preset to destroy him, nor was it structured to support him. He learned that his survival was based completely on the amount of effort he put into his survival. Spencer was able to make the jungle the environment he wanted it to be.

Often people say the world is a jungle, but is it? As Spencer found out and wrote, so too we must see that the world is neutral; it is all up to us how things will go. Today the Christian world enters the discipline of Lent. Let us see this season as an opportunity for true growth. Let us, therefore, make our best efforts to cast off the shackles that inhibit our growth. May we use the righteous gifts of God, prayer, fasting, and almsgiving, to produce abundant fruit so we can proclaim as did Rabbi Moshe, "All that God does, he does well."

Building God's Kingdom:
The Christian Challenge

On December 26, 2004, the greatest natural disaster experienced in the world in over a century struck southern Asia. The 9.0 magnitude earthquake, with its epicenter some 1,000 miles southwest of the island of Java, generated a tsunami that traveled outward at almost supersonic speed in all directions. It created death, destruction, dislocation, and mayhem for literally millions of people in some ten nations that border the northeast regions of the Indian Ocean. Thousands of people, tourists on vacation lying on the pristine white sand beaches in the area, local fisherman and their families plying their trade, children playing in coastal areas, trains ferrying people to many locations, were swept away by a tidal surge that came with a ferocity that can only be imagined. Amateur videos of the wave's progress from sea to land cannot capture the fear nor horror that must have run through the minds of many, who in literally a few seconds, lost everything material and had their lives transformed. This tragedy of biblical proportions killed, in the first month, some 165,000 people, but this was only the start. Millions were left homeless and the destruction was in the billions of dollars. Certainly, life for many will not return to normal, possibly for years, if ever.

The world community responded to the enormous need generated by this disaster in remarkable ways. Governments across the globe pledged money, manpower, and resources to stabilize the situation and prevent further misery from disease. Relief agencies of all stripes, secular and religious, have received record contributions. Churches, schools, and other institutions held special collections. Music, television, and film stars gave concerts and other events to raise additional revenue. All of these relief initiatives were launched without regard to nation, religion, ethnicity, race, or culture. People throughout the world have responded because of the obvious need and the desire to help. The world in a significant way has demonstrated its solidarity, that we are one, sisters and brothers, in the human community.

This world initiative to meet the need after a natural disaster, an example of international cooperation and ecumenical and interfaith spirit should be an inspiration to the Christian community to seek unity and find ways to promote the message of Jesus to those who live in darkness and ignorance. Lent presents an opportunity to share the good news with others, but today's lesson from Paul's letter to the Romans makes it clear that our efforts will be best served by working as a team. As the apostle says, "There is no distinction between Jew and Greek; the same Lord of all is generous to all who call on him. For, 'Everyone who calls on the name of the Lord shall be saved' " (10:12-13). If the world can come together to aid victims of disaster, the Christian community should be able to make significant strides to find common ground with Jesus, as Saint Paul tells us, as our strong and unique foundation.

As many of us know, the Christian community at Rome was unknown to Paul when he wrote this letter. As he tells us in Romans 15, it was his intention to visit Rome on his way to Spain. Thus, he writes this letter to introduce himself to the local community. This was probably awkward for Paul, since all of his other letters were written to communities he had formed during his famous and perilous three missionary journeys through the eastern Mediterranean world. Yet, this, the longest of Paul's corpus, was not written to mollify the people, but presents some of the apostle's most fundamental theology. We hear one of those important topics in our lesson this morning.

Paul wants the Romans to know that Jesus is the center, the foundation, the source of all that he wishes to communicate. Thus, it is imperative that the community's members confess with their lips and believe in their hearts that Jesus is Lord. Paul is asking for a twofold commitment. First, he wants the Romans in speech and action to proclaim their belief in Christ. This exhortation was crucial, especially to those who lived in the imperial capital of the Roman Empire. Surrounded by temples and pagan images and living amongst Gentile nonbelievers, many of whom were most likely hostile to the "new way," the Christian community at Rome was severely challenged. Thus, Paul wishes to buoy their spirits by assuring them that their faith will lead to salvation. Second, Paul challenges the Romans to turn their lives over to Christ. Not only must one confess with the mouth, and by extension action, but one must believe in the heart. This can only happen through a process of conversion, as the Greeks called it *metanoia* or change of heart. This moves a step beyond confession. Paul ends this part of his teaching by saying, "No one who believes in him will be put to shame." The apostle somehow knew what Jesus had taught in his public life, that while the road would not be easy, and many barriers and obstacles would have to be negotiated, those who hold out to the end will be rewarded. We recall Jesus' words (John 16:33b): "In the world you [will] face persecution. But take courage, I have conquered the world."

After exhorting the Romans in their belief in Christ, Paul then challenges the community to place its efforts in solidarity with other believers. As he wrote to the Ephesians (3:6) that the Gentiles were co-heirs with the Jews, as inheritors of God's promise, so now Paul rejects those who make distinctions in the community. One's origins have no bearing; all that matters is belief in Jesus. Salvation comes through Christ. Again, Paul seems to have learned what Jesus told his apostles in response to Thomas' question (John 14:6): "I am the way, and the truth, and the life. No one comes to the Father except through me."

Christianity, as we all know, is a great privilege. We have the privilege of being members of the community of faith, the church. We have the privilege of the sacred scriptures, from which we have just heard and that, if we wish, we can read and meditate upon each day. We have the privilege of the sacramental life, special signs from God of the Lord's presence with us. We have the privilege of knowing that God is our Good Shepherd. Acting like a

"Hound of Heaven," as British poet Francis Thompson put so powerfully in his epic poem, God relentlessly and diligently searches for our souls. While 99 percent will receive a grade of A+ in school, that is not satisfactory for God. God will leave the 99 in the desert and search for the one lost sheep. Yes, we have the privilege of Jesus, the great physician, who is with us every moment and each step of our lives.

The great and multiple privileges of the Christian life come with significant responsibilities as well. Baptism is our common call as Christians to live lives of holiness. We are called as well to be servants, to aid our brothers and sisters as did Christ, who came to serve, not to be served (Mark 10:45). Christianity calls us to be beacons of light and hope to a world often shrouded in darkness. In short, we are called to build God's kingdom through our united efforts. But we, as Paul suggests to the Romans, and Jesus states directly at the end of his Sermon on the Mount, we must build that kingdom, our spiritual house, on Christ, the foundation of life. With Jesus as the foundation, we are the Lord's coworkers. Saint Teresa of Avila, the great sixteenth-century Carmelite nun and church reformer put it this way in a famous prayer: "Christ has no body on earth but yours, no hands no feet on earth but yours. Yours are the eyes with which Christ looks with compassion on the world. Christ has no body on earth but yours." Yes, we are the hands and feet, the eyes and ears of Jesus in today's world. Therefore, we have a significant responsibility to work toward repairing divisions and seeking unity.

How can we construct the kingdom centered in Christ in our world? We do so generically by working together, not as individuals, personally or denominationally, but ecumenically as a community of faith. We begin by fostering an attitude of acceptance, working together and not with antagonism. We are all on the same team, which bears the name Christian, as assuredly as the world is on the same team, called humankind, to alleviate the suffering in south Asia. We must view ourselves, individuals, and faith communities, as belonging to a larger whole, seeking to use our talents toward the common good, not what I, or my specific faith tradition, may deem necessary. We must think globally but act locally, building God's kingdom by applying the message of Jesus. Proponents of the Social Gospel in the Progressive Era, people like Walter Rauschenbusch, Washington Gladden, and John Ryan, and, more recently, in the 1990s college students across the country had it right when they collectively asked, "What would Jesus do?" Our task of building the kingdom will present many challenges and we will be forced to stand against the tide of contemporary life that seeks, like the tsunami, to drown out our voice. This should be no surprise, however. Jesus told his followers, "You will be hated by all because of my name. But the one who endures to the end will be saved" (Matthew 10:22). Thus we must persevere and never lose hope.

Building God's kingdom in our world is not for the faint of heart. It is a task that takes courage, strength, and persistence. Let us never think that if the task is too difficult we can relax and let others take the lead. No, Jesus the foundation of our faith and the one to whom we will return, demands more from us. As the scripture (Luke 12:48b) says, "From everyone to whom much has been given, much will be required; and from the one to whom much has been entrusted, even more will be demanded." Thus, we need to roll up our sleeves and get to work, in a common unified effort. The reality of our call and the need to respond is made clear in a humorous and illustrative story: Fred Everybody, Thomas Somebody, Peter Anybody, and Joe Nobody were neighbors, but not the type that most would want to know. They were odd people and difficult to understand. The way they lived their lives was a shame. These men all went to the same church, but most would not have wanted them as parishioners. Everybody went fishing on Sundays or stayed home and spoke with his friends. Anybody wanted to worship, but he was afraid that Somebody would speak with him. Thus, guess who went to church — that's right, Nobody. Actually, Nobody was the only decent one of the lot. Nobody did the parish census; Nobody joined the Parish Council. One day there was an announcement in the parish bulletin for people to apply for a position as a teacher in the Sunday school program. Everybody thought Anybody would apply; Anybody thought Somebody would apply. So, guess who applied? You are right, Nobody!

Let's not be Everybody, Somebody, or Anybody. Rather, let us seek to be a Nobody, working not for ourselves but for others. Let us take up the challenge of building God's kingdom in our world upon Christ, the rock foundation. We have a good example of how disaster brought the world together. Let us not wait until disaster strikes the Christian community, but let us act now so the scriptures may be fulfilled and Jesus' plan can come to full fruition: "That they may all be one. As you, Father, are in me and I am in you, may they also be in us, so that the world may believe that you sent me" (John 17:21).

Standing Tall In The Lord

History records the expression, *Athanasius contra mundum* —
Athanasius against the world. These words aptly express the situation in the fourth-century church when heresy almost reigned supreme — save Athanasius, a bishop who was a persistent and
staunch defender of the faith. Athanasius was born into a Christian
family in Alexandria, Egypt, in 295 A.D. In his early twenties he
was ordained and entered the service of Alexander, Bishop of Alexandria. He accompanied the bishop to the first ecumenical council of the church at Nicaea in 325 when, among other matters, the
heresy of Arianism, which promoted the idea that Jesus was not
God, was first condemned.

In 326, Alexander died and two years later Athanasius was selected to be the new bishop of Alexandria. It was at this time that
his career as a persistent defender of the faith began. His first opponent was Melitius, a fellow bishop, who believed that it was wrong
for the church to welcome back those who had apostatized. Athanasius triumphed in this struggle through a righteous and dogmatic
campaign. His greatest nemesis, however, was the Arians, who although condemned, continued to grow and attract many to their
theological perspective. In fact, the number of Arians was so great
that Saint Jerome, the original translator of the scriptures into Latin
(the Vulgate), once wrote, "The world awoke and found itself Arian."

Between 335-366, Athanasius, one of the few bishops in the
eastern church who held the orthodox faith, was exiled on five different occasions for a total of seventeen years. Trumped-up charges,
false testimony, and the events of the day combined to work against

him, but each time Athanasius returned from exile he was that much more determined to defend the true faith. During his exiles he wrote many important treatises, including *The Life of Antony*, a biography of Antony of the Desert, one of the first desert monks and a precursor to monastic life. Through tenacity, perseverance, and the fact that he was able to outlive almost all his opponents, Athanasius, in the end, was able to prevail. He died in 373, living his last seven years in relative peace. His greatest triumph came, however, in 381 at the Council of Constantinople when the Nicene-Constantinopolitan Creed, which contains the tenets of the faith Athanasius so staunchly defended, was written and accepted. It was a testimony to Athanasius' persistence and dedication that he triumphed, became a saint, and inherited eternal life.

Saint Athanasius' life stands as an example of the scriptural exhortation to be persistent in what we do in order to receive the gift of salvation. He stood against the tide that sought his demise. These were, as Paul describes them, "enemies of the cross of Christ." The bishop did as Paul suggests to the Philippians today, that is, to stand firm in the Lord. We are called to do the same.

Paul wrote his letter to the Christian community at Philippi from prison around the year 50 during his second missionary journey. He told the Philippians that they must imitate him as he imitates Christ. Like Jesus, Paul has suffered greatly in numerous ways. He had suffered much physical adversity — imprisonment, beatings, and the need to flee from his enemies. Later he was shipwrecked and eventually martyred. He was forced to endure rejection by his peers, from both the Jewish and Christian sides; neither group seemed to trust him. In today's lesson, he spoke of those who are "enemies of the cross of Christ." Most scripture scholars believe he was referring to the Judaizers, a group of very religious, orthodox, and politically conservative Jewish Christians who believed that complete adherence to the Mosaic Law was necessary for converts to the "new way" of Jesus. This adversity was primary in Paul's mind at the time. He stated that their god is their belly and their glory their shame. Like Jesus, Paul stood against the tide and was willing to endure pain and suffering as long as the true word was being proclaimed. As he (or a Pauline author) wrote to his friend Timothy (2 Timothy 4:1c-2): "I solemnly urge you: proclaim the message; be persistent whether the time is favorable or unfavorable; convince, rebuke, and encourage with the utmost patience in teaching." After exhorting the Philippians to be persistent in what they do, he encourages them to keep focused on the prize, the light at the end of the tunnel. One must live, Paul suggests, not on the level of the world, that of the Judaizers, but on a higher plateau. The Philippians are to focus their attention on their citizenship in heaven. As the apostle states, "So, if you have been raised with Christ, seek the things that are above, where Christ is, seated at the right hand of God. Set your minds on things that are above, not on things that are of the earth" (Colossians 3:1-2). Paul wants the community to keep its priorities straight and not be fooled by false doctrines nor transfixed by the world. No, if they keep their lives focused on Christ, then Jesus will transform them into his likeness. He concludes his words through the challenge to stand firm in the Lord. Paul certainly realizes that this is a difficult proposition, but there is a reward. Again, as he or his disciple wrote in the pastoral epistles: "If we have died with him, we will also live with him; if we endure, we will also reign with him; if we deny him, he will also deny us; if we are faithless, he remains faithful — for he cannot deny himself" (2 Timothy 2:11b-13).

The challenge that Paul presented to the Philippians is still present today, only its manifestations have changed. The forces allied against Christianity today are multiple and significant and they come in various forms of darkness. The darkness of ignorance is persistent. We might think with all the advancement in human knowledge, especially the almost unbelievable strides made in technology through the "information superhighway," that there is nothing that humankind does not know. The reality, however, is that we will never know everything and we should not presume as individuals or a community to think we have all the answers. We live in the darkness of arrogance; it is almost pervasive in our society. While it is extremely important to put our best foot forward, to promote our accomplishments, especially in the highly competitive nature of our contemporary twenty-first-century society, we often tend to go too far. We exalt our name, position, or accomplishments to the detriment of others. We become exclusive, in ideas, attitude, and action.

Arrogance can be deadly in the way it kills others' ideas and hopes. The darkness of intolerance is also quite strong today. Business, in fact, every realm of society today, mandates that we perform. We are to do the job well, rapidly, and responsibly; error is almost not acceptable. We forget our humanness and expect others to perform flawlessly. We become intolerant of anything save the best. Certainly we need to strive to do the best we can, but errors of omission and commission are endemic to humanity. We must accept them. Consumerism shadows us in darkness as well. The more things we have the more important we feel and the more accepted we will be to others. Thus, we will only be satisfied with the best and the brightest, the newest and most advanced, when something much simpler, less expensive, and not as flashy would do just as well, if not better. The world is bogged down in the darkness of individualism; the common good has become lost. The priority is me and my needs; the needs of others, individually or communally, always takes second or lower priority. Too often today, people believe the error of sin has taken flight. We live in a pervasive world where one often hears, "I will do 'my own thing.' " People speak and act as if anything goes so long as we don't hurt others or get caught.

In general, secularism seeks to push the sacred away from the light. God is asked to take second place to the world. We concentrate on the here and now; any energies placed toward our external existence with God seem to have no priority. We seem to be foolish to some. But, if we should entertain such thoughts, we can take consolation in an apocryphal story about the Renaissance master, Leonardo da Vinci. When he had completed his masterpiece, the *Mona Lisa*, da Vinci went to a nearby tavern to celebrate the event with his friends. While in conversation and sipping a little of the local wine, Leonardo noticed that many in the tavern were making sport of an ugly fool who made his living going from tavern to tavern, entertaining patrons for a spare coin or a crust of bread. This man truly was an ugly person; he seemed to be more a troll than a man. His small beady eyes were not centered in his oversized head. His ears were like cauliflower and his nose was as large as a gourd, with an ugly mole on its tip. His mouth and jaw were locked in a perpetual grimace.

As those in the tavern continued to mock the fool, a contentious rival artist hurled a challenge to the great da Vinci. "You are a master," said the man, "can you make in paint a beauty of this ugly fool?" Leonardo could not avoid the challenge, to do so would forever place him in doubt with his followers. "Why not?" responded Leonardo. "If I can paint the most beautiful woman in the world in my *Mona Lisa*, then I can certainly make an Adonis of this ugly fool. Return here tonight at the call of vespers and I will reveal the work I have done." Leonardo had little time, far less than normal for such a project, so he began in earnest.

Several hours later, the bell in the cathedral church rang for vespers and the crowd began to assemble at the tavern. It was filled to overflowing; it seemed that the whole city of Florence had heard about the challenge and had come to see what the master had accomplished. Leonardo stood before his new painting, which was covered by a curtain, and called for quiet. Patrons continued to murmur: "What would the painting reveal? Would the fool's eyes now be blue and centered in his face? Would his nose be noble and Roman? Would his lips be gentle but firm? Would his large ears now be petite and soft?" When the noise subsided Leonardo called out, "Behold my masterpiece!" He slowly withdrew the curtain to reveal his work; the crowd held its breath. The painting was an exact image of the ugly fool — not one hair or expression was out of place. The silence in the tavern was deafening. The rival artist cried out, "The ugly fool was too much of a challenge, even for the great Leonardo da Vinci." "Not so," responded Leonardo. Then pointing to the face of the fool he said, "This face was painted by the hand of God and only a fool would dare presume to change or replace the work of the Master." Leonardo da Vinci had used a fool to shame the proud. If we are not careful, God may do the same with us.

This reality is presented forcefully by Saint Paul in his first letter to the Corinthians: "God chose what is foolish in the world to shame the wise; God chose what is weak in the world to shame the

133

strong; God chose what is low and despised in the world, things that are not, to reduce to nothing things that are, so that no one might boast in the presence of God" (1:27-29).

While the reality of darkness is present, we have the solution; his name is Jesus. John the Baptist heralded him, "Here is the Lamb of God who takes away the sin of the world!" (John 1:29b). Jesus was the light who came to dispel the sin, the darkness, of our world. We must place our hope and faith in the Lord, confident as he promised, "In the world you [will] face persecution. But take courage; I have overcome the world!" (John 16:33b).

Christianity calls us to stand against the forces which threaten the message of Jesus. The Lord warned us that this would be our lot. He was rejected. The prologue of Saint John's Gospel sets the stage for Jesus' cross: "He came to what was his own, and his own people did not accept him" (1:11). The forces, enemies of the cross of Christ, were allied against him. Jesus told his disciples, and through them all of us, that we might be betrayed by our brothers and sisters, "but the one who endures to the end will be saved" (Matthew 10:22b). Yes, we have the solution to darkness and the one who can help us to stand firm; his name is Jesus.

It is true — our adversaries are strong, but we must be stronger. We must use the weapons available to fight the darkness of the world. We must be people of true prayer; it must be nonnegotiable in our life. If prayer is central, we can keep our focus on Christ. We must use the community of faith to assist us as well. The community must make the commitment, as individuals and a collective, to seek out the lost, guide the wayward, and provide support to fight the battles we all face. We must seek guidance from the scriptures and use them as our rule of life. In short, as Paul suggests in a later passage in Philippians: "Put on the whole armor of God, so that you may be able to stand against the wiles of the devil" (6:11).

Lent is a period when the darkness of winter gives way, day-by-day, to the light of spring. We are on a trip from darkness to light. At the end of the journey is Jesus, the light that dispels the darkness of our world. As our journey continues, therefore, let us keep our priorities straight, keep our focus on Jesus, and through these stand firm in the Lord. Our reward in heaven will be great.

Minding The Store Of Our Lives

A man lived in an old stone cottage that was badly in need of repair. He made do, day-by-day, and got on with his life, struggling to wrench a living from the meager land. Eventually the rain that leaked in on him got too heavy and the wind around his ears was too cold. He had to do something about the gap in his wall.

Up on the hillside there was an ancient Celtic cross. It had stood there since time immemorial. It was silent and uncomplaining in the Atlantic gales that swept over it, but its very silence said something about continuity, community, and interrelatedness. It had become a part of the local imagination and without ever really thinking about it, the people knew, with a sound instinct, that it was very important. It had something to say about what they hoped to be. It has something to do with the coming of the kingdom.

The man from the cottage, who was a stonecutter, went up to the cross one dark night. One of those stone arcs, he thought, would fit exactly the hole in his wall. He would come the next day with a hammer and a chisel and remove it. He smiled, perhaps uneasily, as he thought of how much warmer his house would be without the perpetual drafts. Almost satisfied with his decision, he turned toward his homeward path, but his plans were rudely interrupted. In the distance he clearly saw flames rising from his cottage. Panic-stricken he ran across the rough field, but when he arrived home, his cottage was still standing as he had left it. The fire had only been in his imagination.

A few days later common sense again reasserted itself and he once again set off up the hill with his hammer and chisel. It was dark, but he looked about warily, lest anyone else should see him there. It was only a piece of stone after all, and he needed it. He started to chip. The sound of the hammer against the solid head of the chisel rang out through the night like the tolling of a bell to alarm the very heavens. But he continued to chip until he remembered the strange events of his previous attempt and looked over his shoulder nervously in the direction of his cottage. And there on the distant skyline, a fire raged. Again, he ran home in terror only to find his cottage unharmed, just as he had left it.

More cold nights came and went; sleep came uneasily to the stonecutter. The bizarre images of dream and nightmare entangled themselves among the pressing urgencies of everyday life. The fierce winds from the sea were stronger by far than the breezes that fluttered through his unease. He made up his mind that the very next day his cottage would be sound again and that no irrational fears would deflect him from his purpose.

He walked up the hill, without looking to the right or the left. He worked quickly and efficiently, closing the doors of his mind firmly against any distraction, real or imagined. Soon the stone arc was in his sack. This time there were no flames on the horizon and, thus, no flash of panic disturbed him. He turned his back on the mutilated cross and walked home through the quiet of the night. And when he arrived home, the cottage was a heap of smoldering ashes.[1]

The stonecutter failed to heed the warnings that he received from his dream. He continued on with his planned destruction, rejecting the opportunity he was given to right the ship of his life as he sailed, possibly unknowingly, into perilous shoal waters. Saint Paul, in a similar way, warns the Corinthians that they must be watchful of their person so as not to run aground on the rocky shoals of the world's multiple temptations.

In today's Second Lesson, Paul begins by reviewing in brief the history of the Jews and their lack of fidelity to God. Yahweh sent Moses to the Israelites to lead them from bondage in Egypt to the promised land. God rescued the community through the waters of the Red Sea by providing a path and destroying Pharaoh's forces. The Lord led the people through the desert by a cloud during the

136

day and a pillar of fire at night. The people all ate the same food and drank from the same spiritual rock. Namely, they had the Law, the Ten Commandments, which God personally gave to Moses on Mount Sinai. In short, the people were given a secure path to follow to reach their destination. Yet, as Paul tells the Corinthians and we too know from our reading of the Hebrew Scriptures, that the people chose another route and most were struck down in the desert. The community wandered rather aimlessly for forty years; even Moses was not granted entry to the land God promised.

The apostle tells the people that these events happened to serve as an example not to follow. The community is to avoid the evil path their ancestors in the faith trod. Paul then gives more details on specific evils to be avoided, providing a short list of past sins and their consequences. He first mentions the idolatry of the Jews. The incident with the golden calf in the desert (Exodus 32:1-35) most assuredly was in Paul's mind, but there were many other manifestations of similar transgressions. Hosea warned the ruling elite in the northern kingdom of their infidelity to God.

The image of Hosea's marriage to Gomer illustrates how Israel was guilty of consorting with many other gods. The prophet wrote: "My people consult a piece of wood, and their divining rod gives them oracles. For a spirit of whoredom has led them astray, and they have played the whore, forsaking their God. They sacrifice on the tops of the mountains, and make offerings upon the hills, under oak, poplar, and terebinth, because their shade is good. Therefore your daughters play the whore and your daughters-in-law commit adultery" (Hosea 4:12-13). Paul next mentions the sin of sexual immorality, an issue he had raised earlier (5:1-12) in this letter to the Corinthians.

Most likely, here Paul was reminding the people of the infidelity of their ancestors in the desert when many had relations with Moab women leading to their worship of Baal (Numbers 25:1-18). Again, referring to the Israelites' sojourn in the desert (Numbers 16:41-49 and 21:5-6 as two examples) Paul tells the Corinthians how the people tested God and complained against Moses, God's chosen liberator. The people tried the patience of God, who it seems was the object of their anger. All of these incidents, Paul suggests, happened as warnings for those living at the end of the ages. Since the apostle, as indicated from his letters (especially 1 and 2 Thessalonians) firmly believed in the close proximity of the Parousia, he issues an important warning: "So if you think you are standing, watch out that you do not fall." In other words, heed the many signs that have been given and do not delude yourselves into believing all is well, personally or communally.

Paul closes this section of his letter with an important note of consolation. He tells the people that various trials and temptations will come along the way. Yes, all will be tested; no one will escape. But Paul also firmly believed that no one is tested beyond one's ability to endure. All are given the strength to overcome the temptations and problems that come our way. Such testing will clearly involve some amount of suffering, but Paul also knew, as did the author of the letter to the Hebrews that it is through suffering that we gain perfection. Speaking of Jesus we read: "Although he was a Son, he learned obedience from what he suffered; and having been made perfect, he became the source of eternal salvation for all who obey him" (Hebrews 5:8).

We should heed Paul's warning to the Christian community at Corinth, but we should also bask in the knowledge that God is on our side, supplying all that we need to overcome any and all obstacles in order to find eternal life. We all find ourselves, at different times in our lives, combating the temptations and evil tendencies we share and experience as humans. But we have had sufficient warning. We have the ethic our parents gave us, a history of Christianity that demonstrates a secure path, and most especially we have the scriptures. Thus, it is all up to us.

Raising our voice to complain seems to be, as they say, "par for the course" these days. Sometimes our complaints are completely legitimate. We may have been wronged; some injustice could have been perpetrated against us. Possibly our opinions or ideas on some issue were summarily dismissed without a hearing. Too often and too loudly, however, we complain for no justifiable reason. It may have been the case that things did not go our way and we think no one cares. We become intolerant and feel wronged simply because our idea or way of doing something was not chosen. Sometimes, as well, we cannot admit that we might have been wrong and, thus, we complain. There are some who cannot accept defeat and when this eventuality happens in our lives we react in less than positive ways. There are times as well that we complain against people whom we feel do not measure up or do things differently or have varied perspectives from our own. If our complaints are legitimate we can stand tall, as Paul suggests, but let us not simply "cry over spilt milk" because we don't like someone or something.

Complaints that have no legitimacy are matched with our tendency to put Jesus to the test, just as the Jews, our ancestors in the faith, did. How many times have we heard one say, "O Lord, grant me patience and grant it to me NOW!" It is a good thing that God is not like us. God has infinite patience with us. Yet, while God's love for us never lies dormant or is lost, surely God must grow weary and become disappointed with us. We know in our hearts and minds what God asks of us; none of us was born yesterday. God has provided plenty of signs and warnings, as well as a detailed and well-lighted path to follow. Yes, as Jesus says (Matthew 7:13-14) it is the rocky, less traveled road we must follow, but we know it is the only proper path. Jesus said, "I am the way, and the truth, and the life. No one comes to the Father, except through me" (John 14:6). We must do what we can to lessen the burdens of the Lord. Jesus said it well to Satan during his temptation in the desert: "Again it is written, 'Do not put the Lord your God to the test' " (Matthew 4:7).

The pervasive nature of today's world allows us too easily to try God's patience through the misuse of our great gift of sexuality. It is easy today to rationalize, to become our own "spin doctors" with respect to our actions. Again, we know what is expected of us. Yet, too often we hide in the closet of ignorance and fake ourselves into believing a reality that does not exist.

Idolatry is still another temptation that is omnipresent in our world. We might mistakenly think that idolatry is not a problem — after all there are few in our society who call themselves people of faith who do not acknowledge their worship of God, but that does not mean idolatry has magically vanished. On the contrary, it is ever-present, but has different names — power, wealth, and prestige, the three great temptations of humankind from the outset. Jesus himself was forced to choose between God and the world when he endured his temptations at the hand of Satan just prior to the beginning of his public ministry (Matthew 4:1-11). He is offered the three treasures of our world, but he never gives in to the temptation. The first temptation of power comes in the offer of changing stones into bread. Power is not necessary for Jesus; concentrating on God's Word is more important. Prestige is the second great temptation seen in the challenge to throw himself from the temple. Satan chides Jesus saying that he is an important person and thus his angels will care for him. Christ responds by saying that he does not need to show such prestige. The fact that Jesus is God is all the prestige that is necessary. The final temptation is wealth in the offer to grant all the kingdoms of the world to Jesus. Just bow down and worship me is the challenge of Satan. Jesus responds that he does not need such riches. Jesus will not honor Satan; God alone is to be worshiped.

While there is more than sufficient reason to be wary of contemporary temptations, we must not live in fear that when such events, people, and ideas come our way we are defenseless. On the contrary, we must, as the Pauline author suggests, clothe ourselves in Christ: "Put on the whole armor of God, so that you may be able to stand against the wiles of the devil. For our struggle is not against enemies of blood and flesh, but against the rulers, against the authorities, against the cosmic powers of the present darkness, against the spiritual forces of evil in the heavenly places" (Ephesians 6:11-12). We must have confidence, as we have been told and have said to others quite frequently: "No testing has overtaken you that is not common to everyone. God is faithful, and he will not let you be tested beyond your strength, but with the testing he will provide the way out so that you may be able to endure it" (1 Corinthians 10:13). Most assuredly this must be a great source of consolation amidst the darkness of today's world.

The stonecutter never heeded the warning and his house burned to ashes. God has provided us through scripture, history, and the experience of our lives, numerous signs, warnings, and opportunities to follow the narrow path to life. Let us not be foolish like the stonecutter, but rather heed the admonition of Saint Paul. Let us do so, however, with the supreme confidence that God is with us every step of the way. As he told his disciples just before he ascended to the Father, "And remember, I am with you always, to the end of the age" (Matthew 28:20b). May this be our hope and consolation as we strive each day to live the Christian life. If we can persevere our reward in heaven will be great!

---

1. Taken from Margaret Silf, *Sacred Spaces: Stations on a Celtic Way* (Brewster, Massachusetts: Paraclete Press, 2001), pp. 49-51.

Be Reconciled —
To Christ And Others

The train clanked and rattled down the tracks one lazy summer afternoon as I traveled from Kyoto to Tokyo. My car was relatively empty — a few housewives with children in tow and a few older folks going to or returning from shopping. At one station the doors opened and suddenly the quiet of the afternoon was shattered by a man who began to bellow violence and incomprehensible curses. The man was big, drunk, and filthy. As he yelled, he swung at a woman carrying a baby. The blow sent the woman into the lap of an older couple; it was a miracle that the child was not injured. The couple quickly moved away, leading the man to follow, but he stopped short and began to again scream profanities. I could see that the man's hands were cut and bleeding. As the train lurched forward, all the passengers were frozen with fear.

I knew this was my opportunity to act, to do the right thing, and teach this man a lesson. I was young and in good shape. Moreover, I had been practicing Aikido for a few hours each day for the past three years. I liked to grapple and throw my opponents; I thought myself to be rather tough. However, my martial arts training had never been exercised in actual combat. As students of Aikido we were encouraged never to fight. "Aikido," my instructor had always said, "is the art of reconciliation. Whoever has the mind to fight has broken his connection with the universe. If you try to dominate people, you are already defeated. Aikido is used to resolve conflict, not initiate it." Despite the teacher's words I wanted to prove myself, to find an absolutely legitimate opportunity whereby I might save the innocent by destroying the guilty.

"This is it," I said to myself and sprang to my feet. "People are in danger and I need to act. If I don't, someone may get hurt." Seeing me rise, the drunk recognized a chance to focus his rage. He roared saying, "You need to be taught a lesson." As I held onto the commuter strap I gave the man a look of disgust, telling myself how I planned to defeat this man and his arrogance. I blew him a kiss in defiance which prompted him to rush at me. Just then someone shouted, "Hey!" The voice was earsplitting and it came again, "Hey!" As I turned to my left and the drunk to his right we both saw an older little man sitting in traditional Japanese dress on one of the seats. The man, who must have been in his seventies, took no notice of me, but focused all his attention on the drunk. "Come here," said the man to the drunk. "Come over here and talk with me."

The drunk responded to the call, as if being pulled by a string. He stood before the older man and shouted, "Why should I listen to you?" The drunk was fixed on the old man. I told myself if he made one move forward or back I would drop him in his tracks. "What have you been drinking?" the old man asked. "Sake," came the answer. "Oh, that is wonderful," the old man said. "I love sake as well. Every night my wife and I warm up a little bottle of sake and take it to our garden and sit on a wooden bench. As we drink our sake we watch the sun go down and we see how our persimmon tree is doing. My great-grandfather planted that tree and we worry with the ice storms that it will survive. Actually the tree has done better than we anticipated. It is wonderful to sit, sip our sake, and watch the sun set each evening."

The drunk began to slowly sway back and forth; his fists unclenched. "I love persimmons, too," said the drunk. "Yes," said the old man, smiling, "and I bet you have a wonderful wife as well." "No," said the drunk, "my wife died several years ago. I have no wife, no home, and no job. I am ashamed of myself." Tears began to roll down the cheeks of the drunk; a spasm of despair rippled through his body. As I stood there in my well-groomed innocence, with my make-this-world-safe-for-democracy attitude, I felt dirtier than the drunk.

The train arrived at my stop and as the doors opened I heard the old man say, "My my, that is a difficult set of circumstances. Sit down here and tell me all about it." I turned my head for one last look. The drunk was sprawled on the seat with his head in the old man's lap. The old man was stroking the drunk's dirty, matted hair.

The young man, skilled at martial arts and perceiving himself to be brave and the bringer of justice, found what the discipline of Aikido was all about, but he learned this valuable lesson, as they say, "through the back door." Reconciliation is something we must learn; it is an active virtue that takes time, energy, and skill. This season of grace, our Lenten journey, asks us to revisit and make stronger our commitment to reconciliation. Paul understood the basic need for reconciliation and, thus, he calls the Corinthians to be reconciled with Christ and by extension to one another. We are called to do the same.

Although Paul had a long-standing and highly significant relationship with the Corinthians, it was not always harmonious. His message in today's lesson serves as a personal challenge as well as a general teaching on the promotion of reconciliation. First, he calls the community to be new creations in Christ. He calls people to forget the past and move forward. Through Jesus a new day has dawned; it is time to seek reconciliation. Jesus is not concerned with the past transgressions of the people; rather he wishes the community to seek a new beginning with him and with each other. Paul rejected the factions that had arisen in the community and preached unity. Similarly, Jesus wants the people to find personal unity by removing obstacles that cause interior division. Jesus has given us the message of reconciliation in order to assist us in this quest for personal wholeness. Once each individual and the community as a collective has found reconciliation with Christ, then we must go forward as ambassadors of the Lord. The Christians in Corinth are asked to bring Jesus' message of peace, love, and forgiveness to others. Once the gift of reconciliation has been received, it must be shared with others.

Paul's exhortation to be reconciled with Christ is a message we need to hear and heed today. Too often we go about our very busy and public lives with a certain sense that all is well; there is no perceived need to look inside and ask the hard question with respect to our relationship with God. But the truth is that we are all sinners and, therefore, in need of the reconciliation that Christ offers to us.

Reconciliation is an active process which must actually start within our own person. The first element is passive but absolutely essential to the process. We need to believe that God never gives up on us. The story in Luke's Gospel (13:6-9) about the barren fig tree demonstrates God's ever-present love. The tree representing Israel has not been fruitful. The owner wants it cut down but the vinedresser says to give it another chance. Some may feel that their relationship with God is so strained that they cannot approach God; we feel paralyzed and unsure which way to turn or where to go. But we must always recall that the invitation of the Lord is ever-present. We should recall Jesus' words: "Come to me, all that are weary and are carrying heavy burdens, and I will give you rest. Take my yoke upon you, and learn from me, for I am gentle and humble in heart, and you will find rest for your souls. For my yoke is easy and my burden is light" (Matthew 11:28-29). Yes, Jesus is present and stands ready to welcome us, but we must respond and open our hearts. As we hear in the book of Revelation: "Listen! I am standing at the door; knocking; if you hear my voice and open the door I will come in to you and eat with you, and you with me" (3:20). Jesus will not break in where he is not wanted or invited; we must open the door of our hearts to his invitation of reconciliation.

The process of reconciliation continues with the discovery of the three active aspects of forgiveness, within self, with others, and ultimately with God. The famous parable of the prodigal son, Luke 15:11-32, best illustrates this second step in the journey of reconciliation. Active reconciliation must begin within our own person. The so-called prodigal son in the story comes to the realization that he needs to forgive himself. He has wasted his father's money; he has lived a wayward existence. Before he could begin the physical journey back to his father, he needed to find a change of heart within himself. He needed to forgive himself, before he would be ready to accept the forgiveness of others.

Reconciliation with others is the second active aspect. The older son in the parable is representative of one who cannot forgive others. He is angry with his brother for his wayward actions. He is even more incensed, however, by his father who has not only forgiven the younger boy's transgressions but has celebrated his return with food and dance. We learn about the need to forgive others in the character of the older son. Since this young man cannot forgive, the process of reconciliation is stunted. As when the weak link in the chain snaps and destroys the usefulness of the whole, so too, if either of the first two active aspects of reconciliation are not found, the final aspect, reconciliation with God, cannot be achieved.

The forgiving father in the parable represents God. His youngest son was barely in sight and the father had the celebration prepared. Reconciliation was achieved as soon as his wayward son realized that he needed to be forgiven, by himself and by others. Similarly, Jesus' arms are outstretched on the cross as a sign of his welcome of us when we have strayed off the path that leads to life. All that is necessary to achieve this reconciliation is for us to ask.

The final step in the process of reconciliation might not seem obvious. God has pursued us and we have found reconciliation within ourselves, with others, and with God. One thing more is required, however; we need to look to the future. The positive message of the prophets is to look to the future. After predictions of doom the prophets say that the people need to forget the past and look to the future. In Isaiah we read, "Do not remember the former things or consider the things of old. I am about to do a new thing; now it springs forth, do you not perceive it? I will make a way in the wilderness and rivers in the desert" (43:18-19). The past actions of the Hebrew people had to be put behind them; they needed to begin anew.

Reconciliation is only complete when we put the sins of our past behind us and start again. If we dwell on the past then it will be impossible to make a new beginning. We carry around our excess baggage; it weighs us down. But as Jesus said to the woman caught in adultery, "Woman, where are they? Has no one condemned you?" She said, "No one, sir." And Jesus said, "Neither do I condemn you. Go your way, and from now on do not sin again" (John

8:10b-11). Jesus' words to the woman point to the future. The past is forgiven. Let us move on, drop the past baggage, and try to do better. Too many times people live in the past; they have never learned to forgive themselves. Reconciliation is very much a desert experience. We may enter the process with some significant reservations. But let us remember that Paul did the same thing in his relationship with the Corinthians. He wrote: "I came to you in weakness and in fear and in much trembling" (1 Corinthians 2:3). Paul's solution to his dilemma was found in Jesus and so too must our answers be sought. Let us remember Jesus' words: "Those who are well have no need of a physician, but those who are sick; I have come to call not the righteous but sinners" (Mark 2:17).

The young man on the train found that reconciliation was not found through a sense of righteousness or aggressive behavior; it could only be found through an active outpouring of compassion. Yet, he had to learn, by observation of the older man, that God was ready and able to be a reconciler. If any of us should have any further need of the reality of God's abiding love for us, picture this image: It is a hot and beautiful summer day and a little girl stands on the edge of large swimming pool. She looks out at the shimmering water and her eyes well up with tears. She is afraid, for she does not know how to swim, but then, she raises her eyes, looks out and sees her mom, with her arms outstretched. Mom says, "Go ahead, jump in, there is nothing to fear. I will hold you up." In a similar way, Jesus has his arms outstretched on the cross and he says to all of us, "Go ahead, take a chance, be reconciled with others. I will hold you up; I will bring you to eternal life."

All Is New In Christ

Running as fast as his feet would carry him, Androclus raced into the forest. He hoped he could survive there, finding roots and berries to eat and avoiding all wild animals. He had few other choices; people were always looking for runaway slaves. He wondered, however, how it would be to live in terror of being discovered. Every pine cone that fell onto the mossy surface of the forest made him jump and look around to see if soldiers were in pursuit. He needed shelter. Rain was in the air and it would soon be dark. Through a break in the trees he saw an opening in the rocks. Thinking it might be large enough for him to sleep in that evening, he headed toward it. However, he stopped short and, looking to the right of the rock formation, he spied a lion. Instinct kicked in and Androclus ran, praying all the while that the animal had eaten recently. Hearing no sound of pursuit, he slowed down and the stopped. Looking back, he saw the lion had not pursued him. Its only movement was to roll its head looking at him with a rather mournful countenance.

Slowly Androclus retraced his steps. The lion was in pain. He spoke softly to the lion, stroking his mane and back, and looking for some injury. Finally he found it — a nasty gash on the lion's left hind leg. It was clear that the wound had been bleeding for some time and showed no sign of letting up. Androclus tore some of the cloth from his tunic and cleaned the wound. The animal shuddered and groaned before falling asleep.

Just then the clouds opened up and Androculus crawled into the cave and immediately fell asleep. Minutes later, however, he awoke when the lion came in, dragging his wounded leg and laid down beside him. The cave was large enough for man and beast to live together, and they did just that for several weeks. Each day they would go out and hunt for sufficient food and water for the day.

One day, when drawing water from a stream, Androclus felt something sharp against his neck. "Don't move," said a voice. "There is a big reward for the return of a runaway slave." Forced back to the city, Androclus often thought of his friend the lion, sad that they would never again see each other. He was taken to see the Emperor who pronounced upon him the sentence of death. Soldiers took him to a stone cell beneath the palace where he was to await the day of his execution. Finally, he was led to the arena. The crowd cheered wildly as a lion, which had not been fed for four days, was let loose on Androclus. The animal roared and ran toward its easy prey. Androclus realized he had no chance and, thus, he closed his eyes and braced for the impact and pain. Instead of searing pain, however, he felt the warm tongue of the lion who playfully licked him until he fell to the ground. Androclus opened his eyes and before him he saw his friend the lion from the forest. Instead of bouncing to kill and devour him, as would be normal, even instinctive, especially after not eating for four days, the lion, once so gently cared for, fawned over Androclus like a friendly dog.

The crowd in the arena was hushed to silence; the Emperor was stunned. He called Androclus to him. He told the Emperor the whole story. "Androclus and the lion are hereby freed," said the Emperor. "Such amazing kindness, gratitude, and the ability to throw away the past must be rewarded."

The captivating story of Androclus and the lion presents many themes to ponder, but it clearly demonstrates the need to forget the past, be converted, and begin anew. Androclus, the lion, and even the Emperor, were challenged to forget the past, their preconceived notions and move to a new, more positive understanding of others. As kindness created a new reaction, replacing fear with love, so we are called in this Lenten season to seek transformation in our lives. Today's powerful reading from Saint Paul provides both the challenge and the answer.

Transformation is certainly a concept that Saint Paul knew quite well from his personal experience. In today's lesson, he tells us that he had every reason for confidence in his earlier life. The Acts of the Apostles and the Pauline corpus verify this claim. He was a zealous Pharisee who was educated at the feet of Gamaliel (Acts 22:3), one of the most learned Jews of the period. He was fervent in his role as Pharisee and took very seriously his responsibility to persecute those who practiced the new way. He was present at the death of the first Christian martyr, Stephen. Luke tells us, "Saul approved of their killing him" (Acts 8:1). Then, almost literally in the blink of an eye, Saul was transformed (Acts 9:1-19) as he traveled to Damascus seeking to continue his zealous crusade against the Christians. Jesus spoke to him and commissioned him to drop the past and take on a new role in life. Paul had previously justified his life and believed himself to be righteous based on the law. Now, after his conversion, all that mattered was faith. Thus, Paul writes to the Philippians that all of his former ways are a loss. Jesus has changed everything for Paul.

Paul had a good life, but Jesus asked him to change. He had all the power, prestige, and presumable wealth that one could seek in his day. Then he was called to become a missionary, to travel throughout the majority of the then-known western world on three dangerous and arduous journeys. He was asked to preach ideas that were not popular to most. He was caught between faithful Jews who saw him as a traitor and Gentiles who found his claim of a slain Messiah now alive to be unbelievable. Yet, Paul says that Jesus was so important to him, that he willingly cast aside all other things, leaving the past completely, so as to have Christ and Christ alone. As Jesus reached out to Paul in a personal way on the Damascus Road, making the new apostle one with him, so Paul tells us, as Christ's emissaries, to reach out to others, and preach the good news. We are to tell them of their need to leave the past behind and press forward to the reward of Jesus. Christ is the one and only prize which has any significance for Paul. It should be the same for us!

Lent is a time for the Christian community, personally and communally, to be transformed, to cast aside the past, to move out from the shadows of darkness and seek the light which only Jesus can bring. We need to put away the old and bring in the new. We need to be transformed in Christ.

First, we must seek transformation in our attitudes. Too often we think in narrow, provincial, and exclusive ways. Jesus clearly demonstrated a more inclusive and broad understanding of life. Rather than restricting people, Jesus welcomed all, but most especially those whom the world had summarily rejected: the sick, the poor, foreigners, and sinners. Jesus never labeled certain people as *in* and others as *out*, a practice in which many of us engage. No one had to pass a litmus test for Jesus. All that was necessary was a sense of openness and a contrite heart. We must cast aside our preconceived attitudes with respect to individuals or groups and find a renewed and more Christlike attitude in our daily interactions with others.

We must be transformed in word, leaving behind both words we have used and those used by others which have been hurtful. As we all know, words are very powerful and can be used for good or evil. We must seek to transform negative speech that tears down into positive language that builds up and reinforces. It is not easy to leave behind the hurt others have inflicted on us by insensitive words or possibly forget how we have willingly damaged others through lack of forethought. But as Paul dropped the past in order to find Christ, so must we do likewise.

Transformation in action is also required. As with words, it is difficult to forgive the injustice that others have perpetrated against us. Our natural inclination is for retribution or revenge. Thus, we harbor evil thoughts against others and await our chance to respond. Similarly, some cannot forgive themselves for past indiscretions. It is necessary to re-evaluate what we do and how we do it; we must transform the way we do things. In the end, however, we need to drop the past and move forward.

Transformation requires us to let go of the past, but we often find this extremely difficult. Thus, we need outside help and there is no better source than God's Word. Scripture provides much evidence of God's willingness to let us start over. We know well that God has always been active on behalf of God's people in releasing us from the bonds of this earth's existence. We remember that God broke the shackles of the Israelites in bondage in Egypt through the work of God's servant, Moses. Later, God sent the judges and the prophets, people like Deborah and Esther, Isaiah and Jeremiah, to guide the people to a better life and understanding of God's way. Ezekiel, one of the major prophets, wrote to the Hebrews when they were in bondage again, this time in Babylon. Yes, the people suffered from physical confinement and isolation from their homeland, but the psychological bonds were probably greater. The people were without hope; they were living in despair. Many of the Hebrews surely thought that God had abandoned them. Ezekiel tells the people that their exile, their captivity, their grave, their chains will be removed. We read, "I am going to open your graves, and bring you up from your graves, O my people; and I will bring you back to the land of Israel" (37:12b). Yes, God will return the people to their homeland. God's faithfulness to God's people will restore hope and break the bonds. A new day will dawn and a new spring will blossom.

The gospel account of the raising of Lazarus from the dead (John 11:1-45) provides the best literal and figurative example of how God alone can set us free from the past. We are not told in the scriptures why Jesus, Martha, Mary, and Lazarus were such good friends, but we do know that they were close. Why then did Jesus linger for three days when he heard that Lazarus, one of his best friends, was sick, possibly to the point of death? Would any of us so linger if we could go to the aid of one of our friends who needed us? Hopefully not. Jesus answers this question. He says that Lazarus' illness was to show God's glory. We might take that one step further and say that Jesus lingered so that the Spirit could set Lazarus and all people free from death, not just physical death, but more importantly the deadness of the past that exists inside each one of us in different ways.

Jesus says, "I am the resurrection and the life." If anyone believes in Jesus, that one will never be without hope. If anyone believes in the Lord that one will never die without the Spirit. Jesus wants Martha, Mary, and all those present, and by extension all of us, to know that his presence is not so much to raise us from physical death, but to restore hope to all and unchain us from all that holds us back from being the fullness of who we want to be. The words of Jesus at the end of this gospel pericope are powerful indeed: "Untie him and let him go free." Jesus has removed the shackles and chains, the cloth of death from Lazarus. It can be that way for all of us as well! We must let go of the past, cut the ball and chain from our leg that impedes our forward movement, and find the newness we seek in Jesus.

Yes, God's rescue of the Hebrew people from the land of Babylon and Jesus' raising Lazarus from the dead demonstrate the faithfulness of God in unleashing us from all that binds us. All of us are bound, dead in some way or another. Maybe some of us are held bound by the cares of this world, which have such a strong and popular attraction these days. For others a burden in our family, at work, or in the community might have hold of us and will not let go. Others are chained by some situation which will not give release. Some may be prisoners of the past, and think that no one cares.

Through our chains, our bonds, there will be a certain sense of dying. Paul knew the need to cast aside his former life if he was to be able to serve Jesus as the "Apostle to the Gentiles." Somehow, Androclus and the lion cast aside their preconceived notions about each other and became friends. The Hebrews were victims of the death of despair, hopelessness, and isolation. Lazarus was caught in the trap of physical death and maybe other forms of death of which we are not aware. Through the action of Christ, the one who brings the light, we are released from all that chains us. All we need is to be open to the action of God in our lives. We know that God sent the Spirit on Pentecost to give us a guide and to renew the people in hope. The Spirit can also release us from all that binds us. The walking dead, those who are held bound are all around us; we are they. There is an answer; there is a release. Jesus says, "Untie him and let him go free." Jesus is the one who can untie us from all that chains us in this life. Let us give our lives over to the Lord so that he can break the bonds that hold us in this life, and, in the end, tie us to God forever in the eternal life that is God's promise to all who believe.

Carrying The Burdens Of Others

There was a man named Sundar, a convert to Christianity who decided to go to India to be a missionary and bear witness to others about Jesus. One day, late in the afternoon, Sundar was traveling on foot high in the Himalaya Mountains with a Buddhist monk. It was bitterly cold and darkness was rapidly starting to fall. The monk told Sundar they would be in danger of freezing to death if they did not reach the monastery before nightfall.

As they crossed a narrow path above a steep cliff, a cry for help was heard. Deep down in the ravine a man had fallen and was severely injured. His leg was broken and, therefore, he could not walk. The monk warned Sundar, "Do not stop. God has brought this man to his fate. He must work it out by himself. That is the tradition. Let us hurry on and continue our journey before we perish." But Sundar replied, "It is my newfound tradition that God has brought me here to help my brother. I cannot abandon him, especially now." So the monk set off through the snow which had started to fall heavily.

Sundar climbed down to where the injured man was lying. Since the man had a broken leg, Sundar had to find some way to carry him. He brought with him a blanket from his knapsack and made a sling out of it. He got the man into the sling and hoisted him onto his back. Then together they began the arduous climb up to the path. After a long time, Sundar, drenched with perspiration, finally got back to the path. He continued to struggle with his heavy burden through the snow which was becoming increasingly deep. It

155

was dark now and, thus, it was hard to find his way, but he continued along the way in the direction of the monastery. Although he was faint from fatigue and overheated from exertion, he finally saw the lights from the monastery in the distance.

Just then he took a step and stumbled, almost falling. He looked down and found that he had stumbled, not from weakness, but from an object lying in the path. He bent down on one knee and brushed the snow from the body of the Buddhist monk, who had frozen to death within sight of the monastery. Kneeling down, Sundar recalled a passage from Luke's Gospel: "Those who want to save their life will lose it, and those who lose their life for my sake will save it" (9:24). At that moment Sundar understood precisely what Jesus was saying and was glad that he had decided to "lose his life" for another.

Years later, when Sundar had his own disciples, they asked him, "Master, what is life's most difficult task?" And Sundar replied, "To have no burden to carry."

Sundar lived his new faith as a vocation. He left behind the ways of the past and adopted the Christian ethic to help others. He took a chance, a big chance, especially considering that the Buddhist monk had warned him of the need to seek shelter in the monastery before nightfall. But he understood that to sacrifice and give of oneself for another was the very heart of the Christian ethic. As the church throughout the world enters this most solemn and significant period of Holy Week, Saint Paul challenges us to emulate the Master, Jesus, by humbling ourselves and to willingly choose to suffer for others.

Scripture scholars tell us that this famous passage was an ancient Christological hymn, probably of Jewish-Christian origins, that was appropriated by Paul and placed into the body of his letter to the Christian community at Philippi. Paul asks the Philippians to consider the humility of Christ and to follow his lead. Even though he was God, Jesus did not in any way exploit this reality to his benefit. As the omniscient and omnipotent God, Jesus could have done many things or nothing to save humanity. He certainly could have escaped the anguish, pain, and indignity of the cross, but he chose to strip himself of all privilege and took on the human condition in all ways, save sin. As the God-Man, Jesus possessed all divine qualities and attributes, but he was also subject to all the pain, suffering, feelings of dislocation, and was forced to negotiate all the hurdles and obstacles of any other human. Jesus was completely obedient to the Father's will, even to the point of enduring an agonizing and ignominious death on the cross. As the author of the letter to the Hebrews tells us, "Although he was a Son, he [Jesus] learned obedience through what he suffered; and having been made perfect, he became the source of eternal salvation for all who obey him" (5:8-9). For a Jew, there was no more undignified way to die. As the book of Deuteronomy states: "Anyone hung on a tree is under God's curse" (21:23b).

The humility of Jesus, leading to great pain and suffering had its rewards. Paul says that because of Jesus' obedience God highly exalted him and his name, for all people for all time. While Jesus was forced to endure much, in the end he received the promised reward. Similarly, in our daily Christian lives we will be forced to suffer much, and often for unjustified reasons. Yet, if we persevere we, too, will gain our promised inheritance. As the Pauline writer states, "The saying is sure: If we have died with him, we will also live with him; if we endure, we will also reign with him; if we deny him, he will also deny us; if we are faithless, he remains faithful — for he cannot deny himself" (1 Timothy 2:11-13). Humility leads to exaltation. As they say, "The ball is in our court."

Holy Week is the culmination of the Lenten season. For six weeks, the Christian community worldwide has been on a special and very important journey. We started this trip on Ash Wednesday, by signing ourselves with burnt palms from last year's Passion Sunday celebration. We were encouraged to fast, pray, and give alms. Even more, we were challenged to not only engage in these traditional practices, but actually to become them. To manifest these virtues in our lives is quite a challenge. We must be willing to give of ourselves, to live lives that are a prayer, that are holy and spiritually exemplary. We must be willing to downplay our own efforts to the exaltation of others. Next we went to the mountain with Jesus, Peter, James, and John. As we witnessed Jesus' transfiguration we were challenged to look inside and find what needs transformation in our lives. What needs to be changed, modified, or even rooted out. Then we were asked to leave the past behind, realizing that former hurts, both those we have inflicted and those we have received, weigh us down like a ball and chain. We are unable to move forward; our growth is stunted. Thus, we were encouraged to break out, let go of the past, and move forward onto new vistas which have so much promise. As we approach the celebration of the paschal mystery, the passion, death, and resurrection of Christ, we are called by Paul to take on the humble attitude of Jesus and through our efforts find the exaltation which is God's reward to all the faithful.

Demonstrating humility in the form of dying to self is a great challenge in today's world. Humans instinctively are fearful of death, in any form, because it threatens their autonomy. A good illustration of this reality can be found in the 1970 Academy Award-winning film *Patton*. The film opens in a rather odd manner. George C. Scott, who portrayed the famous American World War II general, stands atop a platform in full military regalia; he is addressing his troops before they enter battle. In the course of his comments he states, "Some people say it is glorious to die for your country. But I say that the objective of war is to make the other guy die for his country." That simple statement says something very profound about what we, as a society, think of death. We see it as something that is to be shunned and avoided; it is dishonorable to die. Certainly anyone in a normal situation wants to live and desires that all friends and loved ones remain healthy and active. Still, for the Christian, one's attitude toward death must be different. We have been given life by God for the ultimate purpose to return to our Creator. We are on a journey which leads to God, but one can only arrive at the final destination through death. We are called to die to self so others may live.

All of us have witnessed and many have participated in heroic ways in the call to humble ourselves so others may benefit and we may gain the joy of our ultimate Christian hope. Parents sacrifice for their children all the time. Mothers and fathers deny their own needs and desires so that their children may have more and better things and opportunities. Good parents want the best for their children and, thus, willingly give whatever they can, of time, talent, or treasure. Adult children are often called to sacrifice their lives in order to serve the needs of elderly or infirmed parents. Teachers, coaches, and other mentors sacrifice in order to build and/or strengthen a new generation of youth. They teach them not only the three "Rs," or basics of the game, but imbue youth with the virtues and qualities necessary to be active and contributing members of society. Children are called to sacrifice some of their desires and possibly their needs so a classmate or friend will have the basics. Who has not been touched by such an act as a child sharing her sandwich at lunch with a friend who has none?

Our great challenge is to take Paul's message in today's lesson and relate it to similar ideas which Jesus articulated on many occasions during his public life. Humility is found in being a servant of others and gaining our satisfaction from such an attitude. Recall Jesus' words, "Whoever wishes to be great among you must be your servant, and whoever wishes to be first among you must be your slave; just as the Son of Man came not to be served but to serve, and to give his life as a ransom for many" (Matthew 20:26b-28). Humility also means sharing our portion of the burden, even when we might not feel like participating. Again, Jesus points us in the proper direction: "If any want to become my followers, let them deny themselves and take up their cross and follow me. For those who want to save their life for my sake, and for the sake of the gospel, will save it" (Mark 8:34b-35). Humility means that we should never exalt ourselves, and think we are better than others. Jesus challenged his disciples with a parable: "When you are invited by someone to a wedding banquet, do not sit down at the place of honor ... [Rather] when you are invited, go and sit at the lowest place, so when your host comes, he may say to you, 'Friend, move up higher.' ... For all who exalt themselves will be humbled, and those who humble themselves will be exalted" (Luke 14:8a, 10a, 11).

We are called to carry the burdens of our sisters and brothers. Today Jesus enters into the holy city of Jerusalem in great triumph. He is greeted with shouts of "Hosanna" and the local citizens lay palm branches before his path. Yet, we already know the end of the story. In five days he will be sacrificed for the sins of humankind. As Jesus carries the cross, he shoulders the world's burden. We do not have the strength of Jesus and the Father does not expect us to perform such feats or endure such suffering, but we are called to humble ourselves and help others. We must lighten the load of the poor, ignorant, and marginalized of society. We should recall Jesus' famous exhortation: "Truly I tell you, just as you did it to one of the least of these who are members of my family, you did it to me" (Matthew 25:40b). We must lighten the load of those who always do all the work; we must get involved. When we see a need as did Sundar, we must act. Inaction and omission can be as bad as wrong action.

Sundar was willing to do exactly as Jesus, to spend his life for another. Jesus' life and Paul's exhortation to follow the Lord's example must be the model we seek to follow in our lives. Let us faithfully walk the final part of this long journey of Lent. May we voluntarily humble ourselves, to die to self so others may live. We do so in imitation of Jesus, our brother, friend, and Lord.

Sharing God's Love

There once was a king who ruled over a vast empire, but alas, he was rather old and thus decided that he needed to select his successor from his four sons. He called them in, one-by-one, to discuss the inheritance of his kingdom.

When the first son entered the king's chamber, the old man sat down and spoke: "Son, I am very old and will not live much longer. I wish to entrust my kingdom to the son best suited to receive it. Tell me, if I leave my kingdom to you, what will you give to the nation?" Now this son was very rich and so he replied, "I am a man of vast wealth. If you leave me your kingdom I will give it all my wealth and it will become the richest country in the world." "Thank you, my son," said the king, and then he dismissed him.

When the second son entered, the king spoke to him, "Son, I am very old and will not live much longer. I wish to entrust my kingdom to the son best suited to receive it. Tell me, if I leave my kingdom to you, what will you give to the nation?" Now this son was very intelligent and thus he replied, "I am a man of vast intelligence and I love to learn. If you leave your kingdom to me I will give it all my intelligence and knowledge. It will become known as the most intelligent nation in the world." "Thank you, my son," said the king, and then he dismissed him.

Then the third son entered the king's presence. The monarch spoke to him, "Son, I am very old and will not live much longer. I wish to entrust my kingdom to the son best suited to receive it. Tell me, if I leave my kingdom to you, what will you give to the nation?" This son was very strong, so when he heard his father's

161

question he replied, "I am a man of great strength. If you leave me your kingdom, I will give it all my strength and it will be the strongest nation in the world." "Thank you, my son," said the king, and then he dismissed him.

The fourth son then entered and was greeted by his father as had his three older brothers. "Son, I am very old and will not live much longer. I wish to entrust my kingdom to the son best suited to receive it. Tell me, if I leave my kingdom to you, what will you give to the nation?" Now this son was not especially rich, or smart, or strong. So he replied to the king, "My father, you know that my brothers are much richer, smarter, and stronger than I. While they have spent much time attaining these attributes, I have spent my time among the people in your kingdom. I have shared with them in their sickness and sorrow. And I have learned to love them. I am afraid that the only thing I have to give to your kingdom is my love of the people. I know that my brothers have more to offer than I do and, therefore, I will not be disappointed in not being named your heir. I will simply continue to do what I have always done."

When the king died, the citizens of the realm anxiously awaited the news as to their new ruler, and the greatest rejoicing the kingdom had ever experienced took place when it was learned the fourth son had been named by the king to be his successor.[1]

While he didn't believe he had any special talents or gifts that would qualify him to be king, the fourth son was chosen because he possessed the one and only gift that was needed. He was willing to spend his life for others. Today, the Christian world mourns that Christ dies at the hands of cruel men. But as the story of the king and his sons indicates, and our reading from the letter to the Hebrews says, Jesus' action has changed everything. Through his act of love the world has been washed clean. It is a new day as Jesus reigns supreme as Lord and King from the wood of the cross.

Writing most probably after the destruction of Jerusalem and the Diaspora, the author of the letter to the Hebrews had time and perspective to reflect on what Jesus' death meant to the nascent, but burgeoning Christian community. Remembering the plight of their Jewish ancestors in the faith during the period of the Babylonian exile, many Jewish-Christians might have thought God had abandoned them, so severely were they crushed by Jesus' death. All their hopes and dreams for the restoration of Israel were lost. They were confused and most assuredly had trouble making sense of these events. Jesus' death seemed so senseless and unwarranted. Even after the resurrection, the community of faith was still seeking answers; they were trying to make sense of the inexplicable.

The author of the letter to the Hebrews provides some answers to the basic question — what did the death of Jesus mean? Today we are told that because of Jesus' blood we can now enter the sanctuary, that is the eternal reward of salvation. Jesus has opened the way for humankind. As the Hebrews experienced a new beginning after their return from exile, God making all things new, so now Jesus' act has transformed the world. The Lord's act of love has created a new covenant in the minds and hearts of the faithful. It is like that which God proclaimed through the prophet Jeremiah, centuries earlier: "The days are surely coming, says the Lord, when I will make a new covenant with the house of Israel and the house of Judah. It will not be like the covenant I made with their ancestors when I took them by the hand to bring them out of the land of Egypt — a covenant that they broke, though I was their husband, says the Lord. But this is the covenant I will make with the house of Israel after those days, says the Lord: I will put my love within them, and I will write it on their hearts; and I will be their God and they shall be my people ... I will forgive their iniquity, and remember their sin no more" (Jeremiah 31:31-33, 34b).

Jesus' act of love has made us clean. The author of Hebrews tells us that through Jesus' blood, our hearts have been sprinkled clean from evil; our minds and consciences have been washed pure. We are like those mentioned by the seer John in the book of Revelation: "These are they who have come out of the great ordeal; they have washed their robes and made them white in the blood of the Lamb" (7:14). Jesus has shared his life and now his death in a way that has become salvific. Through his death we are made clean; he has inaugurated a new day.

Jesus' act on the cross is not one of defeat, but rather is the apex of his life, his greatest moment. From the perspective of Saint

John in his account of the crucifixion, Jesus begins to reign as king from the cross; the cross becomes his throne. The events of Calvary thus bring a new day for God's people. Jesus initiates this new day, but we, the hands and feet, the body of Christ today in our world, must continue what Christ started. As our reading states, we must use Jesus' act of love on the cross as the catalyst for our own sharing of God's goodness to others. We are called to encourage others to demonstrate love and perform good deeds.

Jesus' salvific death on the cross is an historical event, but our remembrance this Good Friday must be much more than a sorrowful memory. Christ's death obviously has significant theological meaning. His death was the antidote to Adam, canceling our debt. Saint Paul powerfully wrote, "Therefore just as one man's trespass led to condemnation for all, so one man's act of righteousness leads to justification and life for all. For just as by the one man's disobedience the many were made sinners, so by the one man's obedience the many will be made righteous" (Romans 5:18-19). Yes, Jesus is the new Adam who, as the reading from Hebrews says, vanquishes sin. It is through Jesus' action on the cross and his subsequent resurrection that one's faith has meaning. Again, Saint Paul states, "If Christ has not been raised, then our proclamation has been in vain, and your faith has been in vain" (1 Corinthians 15:14).

While Jesus' sacrificial death is laden with theological meaning and significance, what is the pastoral message that we can apply each day of our lives? Jesus' death calls us to be ambassadors of Christ's love to others. As Jesus shared with us completely, so must we share with others. In essence we are called to be bridge builders between Christ and the world.

A short story illustrates our commission. Two brothers owned farms that joined each other. A vast and beautiful meadow kept the two brothers' property united. For many years the two were very close, but disagreements here and there led to some conflict. One day, one of the brothers bulldozed the river levee allowing water to run freely down the meadow creating a natural division between their properties. It so happened that at this same time a traveling handyman came and knocked on the front door of the other brother's farm house. The handyman said, "Have you any work? I am good at carpentry, plumbing, and electrical work." The brother replied, "As a matter of fact, I have just the job for you." He took the handyman to the back of his house and showed him the meadow and the stream that now ran through it. He said, "You see that wood pile over there? Use it to build an eight-foot fence that will separate my property from my brother's." The handyman told the brother, "I will take care of this matter for you. If you wish, you can go to town and run any errands you have. I will finish by the end of the day." Thus, the brother went to the town and the handyman got busy. Late in the afternoon, the brother returned. To his great surprise, the handyman had not constructed a wall, but a bridge over the stream. And on the other side of the bridge, the other brother stood with his arms outstretched. The two men met at the middle of the bridge and embraced.

As ambassadors of Christ's love in the world, we are called to tear down walls that divide and to build bridges that unify. Too often we place barriers between ourselves and others. Hurdles are also placed between Christ's body, the church, and society. We must do what we can to remove these obstacles and share God's love with others. We are called to share the pain and suffering of others, reaching out to those who need us most. We are called to proclaim a new day for strained and broken relationships. We are called to let go of the past and encourage others to do the same. We need to believe and practice, as Jesus clearly did, that the best way to share God's love is through acknowledging our brokenness and weakness. Saint Paul knew this well and thus could confidently write: "I am content with weaknesses, insults, hardships, persecutions, and calamities for the sake of Christ; for whenever I am weak, then I am strong" (2 Corinthians 12:10).

The youngest brother thought he had nothing of value to give to the kingdom, but he really had everything. It was his gift of love, shared with the people, that won the day, not only for his ascension to the crown, but more fundamentally in bringing a new beginning for the kingdom. As we celebrate this solemn day let us join with Jesus and share our lives with others. It is through such action that the world becomes a better place and we find eternal life.

1. Paraphrased from "To Whom Shall I Leave My Kingdom," in Alice Gray, ed. *More Stories for the Heart* (Sisters, Oregon: Multnomah Publishers, 1997), pp. 88-89.

Repairing Our Lives

Once upon a time, there was a king who ruled over a small kingdom that wasn't powerful nor was it known for anything of any great value. But, the king did possess a large and perfect diamond that had been in his family for many generations. He kept it on display for all to see and appreciate and people came from all over the country to admire this rare and precious gem. People from other lands, hearing about the great diamond, also came and they, too, felt some sense of pride simply by gazing upon the unusual gem.

One day a soldier, whose task it was to guard the diamond, came to the king and reported that although the gem had not been touched by human hands it was now cracked. The king ran to investigate and sure enough there was a crack right through the middle of the rare gem. He immediately summoned jewelers from across the land to examine the diamond and see what could be done to repair it, but all the experts gave the same response: it was now useless, irredeemably flawed. The king was crushed and so were the people who felt that they had lost everything. Then, out of nowhere an old man, who claimed to be a master jeweler, asked to see the diamond. He told the king, "I can fix it. In fact, I can make it better than it was before." The king was surprised at the report and was leery of the old man, but he gave him the jewel. The old man said, "I'll have it back to you in a week fully repaired."

Now the king was not about to let the diamond out of his sight, even if it was possibly ruined, so he gave the old man a room and

167

food and provided all the tools he would need to repair the diamond. At the end of one week the old man appeared with the stone in his hand and presented it to the king. The king couldn't believe it. The old man had fixed the diamond and it looked magnificent; it looked even better than before. He had made the crack that ran through the gem into a stem and had carved around it an intricate rose with petals, leaves, and thorns. The king was overjoyed and offered the old man half of his kingdom for he had taken something beautiful and perfect and improved upon it. But the old man refused the offer in front of the whole court, saying, "I did not make something perfect better. What I did was take something flawed and cracked at its heart and turn it into something beautiful once again."

The king thought that all was lost. Since his kingdom was small and relatively unimportant in the area, he perceived his reason for reigning as king, namely the pride he held in the diamond, was gone. The diamond was cracked and beyond repair. Then the old man came along and repaired the great gem in ways that the king could never have conceived. Hope was restored; beauty once again reigned.

The tale of the king's diamond and the gem master is an excellent illustration of the central message of the Easter story. When all hope was lost, Jesus destroyed death through the resurrection. As we celebrate this great event in salvation history, we must rejoice that regardless of the status of our lives, God can repair them and bring us to wholeness. We simply must have trust, confidence, and allow the resurrected Lord to show us the way.

The trust and confidence which the Easter story must engender in us was well understood by Saint Paul from his own experience of conversion. He writes to the Christian community at Corinth and tells them that Christ is the one who repairs our lives, not only in this present existence, but in eternal life. He goes so far as to say that if our hope in Christ is limited to this world alone, we are the most pitiable of people. Yes, the hope that Jesus brought to his disciples, those frightened men and women whose hopes and dreams were smashed on Good Friday, was real and palpable. Jesus' resurrection transformed the sin of Adam and the fall into hopefulness.

While the world was in darkness for many centuries, Jesus, the light of the world, came and through his self-sacrifice of death and resurrection repaired what the fall had broken. The fall condemned all men and women not only to physical death but to spiritual doom as well. But Jesus' death and resurrection has now repaired the breach between God and humankind for all people for all time. We do not deserve this great gift. As part of the human race we deserve the fate that our ancestor Adam generated, but God sent his Son to be one like us, human, as well as divine, so we could be saved by one like ourselves. Now we can stand in the light and rejoice. We can stand before the power of God grateful for what Jesus has done for us.

Jesus' resurrection marked his physical return to life. We might say that Jesus repaired his own life. But this great miracle was not only efficacious for himself, but for all. More importantly for us, he will restore to life all who belong to him. As Paul says, Jesus will repair the whole world until all enemies have been conquered.

Since the dawn of humanity, God has been the one who has been ever present to repair the brokenness in our lives. This is no better illustration than the up and down relationship God has had with the Jews. This relationship can be described as a repetitive pattern of covenant made, covenant broken, reconciliation, and covenant restored. The period of the kings of Israel and Judah was a time when prophet after prophet was sent by God to warn the people that God was displeased with their violations of the covenant. But the warnings were not heeded, neither by the northern kingdom of Israel nor the southern kingdom of Judah. Thus, the Assyrians overran Israel some 700 years before Christ and the religious and secular elite of Judah were exiled in Babylon for fifty years (587-537 B.C.E.). Yet, God never wavered in returning to the people, repairing the breach and proclaiming a new day for the Jews. Isaiah heralded God's message of reconciliation, repair, and hope while the community was in exile: "Comfort, O comfort my people, says your God. Speak tenderly to Jerusalem and cry to her that she has served her term, that her penalty is paid, that she has received from the Lord's hand double for her sins" (Isaiah 40:1-2).

After the community's return to Jerusalem the prophet continued to proclaim God's call for a new day, a fresh start.

> *For I am about to create new heavens and a new earth;*
> *the former things shall not be remembered or come to*
> *mind. But be glad and rejoice forever in what I am cre-*
> *ating; for I am about to create Jerusalem as a joy, and*
> *its people as a delight. I will rejoice in Jerusalem, and*
> *delight in my people; no more shall the sound of weep-*
> *ing be heard in it, or the cry of distress. No more shall*
> *there be in it an infant that lives but a few days, or an*
> *old person who does not live out a lifetime; for one*
> *who dies at a hundred years will be considered a youth,*
> *and one who falls short of a hundred years will be con-*
> *sidered accursed.*   — Isaiah 65:17-20

God was ever ready to repair the breach between himself and his people and the Lord stands ready today to do the same. Jesus was sent into the world to repair our broken lives; he was sent to bring the light. When all hope was lost he came to bring life. As humans we are innately damaged, incomplete and need the great physician Jesus to restore us. At times, as well, we are all lost on the path of life. Sometimes we are so far off course that the ship of our life runs aground, battered by the winds and surf which are the vicissitudes and trials of life. When our lives are so damaged, off track, and even out of control, we are in desperate need of the power of Christ to heal and repair us. We need to re-float the ship of our lives and again start sailing in the direction that leads to life eternal.

The resurrection tells us that Jesus is the one who can repair and restore our lives. Jesus can repair broken relationships. We might be able to physically re-establish lives and friendships that have been broken by death, divorce, or dislocation, but the Lord can only heal how we feel and restore damaged relationships if we are open to change. The Lord can repair damages, dreams, and hopes. Many people see life as a series of disappointments; that is opportunities that got away or were allowed to pass us by. God will provide new opportunities for us, as he provided for the Hebrews in exile, and he will create a new world. Jesus is the one who can restore peace, to our world and to our personal lives. Too often our institutions and officials take all into their own hands and divorce themselves from the power of God. We do the same with our own lives, thinking we can handle things better if we are the ones who control all. The reality is, however, that only Jesus can bring the lasting peace which we seek and need. Jesus restores what is broken; he teaches us how to live with limitations and restrictions, whether these be physical, psychological, or logistical. It is the power of Christ's resurrection that restores all things.

The king felt all was lost, but then the old gem master came upon the scene quite unexpectedly and magically all was restored. Yes, things were different, the diamond was not as it was originally, but it was more beautiful. In a similar way, Jesus rose from the dead, destroying death and restoring life. When Jesus' friends had lost all hope, the Lord restored life in every way. Jesus' resurrection gives joy to the whole Christian world, but it is not only because he conquered the grave, but because his victory can repair the many broken aspects of our lives. The Lord says in the scriptures: "Come to me, all that are weary and are carrying heavy burdens, and I will give you rest. Take my yoke upon you, and learn from me; for I am gentle and humble of heart, and you will find rest for your souls. For my yoke is easy and my burden is light" (Matthew 11:28-30). Let us give our lives to Christ, who rose from the dead and restored life. May Christ repair our lives today and to life eternal.

Jesus Brings Hope

The International Government of the World, or IGW, made its announcement with joy: the last Christian in the world was dead. This last Christian was found hiding in an abandoned mine in South Africa. He was ferreted out, brought to trial, convicted, and then executed, all the while professing Christ. The world state ordered a half-day international holiday to celebrate; the rejoicing grew to a fever pitch. Images of Christ on the cross were burned in sub-capitals throughout the world and singing, which had been banned for more than a century, was permitted this one time to aid the celebration.

Yes, it was a sad and strange day which witnessed these events. The rulers of the IGW were the sons and daughters of those who a century earlier had crushed truth, eliminated all rebellious people, and subjected humans to the monster machines of the age. The founders of the world state had created their empire by the elimination of all adversaries, all ideas, peoples, institutions, and religions. A chemist at that time had discovered a way to combine fuel, food, and water so that it was possible, with the resultant mixture, to control an entire population with a cadre of six. A special gas was developed which destroyed all the fertile land in the world. All vegetation, all trees, plants, fruits, and flowers were destroyed. Even to consider cultivation of these was punishable by death. Breathable air was produced by machines. People no longer had names; they were given numbers. Any children born were raised by the IGW. Those who were intelligent or asked questions were eliminated. The whole world population was subdued and made

173

obedient slaves by the production of one common food for all. It was a thick liquid that was piped into each person's cell; there were no homes. All trains, planes, automobiles, and people operated on the same fuel.

There was, however, an imperfection in the IGW. This godless society of the anti-Christ which had crushed out all truth had a weakness. The weak link was present in the form of a little wiry man, #2,750,300. He lived in the world capital, SC1, a city which a century earlier had been called New York. Now #2,750,300 was a bit different than other slaves; he possessed a twinkle in his eye. Still, he carried the proper credentials and thus was not eliminated by the IGW. Actually #2,750,300, whom we can call Mr. White for short, was a model slave. He did his duty well; he was above all suspicion. On Restday (there no longer was Sunday), White many times left SC1, but where he went no one was certain. He often went to a rural section of the land where one day he found something quite remarkable, a piece of brown earth which had not been destroyed; it was his oasis.

One Restday in the spring, Mr. White journeyed to this little plot of earth. He brought with him a packet which he emptied onto the soil. The moist earth gladly welcomed the offering given to it. "I will bring God back to the world," thought #2,750,300. He left and returned home.

Time passed; spring and summer came and went. One fall day, the season that in earlier centuries was so beautiful when trees existed on earth, Mr. White went to his plot of land. There blowing in the gentle breeze was a crop of wheat. The fact that the IGW had never discovered the plot was a minor miracle. White hurriedly harvested his crop, pounded the grain, and formed it. Using the stubble of the wheat, he built a fire and baked the wheat. The yield was two small wafers. He took his prize home to await his day.

Several weeks later, early one morning, White arose. He gathered his precious wafers and pulled out a box that had remained undetected by the IGW officials. Gathering his things he made his way out into the street and across town. In this early morning hour all was still; the slaves were asleep. He entered the tallest building in the world, found the elevator, and pushed the button for the top floor, more than one-half mile up in the sky. When he arrived on the roof, White disabled the elevator so no one could follow, set up a table, and pulled from his box an ornate cup and plate, two cruets, one with a clear liquid and one with a red substance, and some odd-looking clothes. Yes, there still was one Christian in the world; the last Christian was a priest. When the first rays of dawn were seen in the eastern sky the mass began. A small plane happened to fly close to the building. The pilot observed the scene, and remembering from his history lessons, realized what was happening. He radioed the IGW headquarters; the master was informed. "The mass must be stopped; it must be stopped," he cried. Planes were sent, bombs were dropped, gunfire was applied, but the mass continued. Then the words were spoken, "This is my body, given for you." With that, a crack of thunder was heard and a streak of lightning flashed through the sky. The clouds parted and in the distance could be seen Christ coming toward earth. Yes, it was the end of the world. Jesus had come to claim his own and restore truth to the world.

This apocalyptic story is told by Myles Connelly in his 1928 novelette, *Mr. Blue*. Written during a time of perceived prosperity in the Unites States, one might interpret the tale as a warning suggesting where unbridled wealth and power might lead, but a second interpretation is that the story describes hope. As the Christian community throughout the world enters the Easter season, basking in the light and miracle of the resurrection, we should be filled with hope of what Christ can do for us if we remain faithful. Today's lesson from the book of Revelation clearly demonstrates this same hope.

During this special season we will hear each Sunday from this last book of the Bible. Revelation, or as it was originally titled, Apocalypse, meaning "the message must take place soon," is a confusing book in many ways. It is filled with symbols, namely words and numbers, that have special meanings. In some ways, one needs a list of signs and a road map to negotiate the text. Additionally, the book is written in a prophetic voice. The author, most probably John the Apostle, as judged by its rather unlettered construction and prose, hears God's Word (1:2) and is on eleven different occasions ordered to transmit this word to his brethren.

On four occasions the seer clearly marks the book as a document of prophecy: "Blessed is the one who reads aloud the words of the prophecy, and blessed are those who keep what is written in it" (1:3).

In today's lesson, we initially hear of the universality of God's message of hope. John writes to the seven churches in Asia, a metaphor for the universal church. All are called to hear and heed the message he will present. Then the seer says that the message is sent by the seven spirits who sit before the throne. Again, the universal number seven indicates that the message has authority. But he goes on to say that the message also comes from Jesus under the threefold title faithful witness, firstborn of the dead, and ruler of the kings of earth. Here John is reviewing the Christian understanding of how Jesus brought hope. The three titles represent the passion, resurrection, and exaltation of Christ. When all hope seemed lost at his passion, Jesus restored trust and faith through his rising from death. Now, he reigns over all as Christ, the king of heaven. We can be confident of Christ's power to convert our world for he transformed death to life and finally to exaltation. He can change the deadness of our lives to a hope for resurrection and new life.

The seer, John, sees Jesus coming in the clouds. As Mr. White in Myles Connelly's story saw Jesus coming to claim the world, so John sees Christ coming as just judge. Those who have chosen not to believe are collectively guilty. John says that those who have chosen to persecute the church show their hostility toward Christ. On the other hand, those who have chosen to believe are presented the great hope that through Jesus the world will be saved. Jesus is the alpha and the omega, the beginning and the end, the first and the last. He is the totality that brings hope to an ofttimes hopeless world.

The hopefulness present in Revelation and Myles Connelly's powerful story is present in nature as spring dawns in the northern hemisphere. The deadness of winter and the grip it holds on the land, through cold and darkness, begins to give way to warmth, sun, and the light of spring. The hopelessness of the dark winter is now in retreat; the light of spring has stepped to the front. We see these signs in the landscape — the flowers, blossoming trees, the singing of birds in the morning. We can see changes in people's perspectives as well. The warmth, light, and general beauty of the springtime environment gives new life to how we feel and, therefore, the perspective we take on in life.

The hope of the physical environment is echoed by the presence of God's activity in our world. The Easter season celebrates the triumph of Jesus over the grave. In its wisdom, the church continues to celebrate this most significant event in salvation history for fifty days until Pentecost. It is a time when we can and must concentrate on the great hope which Jesus gives us through his resurrection. Jesus' triumph over death, his ability to make possible the impossible must be our source of hope.

Jesus' great victory must be the counter to our ofttimes natural human inclination to place hope on the shelf. For some, specific problems plague our lives. We may battle with health or finances, whether these be personal or associated with someone close to us. Many people are victims of situations or circumstance. The world situation in which we hear about terrorism, armed conflict, and natural disasters, tends to beat us down as well. We ask, "Why would a good and loving God allow such things to happen?" We are led to despair, disappointment, or even possibly anger. Under the conditions of the vicissitudes of life we seem at times to be barely treading water. We don't seem to be swimming toward our goal. Life seems a day-to-day struggle to keep our head above water and avoid drowning in the rough seas of contemporary life.

Yet, lest we lose hope, we must look to salvation history to see how often and with great power God has restored hope and transformed the night into day for God's people. When the Israelites were in bondage in Egypt and cried out to the Lord, God sent the deliverer, Moses, who led the people through the Red Sea to the promised land and a new day for the people. During the period of the kings in Israel and Judah, God sent a series of prophets who proclaimed God's Word. At times it was a word of warning and others one of condemnation. But the prophets also spoke God's word of comfort, reconciliation, and the dawning of a new day. Even when the people were in exile in Babylon, God spoke through Ezekiel: "Thus says the Lord God: I am going to open your graves, and bring you up from your graves, O my people; and I will bring you back to the land of Israel. And you shall know that I am the Lord, when I open your graves, O my people. I will put my spirit within you, and you shall live, and I will place you on your own soil; then you shall know that I, the Lord, have spoken and will act" (Ezekiel 37:12-14).

It is Jesus of Nazareth, the Christ, who brings this hope to its fullness. As Christ came to restore hope in Myles Connelly's story, so Jesus came to restore life to his nascent group of Christians. By extension, Jesus' hope must be present in you and me. Jesus' conquest of death has restored hope to a world shrouded in sadness and darkness. John, the seer of the book of Revelation, tells us that Jesus transformed the negative to positive, darkness to light, defeat into triumph. If we have sufficient trust and faith, the same will be true for us. Therefore, as we continue to bask in the glory of Easter's light, let us be people of hope, confident that as Christ transformed defeat into victory, he can transform us and our world into a new spring, filled with the hope which God alone can bring!

Death To Glory

Once in a far-off land, there was a great king whose dominion extended far and wide. His power and authority were absolute. One day, as events would happen, a young man, a commoner, committed a grave offense against the king. In response, the king and his counselors gathered together to determine what should be done. They decided that since the offense was so grave and had been committed by a commoner against someone so august as the king, the only punishment that would satisfy justice was death. The king's son, the crown prince, however, interceded on the young offender's behalf — you see, they were best friends. The prince spoke with his father and the counselors; the debate grew rather heated. In the end, the king declared, "The offender must pay a price for his offense. I decree that he must carry a heavy burden up Temple Mountain. If he survives the ordeal he shall live!"

The prince again interceded for his friend. He knew the burden of which his father spoke was the weight of death and he knew his friend would not be able to carry it. Thus, the prince declared, "Royal blood has been offended, therefore, only royal blood can pay the price." So the prince shouldered the heavy burden himself, and with his friend trailing behind him, he began the ascent of the mountain. The task was very difficult. The higher the prince climbed, the heavier the burden became. The prince slipped and stumbled several times, but he always managed to right himself and keep going. When the two friends first saw the summit, their goal, the prince collapsed from sheer exhaustion. He said to his friend, "In order for justice to be served, the price must be paid." The young man understood the prince and, thus, he shouldered the burden himself and, now with the prince following, managed to climb the rest of the way to the summit. When the two friends reached their goal, the prince, with his last ounce of strength, lifted the burden high over his head and then he died.

The king, observing all these events from below, declared, "Justice has been done." Then with his great power he returned his son to life. The prince, now returned to life, said, "Not so, not yet. Justice has not been served. Royal blood received help along the way!" The king had to agree. He pardoned the young offender and the two best friends lived happily ever after.[1]

Although a man of royal blood the prince unhesitatingly went to his friend's aid and shouldered the burden which he knew his associate could not bear alone. He chose to assist one in need and through his efforts that lead to his death, found, in the end, the glory of God. The Easter season celebrates how Jesus moved from death to glory. His life, his death, and his resurrection, provide the example we must follow in our relations with one another. As Jesus chose to die and through that sacrifice found life, so the prince shouldered the burden for his friend and found God. We must do likewise.

In today's lesson from the book of Revelation we hear of a special vision of the seer John. He speaks of myriads of angels who praise the lamb who was slain. This is the same lamb of which John's Gospel spoke when the precursor, John the Baptist, cried out, "Here is the Lamb of God who takes away the sin of the world" (John 1:29b). The sacrifice of the lamb, his willingness to be slain brings him power, wealth, wisdom and might, honor and glory, and praise. This great praise given to the Lamb comes not only from the myriads of angels, but, we are told, from every creature in heaven and earth. Blessings, honor, glory, and might must be given forever. The Lamb was sacrificed, Jesus has been crucified, but he has been raised from the dead and, thus, receives the honor and praise of all the world.

The angels see in the sacrifice of the Lamb the formula necessary for the glory that only God can create, for himself and all those who have followed the path the Lamb has trod. Clearly, the example we need has been provided; now it is our task to do what is necessary to follow. It is up to us how we will respond.

While the book of Revelation, as we heard today, provides ample information and verification that Jesus has passed from death to glory and thus encourages us to do likewise, we should also remind ourselves that the Lord's whole life and ministry proclaimed this same important message. From the outset of his earthly life, it was clear that Jesus was set on a course that would lead from death to glory, sacrificing himself for others and teaching his disciples to do likewise. On numerous occasions in varied ways Jesus played the servant making it clear that such action should be normative for all who wish to follow in his footsteps. Jesus told his disciples, "Whoever wishes to be great among you must be your servant, and whoever wishes to be first among you must be your slave; just as the Son of Man came not to be served but to serve, and to give his life [as] a ransom for many" (Matthew 20:28). Similarly in another context, Jesus taught his followers who were competing for position: "Whoever wants to be the first must be the last of all and servant of all" (Mark 9:35). In still another setting he said, "The greatest among you will be the servant" (Matthew 23:11). The role of the servant, if lived well, is one of dying to self for the betterment of others. If we are to live like Jesus then this must be our goal as well.

Another important aspect of the servant role is the virtue of humility. Jesus certainly taught this important quality by the way he lived and the message he preached. Jesus told a parable about those who sought places of honor at a banquet (Luke 14:7-14). He suggested it was best to sit at the low end of the table, so as to be raised up. Humility was also demonstrated by the younger so-called "prodigal" son (Luke 15:11-32) when, realizing that he had erred, the boy returned to his father seeking to confess his sin and once again to be obedient. Jesus summarized his teaching with the powerful words, "All who exalt themselves will be humbled, and all who humble themselves will be exalted" (Matthew 23:12).

Jesus' ability to pass from death to glory was also demonstrated through his fearless challenge of rules and authority that he believed were misguided and not God-centered. To speak and act

181

against the prevailing Jewish ruling elite, as had the prophets before him, was a dangerous and problematic road to follow. Yet, without thinking about what it might cost personally, Jesus unhesitatingly placed himself in harm's way, allowing himself not only to suffer ridicule and abuse, but ultimately death by crucifixion. Jesus never shied away from his goals nor the challenge necessary to achieve them. He never looked back or questioned his mission, confident that the death he endured would bring the glory and the inauguration of his kingdom in this world.

Moving from death to glory, living the Easter message, is a great challenge. Yet, we know from the experience of Jesus that this is precisely what we need to do in order to find the eternal life which is God's promise to all who believe. Moving from death to glory involves every part of our life and is manifest in multiple ways. First, we can see this transition in carrying the burdens of others.

As contemporary followers of Christ, we have a highly significant responsibility to be Christlike in assisting our sisters and brothers with the burdens they carry. In our various day-to-day work we generally do this very well. Whether we are teachers, nurses, engineers, city workers, or we work at home. Even if we are retired, our ability to carry others' burdens is accomplished with great flair and gusto. The problem comes, for many of us, in our personal relationships. Many times we do not recognize the burdens that others carry. This is not because we cannot see them, but we choose not to see them. It is much more convenient to be like the priest and the Levite in the parable of the good Samaritan and simply "pass by." This type of blindness is self-imposed. Only we can remove the blinders or dark glasses that keep us from seeing or the ear plugs that keep us from hearing the needs of others. If Jesus' resurrection is to have any lasting effect for our world, then we must be up to the challenge to carry the burdens of others and see in that, as did the prince, our true vocation.

Next, our movement from death to glory involves finding new life. Today is our celebration of the new life which God can give to us. No matter our age, status in life, or day-to-day activity, we all can use new beginnings and must rejoice in the hope that Jesus' resurrection brings. Maybe we have felt stagnant in our prayer, our employment, or our relationship with God. Possibly, we seek renewal in a relationship, in our family, with friends, or someone in our office. Some may feel held bound by past hurts, inflicted upon our person or ones we have inflicted on others. Still others may find the routine of daily life a downward spiral from which we seemingly cannot escape. Today, however, God releases us from our bondage, as assuredly as the Jews were freed from Egypt and Jesus was raised from death. The new life is ours for the taking.

Lastly, our movement from death to glory forces us to seek renewal in our lives. Maybe what needs to be restored is our self-confidence. Many people think too little of themselves. Others may think too highly of themselves, their position, or their abilities. In both cases, Jesus' resurrection can restore us to where we should be. Possibly, we feel inadequate, we are not up to the challenge of a new responsibility, ministry, or task. We won't try something new. In other cases we need to restore our attitudes to ones that are more loving, less judgmental, and, thus, more Christlike. Still others need a restoration of faith and confidence, in special people, traditional ideas, the church, and yes, for some, even God.

The Easter story, Jesus' movement from death to glory, is at its essence one of sacrifice. A beautiful story well illustrates the challenge set before us. There once was an ancient temple bell famous for its beautiful tone. It had been commissioned by a king many years ago as a way of showing devotion to the Buddha. The king's advisors had told him that making a bell in honor of the Buddha would save the nation from foreign invasion, so the king approached the greatest bell maker in the realm with this commission. The man worked long and hard and produced many bells, but none had the extraordinary tone necessary for its special purpose. Finally, the bell maker went to the king and told him the only way he could get the bell desired was to sacrifice a young maiden. Soldiers were thus dispatched to find a young girl. Coming upon a poor mother in a small village they took her young daughter. The child cried in vain *"Emille, Emille"* — "Mother, O Mother." When the molten lead and iron were prepared, the girl was thrown into the mix. At last the bell maker had succeeded. The bell, called the Emille Bell, made a sound more beautiful than any other. When it rang, most people praised the artist who had produced the sound, but whenever the woman whose child was sacrificed heard it, her heart broke anew. Her neighbors, who knew of her sacrifice and pain, could not hear the tone without the pain, either. Only those who understand sacrifice can feel the pain. Others just enjoy the sound.

As we continue to bask in the resurrection, let us understand our need to die to self, to be servants, to sacrifice so as to find the glory that can be ours. Let us follow the examples of the prince who shouldered his friend's burden and Jesus who taught us to be servants. Our reward in heaven will be great.

---

1. Paraphrased from "The Burden: A Tale of Christ," in John Aurelio, *Colors! Stories of the Kingdom* (New York: Crossroad, 1993), pp. 130-132.

Enduring The Trials Of Faith

"In the seventh year of his reign, two days before his 65th birthday, in the presence of a full consistory of cardinals, Jean Marie Barette, Pope Gregory XVII, signed an instrument of abdication, took off the Fisherman's ring, handed his seal to the Cardinal Camerlengo and made a curt speech of farewell." So begins the power novel, *The Clowns of God*, the second volume of a trilogy of tales about popes and faith written by Morris West, the Australian-born novelist. In the story, the pope has seen a vision of the Second Coming. He feels that the message of Christ's return must be promulgated throughout the world. Therefore, he gathers his closest advisors, the curia and college of cardinals, and asks their advice. They tell him that such a message cannot be published. "It will throw the world into a panic," they claim. The pope is confused but feels that he has only one alternative. He must be true to himself and, thus, he abdicates his position and places himself under obedience to an abbot in a monastery outside of Rome.

After one week at the monastery, Jean Marie receives his first visitor, Carl Mendelius, a long time friend and former Jesuit priest, who now, as a married man, is teaching theology in a prestigious German university. The two friends speak and begin to map out a strategy whereby the message of Jean Marie's vision can be promulgated to the world. The plan is foiled, however, before it can be enacted. Mendelius, working in Germany on a position paper, is felled by a letter bomb sent by a would-be assassin just as he is ready to present the text of the message to a group of scholars. Jean

Marie, in England to give a speech where the message will be revealed, suffers a severe heart attack. As he clings to life in a London hospital, Jean Marie receives a strange visitor. The man is young, about thirty years old, tall, strong, and speaks with a Middle Eastern accent, although his origin seems a mystery. He wears a beautiful and ancient ring which has inscribed on it the Christian symbol of a fish. This man calls himself Mr. Atha. The stranger tells Jean Marie that he must persevere but that the message which he feels must be told has already been proclaimed, if people will only recognize it.

Several weeks later, Jean Marie returns to his native France to recuperate fully. One day he goes for a walk in Parisian park, sits down, and observes a group of children who are mentally handicapped playing nearby. These children accept their fate without a word of objection. Through this experience Jean Marie begins to realize that the essential message of his vision is to accept God and to endure the trials of faith. The unpretentious lives of these children, whom he calls the "Clowns of God," have made the message crystal clear.

Months later, in a remote mountain villa, Jean Marie joins his newfound friends, the Clowns of God, to celebrate the Christmas feast. To this isolated place, Mr. Atha comes quite unexpectedly. Jean Marie has endured the great trial of faith and discovered Jesus, who has returned to claim the world.

Morris West's epic tale describes how one man was challenged to look beyond the obvious in order to find the presence of God. The former pope was forced to endure a great trial of faith, not because he chose, but out of necessity. Trials of faith are an everyday part of life, although some may not be as obvious as others. We must learn, as did Jean Marie Barrette, to persevere and continue along the road, despite the pain and setbacks that may come our way. We will find, as did Jean Marie, that through the trials and tribulations of life, we will gain strength and be that much better prepared to follow in the footsteps of the Lord.

The trials of faith that come our way are part and parcel of the mission to which all God's children, the baptized, are called. The apocalyptic image that we hear from the book of Revelation today speaks clearly of those who "have washed their robes white in the blood of the lamb." This powerful metaphor of the need to endure the various trials of faith, that is to be willing to move through the hurdles, obstacles, and barriers that often cause us problems, is a great challenge. Can any of us picture the level of persistence needed that allows blood to wash things and make them white once again? It is the image the author of the letter to the Hebrews presents when he says, "Although he was a Son, he learned obedience through what he suffered" (Hebrews 5:8). John, the seer in the book of Revelation, also says there is a very important reward that comes from this high level of faith. These people will stand before the throne of God and worship the Lord day and night. They will hunger no more, nor will the sun strike or scorch them. God will shepherd these people, guiding them to springs of life-giving water. God will wipe away all of their tears.

Jesus' whole life and ministry was, in many ways, a constant negotiation of various hurdles and obstacles of faith. Immediately after his baptism, Jesus went to the desert and was tempted by Satan as preparation for his life's ministry. The Lord was tempted with the three great sins of humanity — power, wealth, and prestige. Demonstrating power by commanding stones to turn to bread was not what Jesus needed or desired. Next, Satan tells Jesus to throw himself from the parapet of the temple, confident that God will not allow anything harmful to befall his Son. Again, Jesus has no need to exalt his position by such acts. Lastly, Jesus rejects the offer of all the kingdoms of the world. He does not need such material possessions. Throughout his public life, Jesus was forced to endure the pain of rejection. Some claimed he was possessed by Beelzebub. He was misunderstood by his inner circle, betrayed and denied by his apostles. During his agony in the garden, Jesus sweat blood (Luke 22:44) as he prayed to his father asking if possible for the cup to pass, but in the end said, "Not what I want but what you want" (Matthew 26:39c). Jesus' crucifixion was his ultimate test of faith, but fortunately for us he never drew back from his task, but willingly, as Saint Paul tells us (Philippians 2:6-11), went to the cross, choosing to suffer so we could find life.

The work we do and the lives we lead are part of God's master plan that necessitates, at times, our negotiation of hurdles that are trials of faith. The image in the book of Revelation of those who have endured their trials of faith, washing their robes white in the blood of the lamb, is, like the events in the life of Jean Marie Barrette, a classic tale of a significant trial. The work that we do, the ministry in which we participate, is a significant part of the life that God gives us, a life that is often dotted with bumps, obstacles, road blocks, and detours. At times its seems that nothing goes right, that the challenges of faith are too great. We must remember the positive story of Jean Marie Barrette and his encounter with the Clowns of God and contrast it with the failure of Thomas, who, as we recall, refused to believe in Jesus' resurrection (John 20:19-29). We must remember this in order to know that there is an absolute need to persevere and maintain faith so as to negotiate the dark tunnels of life and find the light on the other side.

All of us experience trials of faith — how do we fare? Our faith is tried through sickness or death. Do we continually ask why — why my relative or friend is sick, why God chose to claim a member of my family? Or, do we seek ways from which we can draw renewed and strengthened faith from the trial we must endure. Faith can be tried through the pain of unemployment. If we lose our job or cannot find work does it destroy our faith? Do we become angry; do we cry out and ask where God is? Or, does such a trial of faith allow us greater communion and better understanding of the chronically unemployed, those who cannot work because of a mental or physical handicap? Faith can be tested through problems and broken relationships. Does the separation of friends, the pain of divorce, or rejection in love make us "throw in the towel"; do we say, "I can't go on?" Or, does our trial of faith lead us to greater independence; does it allow us to feel better about ourselves? Can we say, God loves me?

We have all had trials of faith and we know others who have had similar experiences. Can we accept the trial and learn, as did Jean Marie Barette that the "Clowns of God," those more vulnerable people in our world, can show us the way that leads to life?

Or, are we like Thomas and refuse to believe? When trials come do we say, I want no part of this; it isn't fair?

Should we need more encouragement to keep moving through the trials of faith in our lives, the true story of Bill Mitchell will inspire even the least confident of heart: On the morning of June 19, 1971, Bill Mitchell was on top of the world. Riding his brand new motorcycle to a job he loved, gripman on a San Francisco cable car, Bill seemed on cloud nine. Earlier that day, he had soloed in an airplane for the first time, the fulfillment of one of his fondest dreams. Twenty-eight — handsome, healthy, and popular — Bill was in his element. In the flash of an eye, however, Bill's whole world changed. Rounding a corner as he neared the cable car barn, Bill collided with a laundry truck. Gas from the motorcycle poured out and ignited through the heat of the engine. Bill emerged from the accident with a broken pelvis and elbow and burns over 65 percent of his body.

The next six months were a period of great trial for Bill. After several blood transfusions, numerous operations, and many skin grafts, Bill was released from the hospital. Walking down the street he passed a school playground where the children stared at his face. "Look at the monster," they exclaimed. Although he was deeply hurt by the insensitivity of the children, he still had the love and compassion of friends and family, and the grace of a good personal philosophy on life. Bill realized that he did not have to be handsome to make a contribution to society. Success was in his hands if he chose to begin again.

Within a year of the accident, Bill was moving again toward the success he enjoyed earlier. He began to fly planes. He moved to Colorado and founded a company that built wood-burning stoves. Within no time, Bill was a millionaire with a Victorian home, his own plane, and significant real estate holdings.

In November 1975, however, the bottom again fell out of Bill Mitchell's world. Piloting a turbo-charged Cessna with four passengers onboard, Bill was forced to abort a take-off, causing the plane to drop about 75 feet, like a rock, back to the runway. Smoke filled the plane and fearing that he would again be burned, Bill attempted to escape. Pain in his back and his inability to move his legs thwarted his efforts.

In the hospital again, Bill was informed that his thoracic vertebrae were crushed and the spinal cord was damaged beyond repair. He would spend the rest of his life as a paraplegic. Although doubt began to invade his generally optimistic mind, Bill began to focus on the cans and not the cannots of his life. He decided to follow the advice of the German philosopher Goethe: "Whatever you can do, or dream you can do, begin it. Boldness has genius, power, and magic in it." Before his accidents there were many things Bill could do. He could spend his time dwelling on what was lost or focus on what was left.

Since that 1975 plane accident, Bill Mitchell has twice been elected mayor of his town, earned recognition as an environmental activist, and run for Congress. He has hosted his own television show and travels the nation speaking to groups about his message of proper attitude, service, and transformation. Bill's message is to show people that it isn't what happens to you that is important, but how you handle the trials of faith in your life. Let us have the courage that he exhibited. Let us triumph over the trials of our lives. Let us be strengthened by our faith. Let us believe that the trials of faith we weather can bring us closer to God and to eternal life.

New Creations In Christ

There once was a very unhappy old man. For him, things were never right and, thus, he grumbled quite a bit. He complained that he had to get up in the morning, and when nightfall came it was too soon. He complained when he had to work, but found it boring when he did not work. He talked about how people paid insufficient attention to him, yet when others spoke to him he seemed annoyed or irritated. He hated it when it rained and found the sun too hot when it shined. In winter, he longed for the summer and in summer for the fall. All-in-all the old man was miserable.

One day he stopped at a fruit stand, but things there were no better. He found some of the fruit was too ripe and the rest was not ripe enough. He left, disgusted, but as he did, the fruit seller said, "I wish you new eyes, sir, child eyes." "New eyes," thought the old man as he walked away. "I have never used glasses; my vision has never been sharper." A week later, he again stopped at the fruit stand. The fruit seller had the fruit he didn't want and did not have the fruit he wanted. As he was leaving the fruit seller said, "I wish you kingdom eyes, sir." "Kingdom eyes?" This puzzled the old man. But no matter, he was busy, and thus let it pass.

Sometime later, the man stopped at the fruit stand once again. It was, however, the same old story. Everything he didn't want and nothing he wanted; some things overripe and others not ripe enough. And as he left the fruit seller told him, "I wish you treasure-hunting eyes, sir." The man was perplexed at the comment, not knowing what the seller was saying. In spite of himself, the old man began to think about what the fruit seller had been saying to him.

What did he mean by new eyes, child eyes, kingdom eyes, and treasure-hunting eyes? The next time he went to the stand, he pressed the fruit seller to to explain. "Well, you see," the fruit seller began, "one day there was a stranger in town. He spoke of many things, but a few things really stuck in my head. He spoke of the kingdom of God being within you and that in order to find it one had to become like a child. On another occasion the stranger was present and so, too, was a man blind from birth. He went to the blind man and asked if he wanted to see and, of course, the man said, 'Yes.' And then the man's eyes were opened and he was delighted in all that he saw. I was confused about all this and thus I spoke to the stranger saying, 'Please, sir, give me new eyes.' And he responded, 'I will. I give you child eyes, kingdom eyes, and treasure-hunting eyes.' I thanked him and he left.

"That was the last time I saw the man, but from that time forward I saw things differently. Where before I saw only darkness, I now saw stars and fireflies. When before I felt only pain, I now discovered a new door to joy. While before I could see nothing worthwhile, now I found much at which to marvel. Where before I lived in a desert of doubt and despair, now I found a fountain of faith, and where in the past I was irritated at people, now I saw something wonderful in them, something that reminded me of the stranger and I rejoiced."

The old man left trying not to think of the fruit seller's story, but no matter how hard he tried he could not shake it off. The more he thought about it the more he wished for new eyes for himself. He began to think about the stranger hoping that he would return. If he did he would ask for new eyes, also. He worried about how he would make his request to the stranger so he practiced. In fact, he found it easy to put his request to music. He sang the refrain all day: "Give me new eyes, sir, child eyes, kingdom eyes, treasure-hunting eyes. Give me new eyes."

Then one day he stopped at the fruit stand and saw the fruit seller was very sad. "What has happened?" he asked. The fruit seller replied, "I have just received news that the stranger has been arrested and will be put to death today." The old man went home and cried for his chance for new eyes was now gone. Yet, because the song had become so much a part of his life, he continued to sing it, and to his great surprise, three days after the stranger was put to death, he suddenly felt like scales had fallen from his eyes, and he began to see things differently. Where before he saw only darkness, now he saw light. Where before he saw only the injuries done against him, now he saw how much he was loved and he was able to demonstrate forgiveness that healed his wounds. Where before he had seen nothing of value, now he found many hidden treasures. Where before he experienced only boredom and suspicion, now he lived in wonderment and trust, and where before people had irritated him, he now saw in them something that reminded him of the stranger. And he knew that the stranger lived.[1]

The old man was bitter, arrogant, and resisted change, but through the persistence and love of the fruit seller he came to realize his need for transformation, conversion, and a new way of thinking. He needed the new eyes which the stranger had given the fruit seller. In the end he found what he needed through the power of the stranger.

This fable is clearly an Easter story of the new life that Jesus' resurrection brings, not only to himself, but more importantly to all of God's people, the faithful who believe. Today, in our lesson from the book of Revelation, the seer John tells us of the new creation Christ will create in us. It is certainly a welcome message amidst a society which often devalues the very virtues Christ celebrated in his life. We, like the old man, must seek the new eyes which only Jesus can provide.

In today's reading from Revelation, we hear that God will create a new heaven and a new earth, and a new Jerusalem will come down from the heavens. John is referring to what he said earlier (20:11) that earth and heaven have fled from God's presence. Those who were not worthy, the wicked, have been driven to punishment into the lake of fire (20:15). Thus, the new creation is the apex of John's Revelation. Those who have survived the great period of trial, the redeemed of humanity, must be received by a creation that is renewed and refurbished. This new creation is manifest in some very specific ways. First, John says the sea was no more. In the chaos of the primeval world, the sea was aroused by brutal forces and gave rise to myths of monsters. God will destroy this sea in the new creation. Brutal power and violence present in the old sea are incompatible with the peace that will come. Along with the new sea comes a new Jerusalem. This new holy city has God as its architect and builder. In this new creation, God will once again be in intimate union with his people. The intimacy that God granted to Adam and Eve, and later to the nation of Israel, when the people traveled through the desert, and through God's presence in the temple, is now granted to all God's people. The former world, with all its repulsive characteristics that gave it the appearance of a creation enslaved to sin, will disappear. No longer will there be tears, death, pain, or mourning. Then, in the only passage in Revelation where God speaks, we hear the Lord say, "See, I am making all things new ... I am the Alpha and the Omega, the beginning and the end" (21:5b, 6b). God is saying that all that was declared earlier in this passage will take place. All will be accomplished.

The message of the book of Revelation is told through the scripture as salvation history, the story of how God has saved his people through many new creations. The story begins as it should at the outset with creation. The creation story in Genesis is laden with hope, possibility, and new life. Each of the six days God created something new, giving the world more and more possibilities. God first created light so that the further creation would be seen. Then God created the oceans and the land, thus providing an environment for what was planned. God then created all manner of vegetation and animals. All was readied for God's greatest creation, that of humankind, made in the divine image.

God next provided new beginnings for the Israelites as they fled from bondage in Egypt. God opened the Red Sea, allowing Israel to escape, but setting a trap for Egypt to be destroyed. The people traveled to the promised land and made themselves into a great nation under David. However, the people often wandered away from God and, thus, the Lord sent prophets who proclaimed God's message. When necessary, it was a message of warning and at times doom, but in the end, God's faithfulness prevailed. God gave the Hebrews new life from their death in exile in Babylon. As Ezekiel prophesied (37:1-14) God would bring new life to the dead bones of Israel. In his letter to the Romans (6:3-11), Saint Paul speaks of how Christ gave us new life through baptism. The final chapter of the salvation history story comes in the paschal mystery, the events we have just recently celebrated, the passion, death, and resurrection of Jesus. Christ makes all things new through his conquest of death. His victory brings the same possibility to all who bear his name.

The new creation that Jesus brings forces us to ask an important question — what needs renewal, restoration, and new life in our lives? No matter our age, status in life, or primary day-to-day work we all can use new beginnings and must rejoice in the hope that Jesus' resurrection brings. Maybe we have felt stagnant in our prayer, our nine-to-five job, or our relationship with God. Possibly we need renewal in a relationship — in our family, with friends, associates at work, or people who live in our neighborhood. Some may feel held bound by past hurts, inflicted upon our person or ones we have inflicted on others. Still others may find the routine of daily life a downward spiral from which we seemingly cannot escape. Today, however, God releases us from our bondage, as assuredly as the Jews were freed from Egypt and Jesus was raised from death. The new creation of Christ is ours for the taking.

The new creation we seek may seem very elusive when we observe our contemporary world. It may seem that God is not creating anything new, but if we believe this to be true, then we are not looking in the right places. In many ways the new creation of Christ is up to us, we must have sufficient trust in God to find and experience the renewal we seek and need. A beautiful little story demonstrates our need to renew our trust in God.

Bert looked into time from heaven and saw the many atrocities perpetrated in the human realm. Absolutely aghast at what he saw, he asked God, "How can you allow this? Look what evil is in motion down there on earth!" The Lord responded, "There is no one better than the devil for creating a tragedy like that." "But," replied Bert, "that man is one of your people." Again God responded, "I gave humankind the freedom to choose between good and evil. Sometimes those who choose my way are injured by those who don't. It is always painful when this happens." But Bert interrupted,

"Those people have no choice. Evil is being crammed down their throats. That isn't a choice!" "Now Bert," God said patiently, "have I ever let pain go unavenged?" "Well, no," came the reply.

"Watch this," God said to Bert. The Lord placed his arm around his shoulders and said, "Look over there. See that man." "Is he praying?" asked Bert. "Ah, yes," said God, "and you should hear his prayers!" Intense love flashed in God's eyes. The Lord continued, "Simple prayers from an aching heart. This is triumph over evil. Trusting me, that is the choice. Isn't he magnificent?"

Together they stood in silence and Bert began to see as God did. "Now watch this, Bert." God spoke softly, never letting his eyes depart from the scene. He called for Michael, the archangel, who immediately appeared. "Go down and get him, Michael," God commanded as tears of divine joy flowed forth. "I will arrange the party."

The old man needed new eyes, but it took some time and the persistence of the fruit seller for him to find conversion and renewal. Jesus' resurrection brings the possibility of new life to us. Let us cast off our slavery to the old world, our old way of life, and place sufficient trust in God's words, "See, I am making all things new." Our trust in God and our surrender to his way will bring us the gift of eternal life, God's promise to all who believe.

---

1. Summarized from "The Old Man with New Eyes," in Jude Fischer, *Be Always Little: Christian Fables for Young and Old* (Combermere, Ontario Canada: Madonna House, 1996), pp.103-108.

Jesus, The Light Of The World

In the beginning when the Great Spirit created all that exists, he gave great gifts to all the animals. The Great Spirit gave each animal a cedar box inside of which were very special and wonderful gifts. And, one by one the boxes were opened. The first box contained water. The second box contained the mountains. The third box contained the seeds of all things that grow. The fourth box contained the wind to carry the seed to the corners of the earth. Thus, one by one all the boxes were opened, except one. This box had been given to Seagull. Seagull took the box, put it under his arm and declared, "It's mine! All mine." This box contained a very special gift; it held the light of the world. Thus, since Seagull refused to open the box, the world remained in darkness.

The other animals pleaded with Seagull, asking him to open the box. Rabbit said, "If there is no light how will the grass grow and how will I eat?" Robin said, "If there is no light, how will my breast become red?" Fox said to Seagull, "If there is no light, how will I see the burr in my tail?" Even bear said, "If there is no light, how can I tell a friend from a foe to invite into my home?" However, the more the other animals asked, the more stubborn and unwilling to cooperate Seagull became. Seagull held the box tighter and tighter.

Finally, the very clever and crafty cousin, Raven, tried his hand to free the box. "What is in the box?" he queried cousin Seagull. "You know what's in the box," Seagull replied, "and it remains mine." Raven simply smiled sweetly and told Seagull how generous, smart, and handsome he was, but this tactic didn't work, either. Finally, Raven grew angry and threatened Seagull, but this, too, did not seem to phase the stubborn sea bird. Nothing seemed to work.

Raven thought and thought about what could be done. Then, he got the answer. "Seagull is causing so many problems he deserves to have a thorn stuck in his foot." And, as we all know when Raven thinks hard and wishes thoughts, things begin to happen.

Then, all of a sudden, Seagull gave a cry. "What's the matter?" Raven asked. "My foot!" cried Seagull, "my foot hurts." "Let me take a look," replied Raven. Raven felt on the bottom of Seagull's foot and found the place where the thorn was located, but instead of pulling it out he pushed it in further. Seagull cried out in pain. "I am so sorry," said Raven. "If I could only see better; if I had some light. Open the box so I can see." Seagull opened the box ever so slightly and a few tiny rays of light escaped into the sky and became stars. Raven hunted around, felt the thorn and pushed it in even further. Again, Seagull cried out in pain. "Oh, I am sorry, so sorry," said Raven, "but there still is not sufficient light. Open the box more so I can see."

Seagull lifted one wing and the lid opened more. A soft light floated heavenward, and lo there was the moon in the sky along with the stars. Once more Raven felt around the bottom of Seagull's foot and he gave such a mighty push to the thorn that Seagull screamed and flapped open his wings. The box fell to the ground, the lid opened, and suddenly the sun streamed out in a great burst. And so in the beginning was the light.[1]

Seagull preferred the darkness; he wished to keep the light for himself. Raven, however, had his method and was able to release the light into the world. The Easter season we presently celebrate commemorates the triumph of light over darkness. While the forces of evil manifested in society sought to shroud the world in the darkness of error, sin, ignorance, and unbelief, Jesus' resurrection brought the light back to the world, and with it the vision we need to find our way home. Today's reading from the book of Revelation speaks in a similar way of the New Jerusalem — Jesus — a light to the nations, who dispels the darkness so common in our contemporary society.

In today's lesson, John speaks of Jesus as the center, the temple of the New Jerusalem. Jesus' return in glory will be obvious for he will be seen as the central figure of the new creation, but John does not stop there. Not only is Jesus the center, the temple, he is also the light of the city. No more will there be a need for sun or moon, for Jesus will provide all the light one could need. The light provides a sense of security, warmth, and welcome. Everyone prefers to walk in the light; it makes us feel better. But Jesus, the light, more importantly provides direction. The light illuminates the path we must follow; it shows us the proper way. On a broader scale, in this eschatological image, Jesus, the New Jerusalem, provides the light and direction for other peoples and nations. As John says, "The nations will walk by its light" (Revelation 21:24a). Jesus is the one who sets the pace, provides the direction, and is the model to follow. The light of the New Jerusalem will shine so brightly that rulers of nations will be inspired to follow as Jesus directs. Again, as the seer John puts it, "The kings of the earth will bring their glory into it" (Revelation 21:24b). With Jesus as our guide, there will be no night.

In addition to direction, the light of Jesus, the New Jerusalem, provides sustenance for our life and all our endeavors. John speaks of the light as the source of goodness and growth. People are attracted to the light and feel better able to do more and move forward in an atmosphere of light. Darkness tends to inhibit our progress. We are then provided a metaphor, an image of a river that flows through the New Jerusalem. The source of life and sustenance provides all that is needed so that trees along its banks can produce fruit twelve months per year. In the environment of the light, with its direction and sustenance, there is nothing unclean nor any person who practices abominations who can enter the city; nothing accursed will be present. Jesus, the light, provides all that is necessary for life; we will need nothing more. If we have the light of Jesus, who comes to us in so many ways, we will be satisfied.

The image of God, and God's Son, Jesus, as the source of our light, our sustenance, in short our very lives, is found throughout the scriptures. The image of how the light of God shatters the darkness is clearly manifest. The message of the prophets is clearly marked by this vision. Isaiah, when proclaiming God's message to the southern kingdom of Judah, spoke of this reality: "The people who walked in darkness have seen a great light; those who lived in a land of deep darkness — on them light has shined." He concludes, "O house of Jacob, come, let us walk in the light of the Lord!" (Isaiah 9:2; 2:5). Micah, a contemporary of Isaiah, but who prophesied to the northern kingdom of Israel, proclaimed, "When I sit in darkness, the Lord will be a light to me" (Micah 7:8b). The proclamation of the light's power to dispel darkness was also heard by the Hebrews when in exile in Babylon. Possibly perceiving that God had abandoned them, the people needed assurance of God's love and care, and Isaiah provided it to them: "I will lead the blind by a road they do not know, by paths they have not known I will guide them. I will turn the darkness before them into light, the rough places into level ground. These are the things I will do, and I will never forsake them" (Isaiah 42:16). God was always ready and willing to provide the light; God has never given up on anyone.

The psalmist also provides many examples of how God provides the light to his children, steering us toward the path of life. We hear, "The Lord is God and he has given us light" (Psalm 118:27). Yes, God who is light, has shared this great gift with us, but this privilege brings with it a great responsibility. The psalmist tells us, "They [those who fear the Lord] rise in the darkness as a light for the upright" (Psalm 112:4). We have the task to go forth in our daily walk with God to share the light we have been given with those, who for whatever reasons, remain in the darkness. This is not an option if we feel like participating; this is our responsibility as those who have been enlightened by God's presence. This is not a burden, however, but a task filled with great wonder and happiness. Again, as the psalmist says, "Light dawns for the righteous and joy for the upright in heart" (Psalm 97:11). Living in, and sharing the light which God brings is not an easy task, but as they say, the reward is worth our best efforts. Saint Paul reminds us, "What no eye has seen, nor ear heard, nor the human heart conceived, what God has prepared for those who love him" (1 Corinthians 2:9).

The image of Jesus as the light of the world is most graphically depicted through the powerful words of John's Gospel. From the very outset in the prologue John clearly shows how the light of Christ is the antidote to the darkness that often pervades our world. The evangelist speaks of John the Baptist, the precursor of the Lord, who "came to testify to the light," but he was not the light. Rather, "the true light, which enlightens everyone, was coming into the world" (John 1:8b-9). On a few occasions, Jesus directly states his association with the light: "I am the light of the world. Whoever follows me will never walk in darkness but will have the light of life" (John 8:12). Again he says, "As long as I am in the world, I am the light of the world" (John 9:5). Jesus describes his mission as one which seeks to dispel the darkness and provide the light: "I have come as light into the world, so that everyone who believes in me should not remain in darkness" (John 12:46).

The scriptural references to Jesus as the light of the world, described by John in Revelation as the New Jerusalem, speak in eschatological terms of Jesus' Second Coming. When this great event happens we will, as Paul says, "meet the Lord in the air, and so will be with him forever" (1 Thessalonians 4:17b). This will be the time of Jesus' final and total reclamation of all that belongs to him. It will be the time when darkness is forever vanquished as only the power of Christ can so control the destiny of time and space.

Yet, as we await this great event which will end life as we know it, we have a responsibility to God and one another to do what we can do to dispel darkness and bring the light to our world. Jesus said in his famous Sermon on the Mount (Matthew 5:14-16), "You are the light of the world. A city built on a hill cannot be hid. No one lighting a lamp puts it under the bushel basket, but on the lampstand, and it gives light to all in the house. In the same way, let your light shine before others, so that they may see your good works and give glory to your Father in heaven." If we are to be the light of the world, we must light the path so that our brothers and sisters in Christ can follow our lead. We must set a good example, in word and action, so others may choose to follow our lead. This basic premise of the life of discipleship to which we are all called, has two significant and related parts. First, we must never cast others into darkness by what we do and say. However, we are called to do more. We must shine and light the way for others. People are not neutral in their opinions of us. Our friends and associates are either drawn to or pushed from Christ by what they see and hear from us. Ours is, therefore, an awesome responsibility.

How can we shine the light of Christ to others? Some may possess the ability, time, and opportunity to take more active roles. Every project and movement needs leaders and some of us will function in this capacity. We may lobby to keep Christ's presence in our ever-more secularized society. We may be frontline soldiers in some campaign to bring the light of Christ to individuals, groups, or institutions that live in darkness. While some may bring the light in more overt ways, most of us are not in positions for such active means, but this in no way means that we are less responsible. Our witness to be champions and disciples of the light is critically important. When we present a positive and happy countenance, making every effort to smile and be friendly in our associations with others, we bring the light. We must avoid the tendency to allow the pressures and problems of contemporary society to preclude the light from shining forth from us. Bringing the light of Christ is the responsibility of all, regardless of our status in life, our age, or what we do for a living.

What we seek to do is not easy, but collectively, our individual efforts become a synergy that can with time and energy lead to systemic change that casts out darkness and restores the light. We have the difficult task to cast out the darkness of error and sin. Too often, especially today, we rationalize everything; nothing is a problem, in error or in sin. But the reality is that darkness lurks and we are called to drive it away with the light of Christ. Casting out the darkness of ignorance is also our responsibility. People need to hear the Word of God and see it put into action in everyday life. This will not happen until we do our part to make Christ more present in our world. Lastly, we have the privilege to assist others in the transformation of our world from unbelief to a true sense of the necessity of the light. We may mistakenly think that idolatry no longer exists, especially in our society of instant and constant communication. However, idolatry is alive and well but masquerades in other less recognizable forms, such as power, wealth, and prestige. These are the contemporary gods to which we often pay homage. We must bring the light of Christ to illumine those in the darkness of unbelief. The resurrection must be the catalyst to renew in us the energy to shine more brightly. Certainly many before us, inspired by the resurrection event, were able to recharge their systems and become the light to others. There can be no better example than Saint Peter. The gospel evangelists portray Peter as one who misunderstands, speaks the wrong words, and even denies Jesus when he needs him most. But Luke, author of the Acts of the Apostles, describes a completely converted man after the resurrection. Peter fearlessly preached to the Jews of his belief in Christ as Messiah and Lord. Similarly, Saint Paul, who as Saul from Tarsus was a zealous persecutor of Christians, was converted by the resurrected Christ on the road to Damascus. The light he received was so bright that his darkness of error, ignorance, and unbelief was dispelled and he was able to become the great apostle to the Gentiles. We must be so inspired so that in similar, but probably not so dramatic ways, we can bring the light of Christ to others and help dispel the darkness of our world.

Jesus, the light of the world, the resurrected Lord, restored the light to a world which had lost hope and direction. Like Raven who forced Seagull to provide the light to the world, so Jesus defeated the forces of evil which sought to destroy the human spirit. Jesus restored confidence; he restored the light. May we have the courage to follow his lead and do the same.

---

1. Paraphrased from "Sea Gull," in William J. Bausch, *A World of Stories for Preachers and Teachers* (Mystic, Connecticut: Twenty-Third Publications, 1999), pp. 79-80.

The Ascension Of Our Lord
Ephesians 1:15-23

Caring For Others: The Christian Vocation In The World

When Bobby Smith was a youngster, his family lived near Mrs. Hildebrand, a widow, who at 95 years of age, was in constant pain and crippled by arthritis, which ravaged her body. Living alone, she could only take a few steps at a time with the help of her cane. Every week when Bobby's mom went to the market, she took her son who would always deliver groceries to the old widow. The family car would pull up into Mrs. Hildebrand's driveway and the command would be heard, "Bobby, here are Mrs. Hildebrand's groceries." That was all the instruction that was needed. Bobby sprang into action, delivering the groceries with a sense of delight. Without fail, Mrs. Hildebrand always gave Bobby a dime for his efforts.

The boy enjoyed the older woman, especially listening to her stories. She told him about her life, a steepled church in the woods, horse and buggy rides on Sunday afternoons, and much about her family's farm which had no electricity or running water. After a short time together, the older woman would offer Bobby his dime, which he would half-heartedly refuse, knowing that she would insist on him keeping it. Usually he walked across the street to Beyer's candy store and bought himself a treat.

One day in mid-December, Bobby was delivering the woman's groceries as usual, but the season's first significant snow was falling and the boy very much wanted to go out and play. He decided, therefore, to make his delivery and refuse to accept Mrs. Hildebrand's weekly offering of ten cents. He could hear the snow beckoning him to go outside. Thus, Bobby delivered the groceries in a bit more hurried fashion. The older woman took the items out of the bag and told Bobby where each went in the cabinets. Normally he enjoyed this, but the snow was calling. Then, somewhat suddenly, Bobby began to realize how lonely Mrs. Hildebrand must have been. Her husband had died some twenty years earlier; she had no children. Her only living relative, who never came to visit, lived far away in Philadelphia. Nobody even called her at Christmas. He noticed that while the holiday was near, the house had no tree, no presents, no stockings. For her, Christmas was just another day on the calendar. Bobby began to think, "Maybe the snow could wait a bit."

Bobby and Mrs. Hildebrand sat and talked about many things, but especially Christmases past. The journey through time must have been somewhat healing for the older woman. Then she said, "Well, Bobby, I bet you want to go out and play in the snow." She reached into her purse, fumbling to find the proper coin. "No, Mrs. Hildebrand," he said, "I cannot take your money this time. I am sure you have more important uses for it." But she replied, "What more important thing could I do with it than give some to a friend at Christmas time?" She placed a *quarter* in Bobby's hand. He tried to give it back, but she would have none of that.

Bobby hurried out the door and ran to Beyer's candy store. He wondered what he would buy — a comic book, a chocolate soda, or ice cream. Then he spotted a Christmas card with an old country church on the cover. It was just like the church Mrs. Hildebrand had described from her youth. Bobby purchased the card and borrowed a pen to sign his name. "Is this for your girlfriend?" Mr. Beyer asked. Bobby started to say no, but responded, "Well, yeah, I guess it is."

Bobby walked across the street and rang Mrs. Hildebrand's doorbell. He handed her the card, saying, "Merry Christmas, Mrs. Hildebrand. Thank you for your kindness." The older woman's hand began to tremble as she opened the card and read its contents. She began to cry. "Thank you very much," and then in almost a whisper, "Merry Christmas to you."

Several weeks later, one cold and blustery day, an ambulance arrived at Mrs. Hildebrand's home. Mrs. Smith told Bobby that she had found Mrs. Hildebrand in bed; she had died peacefully in her sleep. On her night stand was found, still illuminated by a light, a solitary Christmas card with an old country church on the cover.

This very touching story, while centered on the season of Christmas is, nonetheless, a perfect example of what it means to be a Christian. It serves, therefore, as a message for our celebration of Ascension Sunday. Jesus ascends to the Father; he returns to the one from whom he came. But as he instructed his disciples and as Saint Paul instructs us today, we must do as Bobby and Mrs. Hildebrand did: We must live the Christian life and by example encourage others to do the same.

Biblical scholars argue several points about the letter to the Ephesians, most especially its Pauline authenticity and the place of its origin. Many exegetes believe, due to the language used and theology of Ephesians, the letter was not penned by Paul, but rather one of his disciples. Experts also point to the rather impersonal nature of the letter, something that seems odd since Paul used Ephesus as the base of operation for his third missionary journey and spent three years of his life in the city. Thus, this letter, along with Colossians and 2 Thessalonians are often classified as pseudo-Pauline. The author says that he is a prisoner, but we know that Paul was imprisoned in several locations. Thus the letter's city of origin is uncertain, although most scholars believe it was written during the period of his Caesarea imprisonment.

Regardless of its precise Pauline authenticity and its origins, the letter is very important in providing many ideas on the proper Christian life, including this magnificent prayer which we have just heard proclaimed. The apostle prays in thanksgiving for the Christian community at Ephesus asking that God enlighten the people: "I pray that the God of our Lord Jesus Christ, the Father of glory, may give you a spirit of wisdom and revelation as you come to know him." But the Pauline author goes on to say what this enlightened state of God's presence must generate in the Ephesian community: "[That] you may come to know him, so that, with the eyes of your heart enlightened, you may know what is the hope to which he has called you, what are the riches of his glorious inheritance among the saints." Believers have been given great power by God. This power is to be used to build God's kingdom. In essence, God has enlightened the Ephesian community, and by extension all believers, with the power and the opportunity to model for others a proper Christian life. This is our task; it is our common vocation to holiness. And we must realize that nothing can or will stand in God's way to assure this reality. The resurrected Christ, who today ascends to the Father, "far above all rule and authority and power and dominion," leads the way. Jesus is the perfect example for us and thus, as the Pauline writer concludes the prayer, "[God] has put all things under his feet and has made him the head over all things for the church, which is his body, the fullness of him who fills all in all" (Ephesians 1:21a, 22).

The Easter season, celebrating the triumph of Christ over sin and death, now draws to a close and we stand on the eve of Pentecost, the arrival of the Spirit. As we learn from Ephesians today, we have been enlightened by God; next week we will be enlightened by the Spirit. Besides being enlightened, however, we have also been commissioned to go forth and continue Christ's work and mission in our world. We are called to build God's kingdom and we do so by living well and fully the Christian life.

The late Pope John Paul II, who shepherded Roman Catholicism for over 26 years, provided to the Christian community in general a powerful witness of the proper Christian life, from his own actions and certainly his words. What the Pope preached was rooted in the need for us to follow in the footsteps of Jesus, who took on our humanity in all aspects save sin. He often spoke of the need to be disciples of Jesus and to realize that this was the only authentic path to life. In a talk to youth in New Orleans during his 1987 United States visit, he stated, "The true success of our lives consists in knowing and doing the will of Jesus." There is a need, therefore, to pray and reflect sufficiently to know what Jesus asks of us. All of us have different vocations, but each Christian is called to the general vocation of holiness. We live holy and Spirit-filled lives when we are willing to give ourselves completely to the Christian life. Sometimes we hesitate and are filled with fear concerning what God asks of us. The future is uncertain and, therefore, we are rather cautious about our forays into unknown territory. But John Paul II encouraged us to be bold and give ourselves to God, confident that through such action we would know God's will. In a 1996 message on the World Day of Prayer for Vocations, he stated, "Be generous in giving your life to the Lord. Do not be afraid ... The more ready you are to give yourselves to God and to others, the more you will discover the authentic meaning of life. God expects much of you."

A second powerful and important theme addressed by John Paul II on the Christian life was the need to engage the world, not to stand idly by as others build God's kingdom. In a 1996 talk to evangelicals, the Pope articulated the challenge in this way: "True holiness does not mean a flight from the world; rather it lies in the effort to incarnate the gospel in everyday life, at school and at work, and in social and political involvement." Rather than standing aloof from the reality of the world, John Paul II demonstrated, by his own life, of the importance of never shying away, but rather always being one who models a positive and forward-thinking countenance, one who sets the example that others would wish to follow. Speaking to a meeting of the laity in San Francisco in 1987 he stated, "Your great contribution to the evangelization of your society is made through your lives. Christ's message must live in you and the way you live and in the way you refuse to live ... Your lives must spread the fragrance of Christ's gospel throughout the world."

The pope's call to engage society and set the proper example in a society often shrouded in darkness is challenging at the very least, but this should be no surprise to anyone. Jesus warned his followers that suffering would follow those who chose his more narrow path to life. He described families torn apart and delivering each other to the authorities (Luke 12:49-53). But the Lord also brought encouragement: "In the world you face persecution. But take courage; I have overcome the world" (John 16:33). Too often the more difficult path is avoided; we seek the path of least resistance. It is true, the easy path might be inviting; we have too many challenges and do not wish to add more. But in his Sermon on the Mount, Jesus was very clear that only one path leads to life: "Enter

209

through the narrow gate; for the gate is wide and the road is easy that leads to destruction and there are many who take it. For the gate is narrow and the road is hard that leads to life, and there are few who find it" (Matthew 7:13-14).

John Paul II, ever a man of conviction, reminded us "Christians sometimes have to suffer marginalization and persecution — at times heroically — because of moral choices which are contrary to the world's behavior ... This is the cost of Christian witness, of a worthy life in the eyes of God. If you are not willing to pay this price, your lives will be empty." Still, John Paul II, addressing the crowd on World Youth Day in 1996, stated the benefits of this more difficult choice: "The way Jesus shows you is not easy. Rather, it is like a path winding up a mountain. Do not lose heart. The steeper the road, the faster it rises toward ever wider horizons."

Baptism, the basic common denominator for Christian people, calls us to live holy lives that demonstrate our faith and belief in Jesus. Bobby Smith learned the meaning of the Christian life through his encounter with an elderly widow. Jesus, at the time of his ascension, commissioned his apostles to go to all parts of the world, to baptize, and proclaim the good news. The author of the letter to the Ephesians, in the line of the apostles, learned from his experience that his enlightened state, obtained at the hand of God, mandated that he go forward to build the kingdom and encourage his readers to do the same. More recently, the late Pope John Paul II, speaking for all Christian peoples of faith, called us to a full actualization of the Christian life. Let us continue the tradition clearly mapped out as we strive daily to follow in the footsteps of Jesus, the one who died to set us free and will always be our brother, friend, and Lord.

Jesus Rewards The Just

Imagine picking up the Sunday paper, opening it and reading in giant letters, **Jesus Christ Will Return In Two Weeks**. What would we do? How would we react to this astonishing information? I think there would be two basic reactions. Some of us, out of fear, would change our lives immediately. The Lord is coming and we are not ready. We might start going to church more often, probably every day. Prayer would become a much higher priority in life. We would pray not only in the morning and evening, but many times each day. We would seek reconciliation, with a member of our family, neighbor, co-worker, and certainly with God. Others might have a very different response. Some of us might do nothing differently. Some in a defeatist attitude might say, "There is nothing I can do at this late hour. God has already decided my fate. I might as well continue what I have been doing all along." There are still others who might not change a thing that they are doing, but not in a defeatist mode. Some of us hopefully would say, "Isn't this the event for which the world has been waiting? Isn't this the reason for which I came into the world?" Possession of such an attitude would allow us to continue doing what we have always been doing, confident that our preparations have been sound.

Life, it seems, is one big process of preparation. When we are young, each year seems to be preparation for the next. When we are in elementary school, we prepare for junior high, and in junior high, we work hard to ready ourselves for high school. The preparation process continues into college and to our first job, but it does not end there. One job leads to a second or to the promotion that we justly deserve. One might naturally say, "Will we ever be fully ready? The corollary is just as important — what is it for which we are preparing?"

The simple but profound answer is that we are preparing each and every day for our return to God. Thus, we must ask, are we ready for Jesus' return or is there more that we need to do? Most people, I think, would answer that they do not feel ready, even though this is the event for which their whole life should be oriented. We were created by God to serve the Lord as best we can in our day-to-day lives, and then return to the one from whom we came. All of us are on borrowed time; we do not know, as Jesus says, the day nor the hour (Matthew 25:13). But God's promise to be present to, and lead to, eternal life those who follow his lead as disciples must be our consolation when the hurdles, problems, and vicissitudes of life complicate our daily existence. Thus, there is nothing to fear for those who believe. Today's reading from the book of Revelation makes this abundantly clear.

John, the seer of the events recounted in Revelation, says Jesus will return and bring his reward with him. The Lord's master plan was always centered on humanity, God's greatest creation, and finds its apex in the great reward of life eternal. From the very beginning, God provided not only what was necessary, but everything men and women needed. Unfortunately, humanity's response to God has often not been one of gratitude and thanksgiving. Adam and Eve's desire to be like God cost them paradise. The Hebrews failed to uphold the law, leading to the destruction of the northern kingdom of Israel seven centuries before Christ and the infamous fifty-year Babylonian exile for Judah in the mid-sixth century B.C.E. Yet, despite humanity's less than gracious response to God, the Lord never abandoned his people. On the contrary, the whole of salvation history relates how time and time again, despite humanity's response, God always provided the path that would bring people the reward for which they were always destined, namely, the path to life with God. The form was different — the law, secular rulers, prophets, even events — but the message was consistent, God will never abandon his people. God will provide the reward.

Thus, John speaks of Jesus coming at the end of time with the reward of eternal life. Its magnificence is beyond human comprehension. Saint Paul describes it this way: "What no eye has seen, nor ear heard, nor the human heart conceived, what God has prepared for those who love him" (1 Corinthians 2:9).This great gift will be rewarded to those who have washed their clothes white in the blood of the Lamb. Those who have suffered and persevered, those who have successfully negotiated the hurdles of life and have not given up, these are the ones who have the right to the tree of life. This powerful image, which we heard proclaimed a few weeks ago as well, is the proper formula for finding God and eternal life. The Christian life is not easy; if lived properly it will cost us our whole life, as Dietrich Bonhoeffer, the famous Lutheran theologian and pastor wrote back in the 1930s in his popular volume, *The Cost of Discipleship*. Too often when trials come our way we back off; we fail to engage the challenge. G. K. Chesterton, the early twentieth-century British essayist was right when he declared back in 1910 in *What's Wrong with the World?* "The Christian ideal has not been tried and found wanting. It has been found difficult and left untried."

Despite the suffering, pain, and challenges of the Christian life, John assures us that all are invited to the reward which Jesus brings. The Spirit and the bride, an image of the church, beckon us to come. Everyone who hears, and those who are thirsty, must also come. Anyone who wishes to partake of the water of life must come. Yes, Jesus will come and reclaim the world, but we must be ready and we must accept the invitation. God's hand is outstretched in welcome, but the Lord does not force his way into our world. The decision to return to God is ours to make.

John's message in Revelation has been presented in many places and ways throughout salvation history. As a prophet, Elijah had the fundamentally difficult task of proclaiming God's Word to an often unsympathetic and rebellious people. Yet, he carried out his task and mission so well that God rewarded him in a special way. We read: "As they [Elijah and Elisha] continued walking and talking, a chariot of fire and horses of fire separated the two of them, and Elijah ascended in a whirlwind into heaven" (2 Kings 2:11).

When King Hezekiah, who had been faithful to God, was ill, he called out to the Lord, who heard his plea and added fifteen years to his life (2 Kings 20:1-11). We recall in the book of Daniel how Shadrach, Meshach, and Abednego, who refused to pay homage to the gods of King Nebuchadnezzar, were saved by God from death in the white hot furnace, leading the Babylonian king to exclaim: "Blessed be the God of Shadrach, Meshach, and Abednego, who sent his angel and delivered his servants who trusted in him."

As God the Father rewarded the just in the Old Testament, so Jesus in a similar way rewards those who seek him. Jesus rewarded the faith of those who believed in him and his ability. Because of his faith, Jesus cured the man born blind (John 9:1-41). In another incident Jesus encountered two blind men and asked, " 'Do you believe I am able to do this [cure blindness]?' They said to him, 'Yes, Lord.' Then he touched their eyes and said, 'According to your faith let it be done to you' " (Matthew 9:28b-29). Jesus cured the woman with a hemorrhage. He told her, "Take heart, daughter; your faith has made you well" (Matthew 9:22a). Jesus raised people from death, for example, the widow of Nain's son (Luke 7:11-17) and Lazarus, Jesus' good friend (John 11:1-44), based on the faith of their families. We all recall Jesus' promise to Dismas on the cross, "Truly I tell you, today you will be with me in paradise" (Luke 23:43).

Saint Paul echoes the ideas of God the Father and Jesus in his proclamation that God will reward the just. The aforementioned promise of 1 Corinthians continues to sound in our ears. In his letter to the Romans he wrote, "If you confess with your lips that Jesus is Lord and believe in your heart that God raised him from the dead, you will be saved" (Romans 10:9). In the pastoral epistles, the Pauline author continues the theme of Jesus' reward for the just: "If we have died with him, we will also live with him; if we endure, we will also reign with him; if we deny him he will also deny us; if we are faithless, he remains faithful — for he cannot deny himself" (2 Timothy 2:11-13).

The clear reality that God rewards the just, those who walk in his ways and seek to follow his path, forces us to evaluate our lives and ask what is necessary to prepare ourselves for the coming of the Lord. As the banner headline in the paper announcing the Lord's Second Coming would catch our attention, so we must focus our attention and energy on what needs to be done. For some there is a need to correct or make right a relationship that has gone sour. We may be estranged from a member of our family, a neighbor down the street, or a colleague at work. We are not ready for God's reward if we are not exercising love for one another. Others need to release themselves from past hurts, both those inflicted on us and that which we have inflicted on others. Many times these past hurts afflict us like a ball and chain anchored to our leg. We are weighed down so severely that we cannot properly move forward. Jesus says, cut the chain and allow yourself, and others, freedom to resume their normal lives. There are some, as well, who need to make amends or bring restitution for past failures. We simply do not feel complete when we know we owe someone, whether that be our time, talent, or treasure. We must not neglect to assure our relationship with God is in its best possible condition. How is our prayer life? Have we been cooperative with God's plan for our lives, or have we run and tried to avoid what we believe God has scheduled for us, now and in the future? Is our faith strong and can it withstand the many challenges it faces in our ever more rapid, changing, and secularist society? Can we believe that God knows best and allow God to operate? Can we honestly say to God, as did Jesus in the garden of Gethsemane, "Father, if it is possible, let this cup pass from me; yet not what I want but what you want" (Matthew 26:39b).

After we have closely examined what we need to do before Jesus comes, and by that reflection righted our spiritual ship, then we can once again sail freely toward our goal of eternal life. But for many, however, the goal is neither clear nor certain because we do not know the future. Thus, we panic and worry. But there is no need for such consternation. If we are uncertain that God will take care of things and reward those who are faithful, a little story can be helpful.

Once upon a time, there was a boy who was dreadfully afraid of dying. Some folks are, you know. They have never experienced it and thus do not know how it feels. Thus, they are afraid. This boy was this way. Since he was not very rugged and his health was rather frail, he thought about dying even more.

One day as the boy was sitting under a tree crying, he heard a little wisp of a voice, not squeaky, but soft, and he noticed a flower was speaking to him. "Why are you crying?" asked the flower. The boy responded, "I am afraid of dying." The flower gave a hearty laugh, saying, "Dying; you are afraid of dying? Why, I die myself every year of my life." "Die yourself?" responded the boy. "You are alive at this minute." "Of course, I am," said the flower. "That doesn't matter. I have died every year since I can remember." "Doesn't it hurt?" asked the boy. "No, it doesn't," answered the flower. "It's really nice. You see, I get tired of holding up my head and looking pert and wide awake. It gets tiring having the sun shine on you all the time, with the wind beating against you and bees taking all of your pollen. So it is easy to get sleepier and sleepier and then finally you drop off. Then you wake up at the nicest time of the year. Why I like to die, I really do." Some how this did not help the boy as much as one might think. "I am not a flower," he said. "I might not come up again."

On another day, the boy was sitting on a stone in the pasture crying. He heard another tiny voice. It was not like the flower's voice; it was a soft and fuzzy voice and he noticed a caterpillar was speaking to him. The caterpillar said, "Why are you crying?" The boy responded, "I am dreadfully afraid of dying." The fuzzy little caterpillar laughed, saying, "Dying, I am looking forward to it myself. All my family dies once in a while and when they wake up they have wings and sport the most beautiful colors and they fly about giving great delight to all. I would not miss dying for anything. I am looking forward to it." Somehow again, this did not seem to cheer the boy who said, "I am not a caterpillar. I might not wake up."

Well, lots of other plants and insects talked to the boy, trying to cheer him up. They explained that dying and living was part of their existence. The boy did not think that all the conversations helped at all, but maybe they did, as he could not stop thinking about what he heard. Nevertheless, he remained frightened.

Then one summer, the little boy began to fail faster and faster, and one day he was so tired that he could not hold his head up any longer. Thus, he laid down on his bed and he looked out his window toward the east. The sun kept shining into his eyes until he shut them and he fell asleep. He had a really good nap and when he awoke he felt much better and went outside to take a walk. He began again to think of what the flower, caterpillar, and other plants and creatures had told him about dying and how they had laughed at his fear. He said to himself, "Somehow, today I do not feel so scared, but I suppose I am. Then, to his surprise he met an angel. He had never seen one before, but he knew immediately who his guest was. The angel asked, "Aren't you happy little boy?" "I would be happy," he responded, "if I was not so afraid of dying. It must be awful to be dead." But the angel said, "You are dead." And he truly was.[1]

Jesus is coming but we do not know the day nor the hour. Nonetheless, we can be completely confident of God's promise. Therefore, let us entrust our lives and our hopes and fears to the Lord. Let us remember Jesus' promise and follow his lead: "Let anyone who wishes take the water of life as a gift" (Revelation 22:17c). If we can, our reward in heaven will be great.

---

1. Summary of "The Boy Who Was Scared of Dying," in Jude Fischer, *Be Always Little: Christian Fables for Young and Old* (Combermere, Ontario Canada: Madonna House, 1996), pp. 135-138.

Sermons On The Second Readings

For Sundays
After Pentecost
(First Third)

God's Grammar

John B. Jamison

For Pat,
who has kept me going

And for
Jim, Michael, Emily,
Charlie, and Walter,
who have taught me
along the way

Preface

I'll begin with a word of advice. I think you should take a pencil and scribble out the closing paragraphs of most of these sermons. In their place, write your own conclusions, in your own words, that fit the story of the lives to whom you are preaching.

Secondly, you should know that a couple of the stories included are true, although somewhat strange, stories from my experience as pastor. You will see that I've noted those as you read. Again, I offer these stories as the path to get your message out there, but encourage you to find the conclusion that is needed at the time.

For myself, I am a storyteller at heart, and often allow the members of my congregation to write their own "therefore." For those of similar ilk, and for those who prefer to do otherwise, I offer the following stories for your use. I pray that between my writing and your speaking, good things will happen.

John Jamison

The Prodigal Father

It wasn't their first fight. Like most fathers and sons they had their disagreements. But this time, something was different. A line had been crossed that had never been crossed before. They sat there, staring at each other, both realizing they were in new territory, neither of them sure that they really wanted to be there.

No one remembers who broke the silence and spoke first, but it moved quickly from there. No one remembers just how long the fight continued. But everyone remembers that moment when it was clearly over. Words had been said that could not be unsaid. Those words were just hanging there over the kitchen table, and hanging there so loudly that it was clear that no further words would be heard. Instead of speaking, the son pushed his way back from the table, walked over to give his mother a kiss on the cheek, and walked out the kitchen door. He just walked out.

It was over. The fight. The relationship. Over.

Let me stop right here to explain why we are eavesdropping on this family tragedy. You may already recognize it as sounding a lot like the parable that Luke told about the son that ran away and came back later, and you are wondering what that story about the prodigal son has to do with today's reading from Romans. Well, it is not as far a stretch as you may think.

Paul is trying to help the Gentile and Jewish readers of this letter better understand the new relationship they now have with God. Instead of being treated like slaves, and being constantly punished for breaking endless rules and laws, Paul suggests that they are more like adopted children, or sons of God. He even uses the

223

term, *Abba*, which in simple language means "daddy." God is that great, forgiving, loving, caring, daddy-like guiding figure that always has our well-being at heart. Paul was quite certain everyone would understand what he was getting at.

Unfortunately, not everyone gets it.

For too many, the word "father," or even "daddy," brings other images. They are images of disinterest, of absence, or just of confusion. For some, daddy is the one who was never satisfied, never affirming, and never touchable. Dad was always too busy, always distracted, and always disappointed. For some, father left emotional scars that are still felt years later. For too many, the scars are not emotional.

No, for some, Paul's comparing God to daddy was not a helpful thing. And that's why I wanted to help Paul along with this retelling of an old, familiar story, with a slightly new twist. You see, from my viewpoint, the story of the prodigal son isn't really about the son at all. It is an amazing story about what it means to be a father. I think it is the image of "daddy" that Paul had in mind when he wrote this letter to the Romans. Let's go back to the story and I'll show you what I mean.

Many years have passed since that night the son walked out of the kitchen. But rather than worry about what the son was up to, as the story usually talks about, let's keep our eyes on the father. That's the real story in this parable.

As soon as word got out the next morning, the entire village was up in arms. When he walked out on his father, the son not only insulted him, but the whole community. It was a horrendous act of defiance against all of their rules, and their authority. If he got away with such behavior, what would keep the other sons from doing exactly the same thing? It was the prime topic of conversation each morning at the coffee shops and the grain elevators. Obviously, the father had been too soft on the boy, and should never have let things get to this point. Whatever hog-filled, sloppy world the runaway lived in over the years, it was nothing compared to the world of criticism that his dad lived through staying at home.

And then came the day.

The cry first went up from the village gates. Someone had seen dust rising from the road, which meant that travelers were approaching. As the group got closer to town, some sharp-eyed fellow recognized one of the travelers as none other than the, now-famous, runaway son. Word spread like wildfire.

In most every house throughout town, fathers grabbed their young sons and said, "C'mon boy, now you're gonna see what happens to boys who don't behave," or "Grab the boy, Charlie, there's gonna be a whoppin' today!" It was the perfect ending to the perfectly bad situation, with the perfect lesson to be learned in the process, because they all knew exactly what was going to happen.

And the father knew as well. The law was quite clear on this kind of thing. He really had no choice in the matter. The older brother, the one who had stayed home and minded his p's and q's, also knew the law, and on his way out of the house grabbed the big bullwhip hanging by the door, clearly in his eagerness his father had forgotten it.

According to the law, if and when the runaway boy returned home he had to be punished for the insult to his father and the community. The appropriate punishment was a sound public whipping. Everyone knew that, including the boy who was now making his way through the village gate and toward his father now standing just inside. The older brother is just behind Dad. See him standing there holding the whip at the ready? The crowd is gathered. Young impressionable sons pushed to the front of the crowd so they learn their lesson well, and then it begins.

The father walks toward his son, with several years of pain all pent-up inside. He had endured years of shame and of ridicule, all brought on by this one boy, this son who had stormed out the door and changed the entire world forever. He raises his arm, to strike the first blow. And....

Silence.

The blow became a hug. The hug became an embrace. The embrace became almost what you would call a dance. Tears flowed like, well, like tears.

The crowd did what your typical shocked, disappointed, and embarrassed crowd would do. What kind of a lesson was this for their young and impressionable sons? There was grumbling and shouting. There was the shaking of heads and of fists. The anger of the crowd grew, as did the volume.

The father held his son close as he looked at the crowd. He had made his choice. He had just delivered a class on his theory of what it meant to be a father, a dad, and a daddy.

My friends, I believe this is what Paul had in mind as he wrote these few paragraphs to the Romans. When Paul said that we were now adopted as sons of God; this is the kind of father of which we are the sons. The choice between law and love is a simple one. Oh, but there is just one other little piece of the definition Paul knew. That comes at the end of our story.

As the noise and protest of the crowd grew, the dad and son began to move forward, planning to go back home and rebuild their lives. Nothing could stop them now. Except for that other brother; the older son. You remember him. He was the one holding the whip. He also knew the law, and the noise of the crowd was much louder in his ears than the beating of his heart for father and brother was in his chest. He stepped forward and delivered the lesson that the crowd had come to see, the lesson his father was apparently not man enough to deliver. The lesson was delivered to both wayward son and wayward father.

When the beatings and cheerings were over, silence once again thundered through the streets. The older son regained his breath and shook everyone's hands and got his back patted by the appreciative fathers in the crowd. But as the younger brother and dad slowly made it back to their feet and helped each other home, somehow the handshaking and back-patting seemed out of place. Everyone just kind of wandered quietly away, leaving the eldest son standing alone in the middle of the street. With his laws, and his whip.

This is Pentecost Sunday, the day Jesus appeared to his disciples after his crucifixion. Among everything else he said that day, and the disciples said afterward, nothing rings more loudly than the statement that Jesus' father is now our father. We are all adopted sons and daughters of the one Jesus called Abba; daddy. And judging from the story we've shared, we're in pretty good hands.

Boast Of That!

He had been looking forward to Sunday afternoon all week. As a pastor, Sunday afternoons were usually as busy as any time, with youth groups and then preparing for Sunday evening services. But this week, there was no youth group meeting. And this week, there were no Sunday evening services. He had been very careful to protect the calendar so that nothing got scheduled in place of these things, and he would have a full Sunday afternoon, and evening, all to himself — or at least with the family. Who knows? Maybe he would read a book. Or maybe go for a walk. Or maybe he would just sit in front of the television for the entire time and do absolutely nothing. Whatever it would bring, he had been looking forward to it all week, and was going to enjoy it thoroughly.

Then the telephone rang.

The voice on the other end was one he recognized, but he could not exactly place the name and face. It was one of the nurses at the hospital, and her message was brief.

"Pastor, we need you at the hospital. Right away."

No book. No walk. No television. It is amazing how many thoughts can go through your head so quickly at a time like this. But, the thought that came to his tongue and he heard himself speak into the phone was, "Sure, but can you tell me what's going on?"

The voice answered, "Cindy Jones has had an accident. Her family, uh, we need you to come out here right away."

He had received these types of calls before, at all hours of the day and night. The ones he hated most were those that came about 2:30 in the morning. People rarely call you at 2:30 in the morning with good news. And he had become familiar with the tone of voice of the nurses who usually made the calls; the professionalism that came through when the pressure was on. But this time the voice sounded somehow different. It was still professional, but there was something else. What was it? He had never known nurses to panic, but if he had to name it, that was the sound that came over the phone louder than the words; panic.

He made the ten-minute drive to the hospital in six.

As he pulled into the parking area, he saw the nurse waiting at the emergency room door. Yep, he would swear that was panic in the eyes. Red, swollen eyes. This was strange. At the door, she grabbed him by the arm and began talking.

Cindy Jones was a cute, little six-year-old from the pastor's church. Just this morning she had come up for the children's sermon and played along with the story of Noah and the Ark. Cindy was from a very happy family of one three-year-old brother, along with their mother and father. The family was like those in the storybooks, only for real. Both mom and dad worked very hard, but nothing was more important to them than their family. They spent time together, lots of time. In fact, that's what the nurse was telling the pastor at the door.

Cindy's family had taken advantage of the quiet Sunday afternoon as well, driving out the country roads and walking around some of the old cemeteries. Although that may sound a bit strange, cemeteries can be magical places, filled with history and nature. Mom, Dad, Cindy, and little brother walked among the gravesites, rubbing pencils on paper to capture interesting stone images, and talking about the names and dates they saw, and sometimes recognized. They were walking around the third cemetery they visited, one of their family favorites. The sun was shining, and the breeze was blowing the autumn leaves around. It was good.

Someone said they were hungry, so they all joined hands and started walking back to the truck. The next stop would be the Dairy Queen. As they neared the truck, Cindy turned for one last look at the pretty stones as Dad reached for his keys. The next thing he heard was a "thump." He turned to call Cindy to the truck, but she was gone. While his brain attempted to make sense of her disappearance, his eyes landed on one of the large tombstones they had just passed. Only the stone was flat, and not standing up as before, and under the flattened stone he saw Cindy.

Had the autumn breeze been just enough to push the ancient marker over at just the wrong time, or had the six-year-old tried to get one more rubbing before leaving? There just wasn't time. She had just let go of his hand. Now he could only see her face and her feet, everything else covered by the massive slab. Later they would learn that the slab weighed some 300 pounds, but Dad tossed it aside with one hand as he ran to his daughter. There was no time. He scooped her up and yelled for Mom to start the truck, and they began the seven-mile journey to town, and to a hope of help.

Whoever heard of such a thing? This made no sense. Down gravel roads, through stop signs; there just was no time. Cindy was in and out of consciousness. Not a six-year-old! At one point she looked up to her dad and said, "Daddy, I'm dying." This was just too much. Whoever heard of such a thing?

Certainly, no one at the hospital. As Mom and Dad explained what had happened, the medical team sprang into action, doing everything they could to determine how seriously Cindy was injured. At the same time, their minds and hearts were saying, "Whoever heard of such a thing? This made no sense. Not a six-year-old." They were professionals, everyone of them, and darn good ones. But this is just too much. Whoever heard of such a thing?

In the confusion, someone had suggested calling the pastor, so now here he was, standing at the emergency room door. The nurse then said, "The family is in the waiting room. We're glad you're here."

Family members were crying. Nurses were crying. Doctors were crying. Everyone working very hard to make a miracle, but everyone was overwhelmed. The pastor picked up the telephone and called a lay pastor of the church saying, "I need your help at the hospital. Right away." Within twenty minutes, the church had responded with a pastor, three lay ministers, and three or four good souls. During the next four hours every one of them rode an emotional roller coaster as each symptom was identified and treated.

At 9:15 on Sunday evening, the doctor came into the waiting room to say that the vital signs looked good, and they had called the helicopter to transfer Cindy to the hospital in the city an hour away. At 9:30 on that Sunday evening, the doctor returned to the waiting room to say that the helicopter had been sent back, and that they had done all that they could.

Whoever heard of such a thing? This made no sense. Not a six-year-old. This was just too much. Whoever heard of such a thing?

I share the true story of Cindy with you for one reason. When you read those words of Paul that say we should boast of our suffering, don't let them confuse you. Cindy's family found little to boast about that long Sunday evening. And I don't want to hear about how lucky we are when we suffer, since it makes us so much stronger and all. That long Sunday evening makes that argument sound pretty lame.

What is the good news, even in the story of Cindy? I think it's the fact that in the midst of the unimaginable tragedy of a family, God still sent a pastor, three lay pastors, and three or four good souls to care. You are never out of God's reach.

But also be aware. Sometime, when life throws the unimaginable into someone's life, it may be you that God throws in to get them through. It was just a pastor, three lay ministers, and three or four good souls. If you must boast of something, boast of that.

Note to the reader: The story of Cindy Jones is a true story. The names were changed, but the experiences described are just as they happened.

The Dream

It was an October Monday morning. Nothing much happened on Monday mornings, especially during the harvest time. The pastor sat in his office wondering how the sermon reviews were going down at the coffee shop. He would give them another hour, and then stop in for his coffee and wheat toast. He would get the summary of the reviews from Maryanne, the waitress.

The door was open, so there was no knock. The man just kind of appeared, leaning against the sill and looking pretty uncomfortable. The pastor recognized the guy as being from town, knew a little bit about his family and where they lived, but didn't actually know his name. He did know that the guy had never been in the church here, and that was probably why he looked so uncomfortable.

The pastor said, "Hello," and the visitor asked if he could talk for a minute. His hands were shaking, and his voice was quivering. This was not a simple case of the nerves. As he sat down, he explained, "You're probably going to think that I'm crazy, and maybe I am. But I just don't know who else to go to about this."

He was asking permission to talk about something, and the pastor gave it. I'll try to retell the story exactly as the visitor told it.

He began by saying that his name was Fred, and he talked a little more about his family and what they all did. In fact, he talked quite a bit about those things, the whole time sounding like he really wanted to talk about something else. The pastor tried to help him along a bit by asking, "So, what can I do for you this morning?"

Fred sighed, and looked at his shoes. "You're going to think I'm crazy, but I want to talk about a dream. Not one of mine, but a dream my son had a few months ago. Can I tell you about it?"

"Sure."

"Well, it was one afternoon last June. I was out cutting the grass in the front yard. My son came home from work, rode his motorcycle up the driveway, and went into the house. He came back out a minute later with a couple of beers and asked if we could talk. We sat in the yard chairs and had a beer."

His eyes apologized for the beers, but the pastor shook his head and said, "No problem. Go ahead."

"Well, my son started telling me about this dream he had the night before, and wondered what I thought about it. In his dream, he was riding his motorcycle home from work, but was taking a different way home than he usually did, riding down Route 17. Anyway, he was just riding along, there by the grocery store, where the railroad tracks cross the road, you know? So, he was riding along, and this station wagon was coming from the other direction. When the station wagon got to the grocery store, it pulled in the parking lot. Then, for some reason, it pulled right back onto the highway again. But the driver went too far and pulled over into the wrong lane of traffic, right in front of my son. His motorcycle hit the station wagon right in front of the passenger door. My son flew across the hood and landed beside the highway right on the rail-road tracks. He was killed in the crash."

Fred paused.

"Wow, that's a pretty powerful dream," the pastor said. "I can see why you'd be upset."

Fred took a deep breath. "No, you don't understand. That's not what bothers me. You see, I just now came from the funeral home." He looked at his shoes again.

The pastor felt something stirring inside. If it had been a movie, the orchestra would have started playing something really soft and slow, but with definite suspense. Fred continued.

"My son was riding home from work last night on his motor-cycle. He had stopped by to visit at his sister's house and was tak-ing a different way home than usual. He was coming up Route 17, you know, about where the grocery store is? Well, according to the police report, there was a car coming the other way on the highway, a family in a station wagon coming home from vacation. As they got to the grocery store, the wife asked her husband to pull in to the store so she could get some milk. Since they had been gone, they would need some fresh milk for the next morning. As he pulled into the parking lot, she said that she would wait and get milk in town where it would be cheaper. The husband spun the wheel to pull back out of the parking lot, and overcompensated, pulling across the road into the wrong lane."

The pastor almost spoke the rest of the story along with Fred.

"The motorcycle hit the station wagon right in front of the passenger door. My son flew across the hood and landed beside the highway right on the railroad tracks. He was killed in the crash. He landed exactly where the dream said he would land. The police have pictures."

Fred looked at his shoes again. This time he just stayed there. He then looked the pastor in the eyes, and with the eyes of a father who does not understand, asked, "What does it mean? The dream last summer ... why did he have that? Tell me, what do you think about my son's dream?"

The pastor was caught off guard. He had slipped into clergy-mode, and had begun thinking of the funeral service and how it should be done. That is, after all, what Fred had come to ask him to do. Since the family does not have a church, obviously someone recommended him for the task. This one would be difficult. He had begun running through the litany of questions that needed to be answered: which funeral home was in charge, when is the service, where will it be, do you have favorite scripture, or hymns?

But this was no funeral invitation. That would come later, but first, there was something different. Fred wanted to know about the dream.

The pastor found himself mentally running through every seminary theology course he had attended, and every book he had read. He thought of existentialism, and a whole collection of other "isms," but they all seemed to help more with things like funeral plans, and less with answers about four-month-old visions. He tried to find

233

his official clergy response, coming out of his professional training, and personal faith grown out of years of study. Was it a warning to the son? Does God do that kind of thing? If so, why aren't others warned?

Fred watched him.

Finally, the pastor found his answer. What could he say about a dream four months ago, that fully described the event that just took place a few hours ago? What could he say about a young man who appeared to have been given a vision of a life-changing, or more accurately, life-ending event, far ahead of time? What could he say?

The pastor leaned back in his chair and said, "Wow. I have absolutely no idea what that means. What an amazing story."

Okay, so what would you have said? As Paul tells us in the writing today, sometimes the only response to a situation is to point to God and say no more. Sometimes, anything additional we might add is not only unnecessary, but probably just gets in the way of the truth. Sometimes all we can say is, "Wow."

For the record, Fred seemed satisfied with the response. Although he didn't understand much theology, he did understand "Wow." Fred understood that sometimes we are just forced to close our mouths and our minds and sit in awe.

This was one of those times.

Note to the reader: The story of "The Dream" is a true story. The names were changed, but the experiences described are just as they happened.

My Earlier Life

You have heard, no doubt, of my earlier life in Judaism.

Trust me on this one, *everybody* had heard about Paul's earlier life in Judaism. It was one of the most common topics of conversation whenever members of the new church got together. And the opinions about that earlier life were mixed, especially when it came to how it compared with the Paul that was converted. Those opinions were so mixed that it threatened to split apart and destroy the church itself. So when people read Paul's opening line — You have heard, no doubt, of my earlier life in Judaism — he had their attention.

We can make sense of all this; let's remember together just what all the fuss was about. Let's go back a couple of thousand years, to just a few years after Jesus had preached and been crucified. The disciples had accepted the challenge of Pentecost, and had continued preaching and teaching about the new way of salvation. They had been successful; successful enough to rile up the Pharisees and Sadducees, two groups who built their fortunes upon the old way, the way of the temple and the old law. Then, as now, the folks in power were not all that excited to see new groups show up and try to change the way things worked. They began using their powers to put down this new revolution, and destroy this new church before it destroyed them.

These authorities developed a wide variety of methods of finding and threatening Christians. They followed the normal methods of all great oppressors throughout history. First, threaten someone's livelihood, then their family, then their very life. Unfortunately, these Christians were a difficult lot. They were willing to lose live-lihood, family, and even their lives for the freedom to celebrate their faith. And they weren't stupid. Although Christians rarely denied their faith when confronted, they knew better than to run around flaunting the fact that they were believers. No big crosses and religious banners on the front porch kind of thing. They hid. They met in secret meetings. They created secret symbols to com-municate their faith to others who were being threatened. They even spread out, many of them moving from Jerusalem to go to other cities to spread their new gospel. Destroying this new church was not going to be an easy task.

Fortunately for the authorities, they did have a secret weapon. His name was Saul. Today, Saul would have his own reality televi-sion show, something like one of those bounty hunter shows. Saul was indeed a bounty hunter. His area of expertise was locating and capturing Christians, and he was very good at what he did. He was able to work his way inside the secret groups, taking names and then paying late-night visits to homes and carrying away these of-fenders of the faith. But what made Saul so effective was his com-mitment to his work. He believed in what he was doing, and found joy and satisfaction in capturing Christians; you know, doing his part to serve God.

One of the things that really burned Saul was the way so many of these new Christians were escaping authority by getting out of town and going to places like Syria. Damascus had become a hot-bed for the new Christian movement, and was outside the jurisdic-tion of Saul and his expertise. But finally, Saul went to his bosses in Jerusalem, and convinced them to give him papers that would introduce him to the authorities in Damascus, and give him the power to find and bring back those Christians hiding there. His bosses considered it Saul's stroke of genius. Interestingly enough, a higher authority had another kind of stroke in mind for old Saul.

The story goes like this. Saul was on his way from Jerusalem to Damascus. It was a few days' travel, up through the northern country of Israel, up near the border with Lebanon, and then east, over Mount Hermon and then down to Damascus. Our best guess is that it was somewhere on the downhill side of Mount Hermon, a place noted for its furious and unannounced thunderstorms, that God announced his alternative plans for Saul.

We could spend lots of time here, debating over whether Saul really got hit by lightning, or had some kind of inner-flash. We could go on to debate if he was blinded by some actual scales that somehow got on his eyes and fell off later in Damascus. Those are fun things to argue over sometimes, but for today we won't let them get in the way. We want to focus on three simple facts. First, is the fact that Saul had some really great plans in place for his future. Second, is the fact that God disagreed with those plans. Third, is that God won.

Saul was blinded on the road to Damascus. Keep in mind that the Sadducees believed that things happened to people only because God wanted them to happen. The rich were rich because God wanted them rich, and the poor were poor because God wanted them poor. You essentially got what you deserved. If Saul was blinded, he had obviously done something to deserve that blindness. The Sadducees had a field day with that. Although he had been a great force for them, there were jealousies, and many in authority who thought Saul had gotten too big for his britches. His blindness served as a great excuse to turn against him. The result was that Saul found himself in Damascus, rejected by his own, feared and hated by everyone else, blind, and living in a one-room hovel. Those papers he carried from Jerusalem? Useless.

Perhaps the real hero of this entire story is a guy named Ananias. Again, we'll leave the theological debates for a later time, but just know that Ananias was a Christian, and overcoming his fears and the fears of his friends, went to visit Saul. It was during this brief visit that Saul regained his sight, and rebuilt his life. He entered that one-room hovel as a blind, lost man. He walked out of that room as a Christian, with his eyes wide open. However, his mouth was even more open than his eyes, and he began preaching about his experience everywhere he went. He became the Sadducees' and Pharisees' worst nightmare. Now, how cool is that?

Over time, Saul became known as Paul. He traveled thousands of miles preaching, teaching, and leaving a trail of churches behind him wherever he went. His story was one that touched lives. If someone like Saul could start over, maybe we can, too.

Unfortunately, it wasn't quite that neat and clean.

There were many in the church who just didn't trust him. After all, he had often pretended to be a Christian just to finagle his way into the secret meetings, so what made anybody think he wasn't just doing that again? He hadn't really changed at all, and was only preaching things that he had heard the others preach. It was still just old Saul underneath that Paul-disguise.

Overall, it was all just a mess.

And all of that leads up to: "You have heard, no doubt, of my earlier life in Judaism." In his words that followed he simply said: What I have told you is God's truth, so deal with it.

Each one of us here brings our entire life into this place today. Some of us have rather simple stories to tell, never having strayed too far from where we probably should have been. But some of us bring stories that old Saul would understand. However much we may have become something new, people still periodically remind us of what we used to be, and still look for an occasional glimmer of what was. It is hard to allow people to start over.

I look at it a lot like Paul did, and I have a suggestion for anyone who has decided to repurpose one's life, and have left behind some things that were pretty darn creative and hard for those around you to forget. Just keep in mind that because of Paul's earlier life, a church was built and an entire world was changed. In spite of what others may have said or believed, God used that life, with all its bruises and scars, to work miracles.

Why should we expect any less from yours?

Proper 6
Pentecost 4
Ordinary Time 11
Galatians 2:15-21

The Difference Between Knowing And Doing

It is difficult to be the church. What we have been asked to do here is not easy. Jesus' directive to love one another sounds like it should be a fairly straightforward thing to do. Now, I don't want to shock anyone here this morning, but I do have to admit that there have been times in our history that there have been disagreements in the church; disagreements about what it means to love one another. Some of those disagreements are over what it really means to love, and some of those disagreements are over just to whom the "one another" is referring. Paul's writings to the church at Galatia this morning, and for next week, drop us right smack-dab in the middle of those disagreements. Let's read over the shoulder of the Galatians and see if Paul's words can give us direction, as well.

At first, being the church was not so bad. Everyone who was there was pretty much alike. They had all been Jewish, came from the same general area and lived in Jerusalem, and all had joined up at pretty much the same time. They had more in common than they had in differences. Being Jewish, they had all grown up with the same religious laws, and shared the same religious practices and traditions. They were all circumcised. They all ate the same foods, and stayed away from the same foods. Then something very painful happened; something that created all kinds of problems for the early church.

They were successful. It was then that they came face-to-face with the difference between knowing and doing.

It all started the first time that new person who was not from the same side of the tracks came to join the church; he was not

Jewish. He had not been raised in the same traditions, and did not follow, or even understand the laws that undergirded the Jewish tradition. Even worse, he wasn't interested in learning those laws to become a member of the new church. I mean, the new guy wasn't even circumcised.

In reality, there should not have been a problem. Every one of the church members was familiar with Jesus' comment that he had fulfilled the obligation of the old laws, and the only law in effect now was to love one another. They knew that. But they didn't know how to do that. Having lived their entire lives under the myriad of laws, they couldn't conceive of doing otherwise.

Yes, the old laws had been unbearable at times, and had created an inequality in the society that was exactly what Jesus had preached against. But surely he hadn't meant doing away with all of the laws! I mean we have to be reasonable here. Surely we need to do away with those laws that are unfair, and that create injustice; but the others? If Jesus wants us to love one another, then somehow we have to have rules and laws that define just how to do that, don't we! Sure, we need laws so people understand exactly what they have to do to show their love. There's a good case of first-century rationalization. We've been good at that for a long time.

We can do away with those laws that say a guy can divorce his wife by simply writing it on a piece of paper and throwing it at her feet. That's pretty unfair. Besides, there are actually twelve pages of divorce laws in the *Mishnah*, and that's just not necessary. There are another couple of hundred pages of laws about marriage and betrothals, but they are all connected to other religious and political issues that we don't have to worry about anymore, so they're out now. And what about all of those laws about sacrifices at the temple? Now that Jesus has served as our ultimate sacrifice for our salvation, those can go, too. Along with the sacrifice laws, all of those other temple things can go away, also. We have a new temple, one not made with hands. Good, now we're making progress. Let's see, the books of law about the Sanhedrin, the Sadducees and Pharisees, nope, don't need them anymore. There must be thousands of pages of laws about cleanliness and uncleanliness. Those have been some of the most oppressive laws of all of them. Jesus made it clear that those laws just don't apply anymore, so we'll consider them gone.

Well, wait a minute.

Except for a couple of those laws about food. Some of those probably ought to stay. You know, some of those that tell us which foods are clean and okay to eat, and which ones we should stay away from. I'm sure Jesus didn't mean for us to stop following those laws. Actually, those were some of the laws that really set us apart from all those other folks. They would eat anything. So the laws about what food we can and cannot eat stay. But all the rest of them are finished.

Except of course, for the law about circumcision; we really ought to keep that one, too. Circumcision is what has set us apart since the days of Abraham. It is what has identified us as God's chosen people throughout history. Besides, Jesus grew up in the tradition and was circumcised, so I'm sure he expects us to continue that.

So, we're agreed then. All of those joining the new church can celebrate the fact that, through his death and resurrection, Jesus has freed us from the bondage of the old laws; except for those rules about what we can and cannot eat, and for the fact that all the guys have to get circumcised.

If it sounds like I'm making light of all of this, that is not the intent. But it is interesting to note that the early church had such a hard time creating its own identity that until the year 130 A.D., Christianity was still considered a Jewish sect. However much they knew that they were justified by faith alone, they still relied on works to get it done.

As new people responded to the call, they were met with the demands to follow the old laws that remained. If you were Jewish to begin with, there wasn't much problem. But if you were not Jewish, to become a Christian you first had to be circumcised as a Jew. This might have worked for a while, but as Paul and others traveled the world bringing more and more to Christ, the questioning about food and circumcision grew. Eventually, a split developed among the early disciples. Those remaining in Jerusalem maintained that circumcision was non-negotiable, and the only way into the salvation of the church. Those preaching from other corners of the world insisted that such laws were unjust, and the acts of false believers.

At one point, Paul met the Apostle Peter, one of the original disciples, and ended up in a yelling match with him. It seems that Peter, who was one of the Jerusalem boys, had had a dream about the laws regarding cleanliness. In Acts 10, we read that Peter had a dream about a big white sheet being lowered from heaven, and in the sheet were animals and foods of all kinds. It might help this make sense if we understood that when the ships docked at the port and unloaded their animals and cargo, everything was just loaded into the big white sails and hoisted over the side of the ship. Peter had seen that happen at Caesarea, and got the point of the dream. God told him to go ahead and eat anything he wanted out of the sail; clean, unclean, it just didn't matter. Peter got the message and began preaching it, which made Paul and the other non-Jerusalem folks happy. But after getting a chewing out from his friends back home, Peter dropped the sail story from his sermons and went back to warning people not to eat unclean things. Paul was so angered over this about-face that when he ran into Peter in the city of Antioch, he called him a hypocrite and put him in his place.

This food and circumcision argument may sound somewhat overblown to us today. But what it meant at that time was that if you ate the unclean foods, which most everyone outside of Jerusalem did, and if you were not circumcised, which most everyone outside of Jerusalem was not, then you were yourself unclean. And if you were unclean, you could not join the church. You could not have salvation. You were lost.

Yes, it is difficult to be the church. Paul's writing in this morning's message was a reminder to the church of Galatia that no one was to be excluded because of some nonsense about eating unclean food or being uncircumcised. He also reminded them that salvation came from what people believed, and not from following some laws established by a group of people, no matter how well-intended.

As we continue to try to create the church that Paul envisioned, it might do us well to periodically read these words as if they were written to us today. It might do us well to look upon ourselves to see if we are excluding anyone because of our laws, written or unwritten. We know what we should do, but how is our doing, doing?

If Paul will stand up and tear into Peter, the disciple upon whom Jesus said he would establish his church, I'd rather not see how he might deal with us. Yes, it is difficult to be the church.

God's Grammar

In the last reading from Paul's letter to the church at Galatia, he addressed the ongoing feud in the early church and reminded the folks that salvation comes from faith alone, and not from working to follow some collection of man-made laws. This week's reading continues Paul's warning to the Galatians. But if he faced strong resistance over the issues of clean and unclean foods, and the issue of circumcision, it was just a dress rehearsal for the real battle he faces now. As we did last week, it might be wise for us to keep an ear tuned to the conversation, and see if Paul's words have any meaning for our attempts at church-building here today.

Let's begin by accepting the reality that the church was originally created by a group of good Jewish boys. I mean absolutely no offense in making that comment, but it is important to start there as we try to understand what is to come. The twelve disciples selected by Jesus were all from the Jewish tradition, and all from fairly well-established families. When they decided to follow Jesus, they left behind boats and businesses, some of them giving up rather sizeable and respected positions. They each would have been well-reared in the traditions of the Jewish community, and most likely all full practitioners of the matters of the faith, as were their ancestors before them. We see this fact demonstrated several times throughout the gospels. We see it most clearly in those situations when the disciples are faced with interacting with those people who come from outside the Jewish faith; the unclean.

On one occasion, Jesus sent a group into town for food, and he was met with real protest. The protest was not because it was a

245

long walk to town, or they just didn't want to go shopping, but because they would probably run into unclean people there, and they just didn't want to do that. It is interesting to remember that to finally get them to go, Jesus sent twelve of them to go do the shopping for only thirteen people. The old security in numbers thing?

Even Jesus himself seemed, at times, to follow that lead. Jesus spent years living and preaching around the northern country of Galilee. There were seven major non-Jewish cities around the Sea of Galilee, yet we have absolutely no biblical reference of Jesus ever entering one of those cities. It would not be at all uncommon for that to be intentional, and for Jesus to avoid visiting the unclean cities of the Gentiles. Whatever he personally believed at the time, his visit to those places would have raised so many religious and political issues that it may have interfered with what he understood that he had to be doing.

The gap between Jew and Gentile, or anyone non-Jewish, was tremendous. The disciples would all have been raised to believe that if the shadow of a Gentile fell upon you as you walked by, you must go take a ceremonial bath to remove the uncleanliness from you. If you had to pass through Gentile land, you did so quickly and without turning to the left or right. You did not enter the home of a Gentile, and you most certainly would not sit at a table with them. Each disciple knew that you just don't mix with non-Jews.

Most despised among the Gentiles were the Samaritans. Now living in the area just below the Sea of Galilee, the Samaritans were descendants of the Jews who stayed in the land of Israel during the Babylonian exile many years before. While the rest of the Jews were sent off to live in Babylon, the Samaritans stayed behind, and worked with, and intermarried with the non-Jews who moved in. Their offense would be carried down from father to son, and was cause for the breach between the two groups now.

If you ran a business and a Samaritan was to pay for your product or services, rather than touch the money they had held, you had them drop their money into a bucket of water, to remove the uncleanliness before you handled it. In some parts of the country even today, if a Jew happens to walk across the property of a Samaritan, the Samaritan will run outside, throw a handful of straw on the spot walked upon, and set it on fire to burn away the uncleanliness.

This may help us to understand some of the outcry of the disciples when Jesus approached the woman at the well. First of all, she was a Samaritan, and the disciples simply could not understand why in the world Jesus would want to be seen talking to a Samaritan. Secondly, it was a woman.

Yes, the disciples had just as clear an understanding of the role of women. Though we today fully understand the depth of the misperceptions they held, let's suffice it to say that the disciples were as seriously in error with this as they were with the issue of the Gentiles.

But there were more.

This group of disciples had very clear understandings of people such as those who were called the "demoniacs." The term refers to a large group of people who would have suffered from a wide spectrum of illnesses, both physical and mental. Their symptoms were seen not as that of illness, however, but as signs of possession by spirits or demons. And the possession was clearly understood as the result of some behavior or act that was being punished. They were clearly unclean beings, and definitely to be avoided. The fact that Jesus not only sought to heal these demoniacs, but actually went to the places where they hung out, and had the nerve to even touch them, was just too far beyond the comprehension of our good collection of disciples.

Of course, they knew about Romans. Every Jew knew about the Romans. Unless you were a Sadducee, making a good living in support of the Roman authority, there was not one positive word in the entire Jewish vocabulary that could be used to describe a Roman. That one group of Jews, known as the Zealots, had as their number one goal in life to take the life of a Roman soldier, and they always carried a dagger under their cloak just in case fortune would smile upon them. It is good to keep in mind that at least one of these Jewish disciples of Jesus was a Zealot.

I tell you all of this background on the disciples and the people around them to simply set the stage for what happens when the beginnings of the new church is placed into their hands. They have spent years following and listening to Jesus, and they met his Spirit in the upper room and received his command to create the church. But inside, in their heart-of-hearts, however much a disciple they may have been, some of them were still Jewish disciples.

As long as newcomers to the church were like them, there was no problem. They did pretty well when the women got more involved, but then, there were plenty of tasks for them to perform that were more appropriate for women to perform. In fact, since the women were there, it would spare the disciples the embarrassment of having to perform those tasks themselves. Yes, sometimes God works in mysterious ways.

When the Gentiles started attending, some of them even Samaritan Gentiles, we had some problems. Then a few of the disciples, and people like Paul, went out there running around, opening the membership to all sorts of people, even, if you could imagine, to Romans.

Houston, we have a problem.

As you would expect, there was a split. Some of the disciples had left Jerusalem, and along with Paul, Silas, and many others, preached a gospel of salvation to all. They offered baptism to any and all who would come. The disciples who remained in Jerusalem, those well-healed traditional boys, fought this move tooth and nail, and insisted that all newcomers first be circumcised as Jews before being allowed to join the church. They also insisted that Christians could not eat unclean Gentile food, eat any food with a Gentile, and definitely not enter the city or home of a non-Jew. They also kept up their attitude toward women and demoniacs, in case you were wondering.

The church at Galatia was one of those that Paul had started some time ago, and it had received Jew and non-Jew into the fold. But they were now under attack by the Jerusalem group, and were being told that they were not only wrong, but condemned because of their acceptance of the unclean.

So Paul wrote to the Galatians about God's rules of grammar.

For those unfamiliar with those rules of God's grammar, let me explain them. Most groups, including the early church

248

members from Jerusalem, spend most of their time using nouns. Nouns are words that declare things. Things like Jew, Gentile, Samaritan, Roman, woman, and demoniac. These are words that define things. If you are described as a noun-Gentile, it establishes boundaries and limits for you, and it puts you in a little box that determines not only your past but your future. Although few of us have used the word Gentile as a noun, perhaps you have used the noun woman, or black or white or rich or poor or sick or crazy. When we use those words as nouns, we kill the individual, and replace it with a concept.

God is in the business of changing nouns into adjectives.

Adjectives describe something about an object, but not the entire object. Something might be big, and yet be many other things as well. Adjectives don't limit like nouns do. In God's perspective someone might be a Gentile, and be a number of other wonderful things as well. Someone might be a woman, or homeless, or even mentally ill, and still be many other things of great value besides.

As a church, it might be an interesting way to spend our energy. What if we accepted Paul's challenge, and began teaching the world some new lessons in grammar? I invite you to accept the challenge to turn nouns into adjectives. I challenge you to no longer see people around you as Christian, as Arabic, as women, as men, as homeless, as sick, as democrat, as republican, as any noun; but to see them as God's creation with many tremendous abilities and gifts.

Come on, try God's grammar and change some nouns into adjectives. Let those people out of the box.

Church Potluck

It was the pastor's first Sunday at the church. She had just finished the morning services and was making her way down the aisle to the door at the rear of the sanctuary for the traditional handshakes and "nice sermon, reverends." She thought she had done a nice job, and most folks had seemed to enjoy it.

She took her place at the door, next to the choir director and a few others who always stood there for some reason or another. The first person to greet her was a nice looking, older lady, looking rather short and frail, but with a wonderful smile on her face and a gleam in her eyes. She took the pastor's hand, shook it gently, and quietly leaned forward and bit the pastor on the thumb.

The pastor jumped back about five inches and yanked her hand away from the lady. Her eyes still gleamed and she still had that wonderful smile on her face as she nodded and turned to walk out the door. Fortunately, the lady apparently wore dentures, and they were loose enough that the bite was rather soft and did not break the skin. What was most amazing to the pastor was that no one else seemed to notice, and everyone smiled and talked about this and that.

A bit later in line was a kindly looking, young man. She remembered him because he really seemed to be paying close attention to her sermon, frequently nodding his head and smiling just at the right times as she made her points. He walked up to her and took her hand and shook it. Then gently bowed forward and bit her just above the wrist, right there in front of God and everybody. Again, no one seemed to notice as she yelped and jumped back from the handshaker-biter. And this one left a mark. She turned to the choir director standing next to her, and only then noticed the scars. Little marks on her hand, and her arm, some of them pretty darn big, too. But the choir director just nodded, and gave one of those "what are you going to do?" kind of smiles, and went back to shaking hands — and getting bit.

By the end of the greetings, she counted eleven nips and three or four actual bites that left marks. Two even broke the skin and probably needed some treatment of some kind. But there were many more sincere handshakes, and some really wonderfully kind and supportive words for her sermon. Overall, it felt like a really wonderful place to be. Except for the biting, that is.

The next evening happened to be the regular monthly meeting of the church council. It would be a great opportunity to meet people, and get a better understanding of just how the church worked. As she entered the room for the meeting, everyone was happy to see her, and made her feel right at home. All looked normal. They sat around the three big cafeteria tables that had been pushed together to form one big table. There were probably 25 chairs around the table, and by the time the meeting started most all of them were filled. The only thing that seemed unusual was the Kleenex box, or boxes, on the table. There must have been ten or eleven of those boxes around the table, all of them freshly opened and full. But the conversation was good, and promptly at seven, the council chair called the meeting to order.

The chair turned to the new pastor and asked if she would be willing to open the meeting with a brief prayer. This was not unexpected and she had come prepared for this. But as she spoke the few words, she was not prepared for what happened next. Just as she ended the prayer with an, "Amen," the little man sitting next to her leaned over and bit her on the arm. It was a real bite, too. It broke the skin and began bleeding. Before she could do anything, the woman on the other side reached for some Kleenex and pressed it upon the pastor's arm, stopping the bleeding. "Just hold it there for a few minutes dear, and it will be all right."

The pastor was too overcome with shock to even respond. Everyone had seen what had happened, just as they had yesterday morning in the greeting line. But while she tried to regain some of her senses, the meeting continued.

The minutes were read and accepted without comment. A few letters were read, and the new pastor was formally introduced. All applauded and smiled. Her arm still ached a bit, but the bleeding had indeed stopped. Her friend on her left had slid the Kleenex box closer to her, just in case she needed a fresh bandage.

It was as the meeting continued that the pastor began looking around. She began to notice, once again, the scars. Lots of scars. And she was curious about the number of crutches leaning against chairs. There must have been half a dozen people there using crutches.

The discussion then turned to the work being done in the church basement. A woman on the far side of the table was describing the new colors that had been selected for the women's bathroom, currently being renovated. Just as she began passing around paint chips, the woman sitting on her left leaned over and bit her on the shoulder; bit her hard. Another neighbor reached for a Kleenex box, and the discussion never wavered. The paint lady did waver though, in fact, she started to swoon from the attack. Someone walked over to her and helped prop her up in the chair, as they all continued the debate of the new colors for the downstairs women's restroom.

The new pastor was overcome to the point of standing up in her chair and asking, "What in the world is going on here?" Everyone looked totally surprised by her outburst. They all glanced around the table in obvious confusion, before finally all turning to the council chair for some direction out of this distraction from their church business. The council chairperson began explaining that everything was just fine, and that sometimes we disagree about things in the church, but that we handle those disagreements and move on.

It was then that she noticed his thumb. Or I should say she noticed his absence of a thumb. And the second finger on his left hand. There were also scars on his arms, and a couple visible on his neck as well. He noticed her checking him out, and went on to explain that sometimes even church people have disagreements, and that they really do love each other, and just want to help each other do the right things. Just as he finished, the council co-chair, sitting on his right, leaned over and took a big bite out of the council chair's left wrist. And the treasurer immediately slid a box of Kleenex over and offered the first handful.

Okay, let's end this silly story right here. Whoever heard of such nonsense? People taking bites out of other people. In church no less. Impossible.

Nonsense perhaps, but impossible?

In today's reading from Paul's letter to the churches of Galatia, he urged them to allow themselves to be led by the Spirit, and not by the flesh. He explained what he meant was that they should focus on things like kindness, generosity, patience, gentleness, and self-control, and not spend their time in jealousy, anger, quarreling, and arguing. What has always fascinated me is his little comment that if, however, we continue to bite and devour each other, we should take care that we are not totally consumed by one another.

Perhaps, today's story is a bit over the edge, and far too close to nonsense. But don't fool yourself. There are people here today wearing the scars from the bites of others. Oh, they are invisible scars perhaps, not requiring boxes of Kleenex to stop the bleeding, but they are scars. They are scars that hurt and frighten and sometimes even do fully consume us. And there are those among us who have wonderful smiles, and speak kind and gentle words of support, while at the same time biting pieces out of our spirits, all the while believing they are helping us.

What could be more nonsense than that?

Sowing And Reaping

These words certainly sound like a threat, don't they? You will reap what you sow! So you'd better watch out! Don't think you can mock God and get away with it. God is watching with this big club, and if you get out of line, *Whap!* It may be sooner or it may be later, but you won't get away with it, that's for sure. One of these days ... *Pow!*

Sorry. I kind of got carried away there. But is sure sounds like that is just what Paul is saying to the Galatians. You will reap what you sow. These were not new words. The Sadducees had built their empire upon these words, saying that God gave people exactly what they deserved; you reap what you sow. Therefore, if you were rich, like the Sadducees, you must be an especially good person, since you were reaping such nice stuff. If you were poor, you obviously deserved it. The Pharisees liked those words, too. If you break the rules, you will be punished. You reap what you sow. Of course, nobody understood all the rules as well as the Pharisees did, because the Pharisees wrote the rules and changed them regularly just to keep ahead of the game.

So reaping what you sow has usually come across as a threat, just as it usually does today. But what if I told you that was not what Paul had in mind when he wrote those words to the Galatians? Instead of issuing a threat, Paul was actually trying to make them feel better, and probably did. Just before saying the reap what you sow phrase, he said something about how they should all share in the good things with their teacher. This was a good thing? To understand just what Paul was getting at, we have to imagine a world in which that rule did not apply. Imagine what it would be like if we did not reap what we sow.

Imagine the young child growing up in a house where you did not reap what you sow. The poor child never knew what was going to happen next. No matter what he did, he could never predict the outcome. He could behave as a perfect gentleman, only to end up getting yelled at and sent to his room, or worse. When he misbehaved, even in some really horrendous ways, it might be overlooked, or even somehow rewarded. Acceptance and rejection were given out randomly. Attention was paid or not paid, but with no clear rhyme or reason for either. Can you imagine that child trying to make some sense of his life?

Can you imagine the woman working in the job where you do not reap what you sow? Her performance and behavior had no connection with her evaluation or treatment by the company. She could work hard, and put in extra hours to do a great job, only to see the recognition and promotions go to those who come in late and leave early. She never really knew how she was doing. Every day she went to work could be her last, and every summons to the office could be a promotion or dismissal. Can you feel the energy being sapped out of her?

How about the marriage in which you don't reap what you sow? Kind words spoken out of love are responded to with anger, or ignored completely. One person does something completely cruel and abusive, and the other doesn't get upset, or even worse, doesn't even seem to notice. How do you survive in that relationship? How do you know if anyone really cares?

Now imagine if your entire world operated without the reap what you sow principle. Your home, your job, your marriage, and even your God, all of it. This was exactly the situation of the folks Paul was writing to in Galatia. They lived in a world that worshiped many different gods, and most of those gods followed the Greek approach to the job of a god, being an aloof kind of role that pretty much did whatever it wanted to do. Their gods would answer prayers, or not answer prayers. It all just depended upon, well, upon whether they wanted to answer or not. Their gods would give out rewards and punishments pretty much as they wanted, and sometimes did so just to see what would happen as a result. Like playing checkers.

Religious leaders followed the practices of their gods, giving favor to some and punishment to others, but all pretty much unrelated to the behavior or the recipient. In reality, those Sadducees sowed some pretty nasty stuff. They mistreated the poor, and that's how they stayed so rich. Surely the Pharisees made people reap what they did sow, because they had the books of law as their guide. Surely that was some stability? Just for fun, listen to one of the laws from the Pharisee's books. One sentence out of a six-paragraph-long law about how to offer a bird as a proper sacrifice says that if you had wrung off the bird's head with your left hand instead of your right, or used a dull knife, or had done it at night, or if you had offered a bird that was not properly consecrated, or did have the bird consecrated but had it consecrated by the wrong guy or on the wrong side of the building, or if you goofed and brought turtledoves instead of pigeons, or if its wings were too dried-up, or if it was partially blind, or if it otherwise did not meet the approval of the chief bird-burner, you were just out of luck. In reality, no matter what you sowed, the reaping was pretty much under someone else's control.

Political leaders followed the same practices. Rulers like Nero and Caligula made decisions that impacted the lives of every person in their land, but paid little attention to what those people had sown. People's lives were altered or destroyed daily, not because they had sown something they should not have, but because their land was governed by some guy who lived a couple of thousand years before the appropriate medications were available to treat whatever mental illness he suffered from.

So, what is it like to live in a place where you do not reap what you sow? You can count on nothing, and no one. You do not know what the next day will bring, and have no ability to influence it. Neither you, nor anyone around you, has any reason to behave, or to be fair, or honest, or much of anything else. If you can imagine even just a taste of what that life would be like, you can imagine what Paul's words might have meant to those people of Galatia who were reading this letter. Rather than threatening them, Paul was offering them a promise. Rather than describing a God with a big club, Paul was telling them about a God who could be trusted. He was describing a God who was fair, and actually gave reward and punishment where they were deserved. He was writing about a God that was the same when you got up in the morning as when you went to bed the night before. Paul was offering a life that was not out of control, one that actually made some sense, and gave you the ability to chart your own course.

The offer still stands.

Something To Whistle About

It was back in the days when the railroad was the most common mode of transportation. There were automobiles, and some airplanes, but the steam locomotive was the way most folks traveled and the way that most of the goods were distributed around the country. After dinner, people sat in the drawing room and listened to the radio programs, fading in and out from some faraway location, over the magical broadcasting signal. Later at night, as they lay in bed, they listened to the roar and squeal of the old steam whistles, telling them that the Old 97 was heading out of town for the run to the city, and wishing each and everyone a good night.

Charlie was an engineer on the old steam locomotives. He had spent most of his life riding those rails, first as a child, hopping rides out to the swimming hole, and now as the man driving the engine, blowing the whistle as he drove past the next generation of children hoping to hitch a ride out to the same old swimming hole. Charlie had raised a family on the railroad. Two sons and three daughters all grew up in a nice wood-frame house with a big garden in the back, a little cement pond for Charlie's goldfish, and the occasional bluegill he caught on his old cane pole.

Oh, there had been hard times, don't get me wrong. There had been hardships both at work and at home. But overall, it just seemed that the good outnumbered the bad. And after all, whether driving a steam engine, or raising a family, there were just some things that there weren't much you could do about. You just had to accept them. Sometimes you spent hours sitting on a siding, waiting for that slow freight to move past you. You had schedules to keep, and deadlines to meet, but what could you do? You just waited. And sometimes you spent hours trying to help your children understand the *whys* of life. Or you sat by their bedside waiting for that fever to break, and the whole time all you could do was pray that it would. Charlie had learned how to accept it all, just as it came.

That's probably what turned Charlie into a whistler and a story-teller. Wherever he went, he whistled as he walked. Usually it was a nice, slow tune that set the pace for his journey. Whether it was to an important meeting across town, or to the icebox for a glass of milk, there and back he announced his approach to life through his peacefully whistled tune. And whenever the opportunity presented itself, which was most of the time, Charlie was ready with a story. Whatever the occasion, but especially on those occasions when he found himself talking to someone who was hurting, or afraid, or just unable to keep up a good whistle because of some problem in their life ... he gave them a story. And he usually left them feeling better than he found them.

In fact, if Charlie were here, he might end up telling us about that time he was walking home from the roundhouse late at night. He had taken a few runs on the late shift, to cover for a good friend who was down with the grippe. Well, as Charlie told it, he was just walking and whistling his way home, some twelve or thirteen blocks in all. For some reason, that night he decided to take a different route home, no particular purpose in it, just because there was no hurry and it was a path not yet taken. So he turned at a new corner, and as soon as he made the turn, he could hear the barking. At the far end of the street, a whole block away, was this big dog tied up in the yard of the house on the corner, letting Charlie know that he was unwelcome at this hour. Charlie crossed to the sidewalk on the other side of the street and walked on. As he neared the dog, the barking and growling got more ferocious. When he found himself directly across the street from the beast, Charlie stopped. He just stood there for a few minutes, whistling his tune, perhaps trying to teach it to his new friend. Finally, with the dog growing almost frantic, Charlie headed on home.

Until the next night.

This time as he came to the spot across the street from the barking dog, Charlie stopped and sat down on the curb. Across the street, the dog continued his protests, as Charlie whistled a bit, and told his new friend about some of the things that had happened that day at work. After fifteen or twenty minutes, fully filled with growls, snaps, barks, and howls, Charlie got up and went home to bed.

After four or five nights of this, Charlie's partner began spending more time listening than protesting. They sat on opposite sides of the street, one whistling and talking, and one staring and wondering. The next night, part way through the conversation, Charlie reached into his pocket, and pulled out a piece of doughnut he had saved from his dinner, and tore it in half. One half he plopped into his mouth, and the other half he tossed across the street. It was clearly appreciated.

Each night for the next week or so, Charlie sat, whistled, storied, and threw pieces of doughnuts, hotdogs, cookies, or whatever else he had brought along. Did I mention that a few nights earlier Charlie had crossed the street and now sat on the curb on the dog's side of the street? He also noticed that as he made his turn around the corner, his buddy was straining at the leash to see him coming. The barking and growling was replaced with tail wagging.

By the time his late-shift duties had ended, Charlie's walk home included a twenty-minute stop, as he sat in the yard rubbing the belly of a big, yellow dog, and telling him about the many adventures of riding the railroad and raising a family.

Okay it is fair to ask just what all this has to do with anything, and how it could be considered a sermon. It is a nice story, for sure. Kind of makes you all warm inside. That is exactly the point.

The lesson this morning is from the introduction of the letter Paul wrote to the church at Colossia. Did you hear the words? They almost sound like the story of Charlie. Paul is writing to a group of people who have been there for him. He has spent time running from mobs, defending himself from other church members who were threatening to destroy everything he had created, and had already spent more than enough time in prison. Throughout it all, the Colossians had supported him, cared for him, listened to him, and truly followed him. That created a warmness in Paul that he found almost nowhere else.

The point is, my friends, that sometimes, like the Colossians, we do it right. Sometimes, in the midst of all of the nonsense and craziness, the noise and the rush, sometimes, we, as a church, really do take our time and do it right. And when we do, we create a warmness in the people we care for that changes lives. Charlie was just a railroader, but he understood something that Paul was expressing to the folks at Colossia. It really isn't that difficult to care. And sometimes, caring isn't all that sophisticated. It may be as simple as sitting in the yard for a while with a barking grouch.

Yes, my friends, sometimes we do it right. And that is something to whistle about.

Note to the reader: The story of "Something To Whistle About" is a true story. The names were changed, but the experiences described are just as they happened.

Be Real

The old story is told about two painters; two artists. Now, the story may be from Greece and may be true, or it may be from some other place and be even more than true. I'm not sure. But the story goes like this:

Each of our two artists was extremely talented and each had their own audiences of followers. As you might expect, and maybe even have experienced, it is difficult for two people to be seen as the best at anything. So eventually, the decision was made to host a competition to determine which of the two was truly the best. A panel of experts was selected who would serve as the judges. Once and for all, the question of "best" would be put to rest.

On the day of the judging, so many people had come to watch that it was decided to hold the contest outdoors. Because of the sun and wind, and perhaps to raise the suspense just a bit, both paintings were to be covered with draperies until each was revealed and judged, one at a time.

The drapery was removed from the first painting.

The judges and the audience gasped as they looked at the image that appeared on the canvas. It was a still life of flowers and fruit. And it looked so real. The colors and the shading were so authentic. In fact, after a few moments, some birds even flew down from the trees and tried to pick the grapes that were painted on the canvas. The crowd cheered as the artist smiled and nodded to the judges who were clearly shaken. All were overcome by the obvious talent of this artist. There was even some discussion as to whether it was even necessary to look at the second painting. But it was decided that they did have to be fair. Even if it was a waste of time.

The drapery was removed from the second painting.

Or at least a judge tried to remove the drapery from the second painting. But as he looked closer, he found that he could not remove the drapery. The drapery covering the second painting was, in actual fact, the painting itself. As the judges and the audience began to realize what was happening, they grew silent. Then a cheer erupted that echoed through the courtyard. The best artist was selected. One painting looked real enough to fool birds, while the second was so real it had fooled everyone.

Sometimes, we all have trouble picking out the real from the unreal. The true from the untrue, or only partially true. There are some thirty different news channels on television today. Many of them are openly biased to a particular political or cultural agenda, so we clearly understand that what we are hearing may reflect that bias. Some channels claim to be bias-free, presenting events "just as they happen," but when we listen to the same story on two different channels, they are often different. Which is real? Which is the truth? How do we know?

Those who are tapped into the digital world have even more problems finding truth. The internet has created a culture in which everyone is an expert; and anyone can publish their thoughts, beliefs, and opinions, with the same level of apparent credibility as anyone else. How do we sort through all of those words and identify what is real? How do we find the truth in the mix of untruths, partial truths, and just complete nonsense?

Don't misunderstand; I'm not bashing either television news or the internet. The problem I am describing is not new, is not the result of some evil technology, or some sign of the end of the world. The people of Galatia had exactly the same problem some 2,000 years ago. There was no television news, and no internet, but the truth was no easier to find just the same. Every street corner had another temple and a street-corner preacher announcing his reality and the one sure way to truth. Imagine for a moment a walk down one of those streets.

There's one guy, over on the left. He is preaching that the truth was to be found through burning incense to the statue of a bull. Come inside and pay your money, burn your incense, and find the answers you seek. You will probably have a decent wheat crop as well. And he explains how he knows this is the truth. Worship of the bull comes from far off Babylon, and has been around since before the time of Abraham. Anything that old has to be true.

There, on the corner across the street, is a man standing on the steps with the pretty girls. That's one of the Greek temples. He is inviting people in to also burn incense, but then to have sexual relations with the temple prostitutes to guarantee the fertility of the flocks and fields. He knows that this is the one true way to worship, because it was written in the story of the goddess Isis, and everyone knows the truth of that story.

We're not going to go down that side street. That's the temple of Dagon. It is a dark place, where the man outside invites you inside where you will present one of your children to be offered to the god of thunder. Anything serious enough to call for child sacrifice has to be true, doesn't it?

But back over here is the Jewish synagogue. They have lots of rules to follow, and they don't mix much with other people. They talk about a God that has led them through trial after trial, and has brought them out of some amazing situations. They talk about that one God, who created the entire world. They say you should occasionally sacrifice a dove or a goat, but just at certain holidays, and they don't believe in things like temple prostitutes and child sacrifice. They talk about how their God actually spoke to them through Abraham, and then God's words were passed down through a long line of people, down to Rabbi Horam, then Rabbi Ezra, and even old Rabbi Gamaliel who lives just down the street. The story they all tell sure sounds real.

Then there is Paul. He came to town a few years ago talking about the new group following Jesus, whom they say is the actual Son of God. He has visited several times since, and has written us a number of letters telling us more about what he has experienced, and how Jesus has completely turned his life around. Paul says that he is offering us the one true way.

So, how do we know? How do we determine the truth?

There is a way. We refer to it as going to the original source. As you listen to the news look for those broadcasts that present the people actually involved in the events being described, and not just a news "analyst" giving an interpretation. We are attempting to teach our children that as they search the internet to try and find out who is actually writing the information they are reading. Is it someone who has the real expertise to understand what they are writing about, or are they just some unknown person giving an uneducated opinion. It is an important skill to learn.

The same approach works for our questions of faith, and this is the one thing that sets Paul apart from the other faith vendors we face each and every day. Paul is not asking us to follow some God that existed in Babylon, and is written up in the old stories. He is not asking us to follow some God that the Greeks admire, or a God who once did some amazing things for a bunch of people who sacrifice the right stuff. Paul simply stopped by the house, and wrote to us in some letters, to tell us what God had done in his life. It's that original source thing. Others can speak from tradition and stories and hopes, while Paul speaks to us from his own personal experience. And there were enough folks around who knew Paul back when he was Saul, to know that the change that had taken place was indeed real. It was the truth.

This is important for us to know as we choose which path we are going to follow as we go through each day. It is even more important as we think about how we will share what we believe with others. We can work to memorize stories and scriptures. We can study theology to be prepared to hold our own in any argument. Or, we can figure out how to simply tell what we have experienced. I have my own hunch which is more valuable. If I were in trouble, and you came to me to help me through, I'll tell you what I would prefer. Rather than hear you say to me, "Here is what I've been told God will do," or "Remember that passage that says ..." I think I would be much more interested in hearing you say, "Let me tell you what God did for me...."

One sounds more like an opinion. The other sounds like the truth. One sounds more like a painting. The other sounds really real.

Real is better.

Sermons On The Second Readings

For Sundays
After Pentecost
(Middle Third)

God Is Rock Solid

Clayton A. Lord, Jr.

Proper 12
Pentecost 10
Ordinary Time 17
Colossians 2:6-15 (16-19)

Claiming Our New Life In Christ

I heard a story about a man who decided that he wanted to live a good life. He set his mind to developing healthy habits. He read every book he could find that laid out the path to a long and productive life. He never smoked, drank, or overindulged at the table. He ate fresh fruit and vegetables and stayed away from anything with preservatives in it. He exercised every day and got his eight hours of sleep each night. He lived in the country and avoided going into the city with its smog and high incidence of crime and disease. He visited his doctor regularly and he was set to live to be 100 years old.

I am told his funeral was last Wednesday. He was only 53. He is survived by eighteen specialists, four health institutions, six gymnasiums, and numerous manufacturers of health foods and drugs.

If only the secret to a long and happy life was that easy. We can follow all the rules and still come up short. No one has all the answers. Yet we keep looking for them. Just check out the shelves of the local bookstore and you will find best-selling books by modern day gurus telling us how to please God, live long, and prosper. We may think it is a modern phenomenon but things haven't changed over the centuries.

Even in Paul's day there were people who made their mark in the community by selling people on the idea that if you did certain things you could earn God's favor and live prosperous lives. In our text today, Paul addresses this situation head on. He calls these spiritual profiteers false teachers and tells the Colossians that what they are hearing from them is hollow and deceptive philosophy, which is based upon human tradition and follows the principles of this world. He goes on to encourage them to compare what they are hearing to the truth that they received when they became one in Christ.

You see, the Colossians were being told that if they followed a strict set of rules and regulations they could be assured of being accepted by God as pure and holy. The Colossians were being told that their future salvation depended on what they did and how they lived their lives. These teachers went so far as to say that the only way one could be saved was by a strict adherence to the law.

It is easy to look at the situation from our vantage point today and wonder how the Colossians could forget the fact that in Christ their sins had been forgiven and that they were a new creation. But think about it for a minute.

There have always been rules set down to serve as boundaries for all of our human interaction. Rules govern how we behave at work, at school, in our homes, and even at church. The rules allow us to live together in an orderly society. If you want to take it a step farther, just look at the Old Testament and you will see a myriad of laws (rules) that regulated every aspect of life for the Israelites. The laws regulated relationships between husbands and wives, merchants and consumers, masters and slaves, and everything else.

Almost from the beginning of their walk with God, the Israelites had asked for a list of rules so that they might know how to find favor with God. That's where the Ten Commandments have their roots. The people wanted to know exactly what God expected of them and how far they could go and still remain in his favor.

I heard a cute story about one pastor who told his congregation that there were 700 different sins listed in the Bible. That afternoon he received three dozen requests for the list. Everybody wanted to know what they were missing out on!

Paul tries to turn this whole thing around and calls the people to forget the notion of rules and to simply begin living in relationship to Christ. Paul tells them that rules have no ability to change the heart, but a life that looks to Christ will soon turn around and reflect his glory.

Paul uses several images to make his point. He begins with the image of being "rooted in Christ." In other words, we are to be like a tree that puts down deep roots in order to find nutrition and find stability. Jeremiah 17:7-8 comes to mind where the prophet says, "Blessed are those who trust in the Lord, whose trust is the Lord. They shall be like a tree planted by water, sending out its roots by the stream. It shall not fear when heat comes, and its leaves shall stay green; in the year of drought it is not anxious, and it does not cease to bear fruit." When we go deep in Christ, we will find all the resources we need to find joy in life and remain confident even when trials and seasons of difficulty come our way.

Paul continues with the image of building on the foundation we have received in Christ. With this construction image, Paul lifts up the idea that with Christ as the cornerstone, the life we are building rests on the most solid foundation. Jesus holds everything together in a way that nothing else can. Today, a lot of people throw around the saying "What would Jesus do?" You may think it is trite but when we begin to look to Jesus and build our lives on his words and actions, we begin to find joy in everything we do.

Paul continues by saying we must be students of the scriptures. I think the reason that so many people in Paul's day, and in our own, get confused about the Christian life is that they have stopped studying God's Word. If you do not know what the Bible says about God then you can be easily misled. We need to be in worship and Bible study, discussing and praying over the scriptures. We need to be talking about our experiences in Christ so that we can learn all that he has to teach us. If we are rooted in Christ, then study will be second nature.

Think about a person in your life that you care deeply about. Haven't you made it a point to learn all about them? Don't you want to spend time with them, listening to what they have to say? It is natural to want to be with the one you love and know all about them. So it is with Christ. When you stop wanting to know all there is to know, you better watch out. It is a sign that the embers of love are beginning to burn out. Paul reminds us that if we want to find out what pleases God, then we need to be sitting at his feet.

271

Paul has often been accused of being blunt when he addresses his audience. He makes statements that seem a bit presumptuous. But you see, Paul believes that when you invite Christ into your life you will change. He says in 2 Corinthians 5:17 that, "if anyone is in Christ, there is new creation...." He firmly believes that a transformation is in process and that if we go along with it then we no longer need to look to the old ways to know what we are called to do. It will become second nature.

We know that Paul is right, don't we? Something has changed inside of us. We don't need the old laws to tell us how to please God. Our sins have been forgiven. Our hearts have been filled with Christ. We have been given a new life and the promise of a home in eternity. So now we can begin to live a life that pleases God simply out of our gratitude and desire to please him. We can live a good life simply because we want to.

A friend of mine sent me a story that Bill Bright, founder of Campus Crusade for Christ, used to tell about the transforming power of love.

It seems that there was this woman who was married to a tyrant of a husband. She could never please him no matter how hard she tried. He didn't like the way she kept house. He didn't like the way she did laundry. He didn't like the way she ironed his clothes. He didn't like the way she dressed. He didn't like the way she conducted herself in public. He constantly criticized her for everything.

Early in their marriage, he handed her a list of 25 rules for her to follow. She hated it and she hated him. You can imagine how frustrating it was to her to have to constantly check her list to see if she was pleasing him — and to stay out of trouble. But, she usually failed miserably — and each time, she got a tongue lashing from him — he made her feel miserable and small.

Then one day, much to her great joy, the abusive husband died. Soon, she fell in love with and married a wonderful, loving man. They loved each other very deeply. She practically broke her neck to please him. She wanted to do everything for him. She even brought him breakfast in bed.

One day as she was busy cleaning up, she ran across that old list and the feelings of anger and inferiority returned. As she looked at the list, something happened within her and she began to laugh! She realized that she was now doing all of these for her new husband and many more. And she did these tasks now with great joy because she loved this man.

Love makes all the difference in the way we live and serve. This is what Paul is trying to tell the Colossians. They are free from the law now. They are free to live and love Christ with all their hearts. They have been released from their sins and can now start life over. Now they are truly alive and able to live to the glory of God.

I want to close with a story I heard about a man named Jeff. He was an Atlantic fisherman living on the coast of Rhode Island. He was a tough guy. He had to be to in order to survive the severe weather and the cruelty of the sea. The job demanded long hours and cramped quarters. He often would be away from home for weeks at a time. He never married and wasn't much for relationships. One Sunday though, something prompted him to attend the local church.

All heads turned when he walked in the door. He was quite a sight with his rugged skin and long hair. He had on a plaid shirt, a pair of jeans, and workman's boots. He looked totally out of his element.

As the service began, he fumbled with the hymn book and tried to read along with the scripture. When the preacher began to speak, he appeared to be distracted and did not look at him once. If you looked at the fisherman you might have thought he wasn't paying attention. No one would have guessed that when the invitation was given, that this big man would come forward with tears in his eyes and give his life to Christ.

The next week the fisherman was back again. This time he was clean shaven and dressed in his Sunday best. When the preacher commented about his appearance the man simply said, "Jesus changed me on the inside and I want people to know it. So I changed the outside."

Has Christ changed you on the inside? Then claim that new life today. Forget about trying to follow rules and regulations. Simply let his love flow through you so that the world can see it and live to the glory of God. Amen.

Wearing The King's Clothes

There is nothing like putting on a new shirt and pair of pants. Just ask any of the children who are getting ready to go back to school. The best part of that first-day experience is showing up in a new set of clothes. Admit it. We all feel better about ourselves when we put on something new. We have more confidence. We have more energy to tackle and complete our assignments. We feel more comfortable and better received among our peers. The saying, "Clothes make the man (woman)" is true.

In our text today, Paul encourages the Colossians to change their wardrobe, if you will. In effect, he tells them that since they now belong to Christ, that they ought to look the part.

Paul is not literally telling them to go out and buy a new wardrobe. What he suggests is that the Colossians begin living lives that reflect the glory of God. He calls on them to take advantage of their new estate and make the changes in their lives that will allow them to fully reflect the love of God that they experienced in Jesus.

This was a radical concept for the people back then. In the *Bible Exposition Commentary*, Warren Wiersbe reminds us that the pagan religions of Paul's day taught little or nothing about personal morality: A worshiper could bow before an idol, put his offering on the altar, and go back to the same old life of sin. What a person believed had no direct relationship with how he behaved.

No doubt there were many who heard the gospel and felt good about it. That is where it ended, though. Luke tells of an occasion where several people came to Jesus and declared that they would follow him, only to make one excuse after another. One man says

"I will follow you wherever you go." He is easily put off when Jesus says that he will have no place to lay his head. A second man says he will follow "right after I bury my father," and Jesus sees right through him. A third man says, "Let me first say farewell to those at my home," and Jesus sends him away. That still happens today. We have people sitting in our pews who love Jesus on Sunday but go right back out and do whatever they please on Monday.

Paul says to love Christ is to be a new creation and to be crucified and resurrected with him. Therefore, we need a set of clothes, a new look, a new appearance when we begin walking with him. There should be a difference between us, as Christians, and the rest of the people in the culture in which we live.

Ask your kids who their heroes are and you will get some surprising answers. They may point to the president or some sports superstar. They may point to a popular singer or movie star. Look at their wardrobe and you will see who influences them the most. Look at the way they wear their hair and you will see who they want to be like. We become that which we worship. Paul encourages us to "set your hearts on things above." He wants us to keep our eyes on Jesus so that we can emulate him in our lives.

The first step in doing this is to get rid of our old ways. Someone said there is nothing as comfortable as an old shoe. There is some truth in that. Many of us enjoy wearing an old pair of jeans or our favorite T-shirt. As a matter of fact, I know some kids who go so far as to buy some jeans with holes already in them. I'm told it is the style.

As much as we like to put on new clothes, some of us have a hard time getting rid of the old ones. Paul addresses that in the next part of the text. He lists out several habits that we should abandon. As we look at the list, it becomes obvious that it is easier said than done. Some of these sins have established strongholds in our lives. We may have even justified some of them and found ways to make them look acceptable, but Paul reminds us that they are to be dealt with by the wrath of God.

You see, we can make all kinds of excuses for what we do. We lie to each other and pretend that God doesn't care. Paul tells us otherwise. God cares. I heard a story about a man who went with some friends to an amusement park on a hot summer day. They decided to go on a white water rafting ride so they could cool off. Lo and behold, they got soaked. As they got off the ride, they looked at each other and began debating whether or not to go back to the car to get a change of clothes. No one wanted to admit just how uncomfortable they were, so they decided they would continue on. They spent the next two hours feeling gross and washed out. Whenever one of them would ask another if they wanted to go back to the car, the reply was always the same. "I'm okay. Did you want to go back to the car?" "No. I'm okay." Back and forth it went.

That night as they were driving home, the man said to his friends, "I can't wait to get home and get changed. I have been miserable all day." One by one, they all confessed the same thing. What we are wearing can make us miserable. So it is with sin.

Annie Dillard, in her book *Pilgrim at Tinker Creek*, writes:

At the end of the island I noticed a small green frog. He was exactly half in and half out of the water. He was a very small frog with wide, dull eyes. And just as I looked at him, he slowly crumpled and began to sag. The spirit vanished from his eyes as if snuffed. His skin emptied and drooped; his very skull seemed to collapse and settle like a kicked tent.

An oval shadow hung in the water behind the drained frog: then the shadow glided away. The frog skin bag started to sink.

I had read about the water bug, but never seen one. "Giant water bug" is really the name of the creature, which is an enormous, heavy-bodied, brown beetle. It eats insects, tadpoles, fish, and frogs. Its grasping forelegs are mighty and hooked inward. It seizes a victim with these legs, hugs it tight, and paralyzes it with enzymes injected during a vicious bite. Through the puncture holes shoots the poison that dissolves the victim's muscles, bones, and organs — all but the skin — and through it the giant water bug sucks out all the victim's body, reducing it to liquid.

Sin can suck the life out of you. You cannot walk with Christ and at the same time do things you know are contrary to what the Bible teaches. Your spiritual life will be sucked out of you. Your walk will be filled with disappointment, guilt, and discouragement. That is why you must confront it. One of the basic principles in a tewelve-step program is admitting that you have a problem. Recovery cannot take place until you are honest with yourself and confront your failings. Once you do, then you can begin dealing with it and reclaim your life. At that point, you can put on the new wardrobe that God provides through his Son, Jesus Christ.

Jesus shows us the way to live a life that is both meaningful and joyful, as well as, pleasing to God. When Paul says, "Put on Christ," he is saying that we should live life as though Christ were living through us.

Again, it all goes back to asking the question, "What would Jesus do?" It is not only a moral imperative, it is also a way to find joy and happiness in life. Jesus shows us the way to live a completely satisfying life. He offers us everything we need to find our fulfillment without having to revert back to our old lifestyles. Your life will never be the same when you accept Christ and decide to walk with him.

I came across a story on the internet about a man named Don Calhoun. Have you ever heard of him? He worked for five dollars an hour at an office supply store in Bloomington, Illinois. Tickets to a professional basketball game were so expensive that although he lived close enough to the arena, he had only attended two Chicago Bulls' basketball games in his life. It was a pretty special moment when he arrived for his third game ever. A woman who worked for the Bulls' organization walked up to him and told him they were selecting him to take part in a promotional event during the game called the "Million-Dollar Shot."

The shot came after a time-out in the third quarter. If Calhoun could shoot a basket standing 79 feet away — meaning he had to stand behind the free-throw line on the opposite end of the court and throw the ball three-quarters of the length of the court — he would win a million dollars.

Calhoun played basketball at the Bloomington YMCA, but he had never tried a shot like this before. He took the basketball in his hands and looked over at Michael Jordan and the rest of the Bulls. He could see they were pulling for him.

Calhoun stepped to the line and let it fly. As soon as the basketball left his hand, coach Phil Jackson said, "It's good." Indeed, the ball went through the basket with a swish. The stadium crowd went wild. Calhoun rushed into the arms of Michael Jordan and the rest of the Bulls' players crowded around slapping him on the back.

When Don Calhoun went home that night, he had only two dollars in his wallet, but he would receive $50,000 a year for the next twenty years of his life. His life had been changed in an instant. Can you imagine having that kind of life-changing experience?

That is exactly what will happen to us when we accept Christ into our hearts. We may look the same, but we are a new creation. We are living with a promise. We are joint heirs with Christ and therefore we can proudly begin to live the life and take on a wardrobe that befits a king. Amen.

279

Where Have All The Heroes Gone?

I want to talk about heroes today. We all have them. Our heroes are men and women that we look up to. Our heroes are those individuals that inspire us and help us to strive to be our very best.

There is a cute story about a Texan who was trying to impress on a Bostonian, the valor of the heroes of the Alamo. After finishing his story about Sam Houston, Davy Crockett, and countless others, he says "I'll bet you never had anyone so brave around Boston."

"Did you ever hear of Paul Revere?" asked the Bostonian.

"Paul Revere?" said the Texan. "Isn't he the guy who ran away looking for help?"

Heroes are important even if we disagree on the interpretation of what makes them heroes. Fred Smith in his book, *You and Your Network*, says:

> *We cannot live fully without heroes, for they are the stars to guide us upward. They are the peaks on our human mountains. Not only do they personify what we can be, but they also urge us to be. Heroes are who we can become if we diligently pursue our ideas in the furnace of our opportunities. Heroes are those who have changed history for the better. They are not always the men and women of highest potential, but those who have exploited their potential in society's behalf. Their deeds are done not for the honor but for the duty. Through our study of heroes we enter the realities of greatness.*

Heroes are the personification of our ideals; the embodiment of our highest values. A society writes its diary by naming its heroes. We, as individuals, do the same.

Dr. J. C. Cain of the Mayo Clinic had difficulty selecting the young medical men to be trained at the clinic because of the exceptionally high caliber of all the applicants. All had excellent grades, fine discipline, high motivation, and good work habits. In searching for some question that would differentiate between them, he chose to ask this question: "Young man, tell me of your heroes." Dr. Cain found this was the best clue to their value structure.

Our heroes tell us much about our values. Those who have no heroes probably have not yet identified their highest ideals. Heroes not only inspire us, they also prove the greatness of which the human spirit is capable.

Who is your hero? Think about it.

While you do, I want to tell you that researchers for the *World Almanac and Book of Facts* asked 2,000 American eighth-grade students to name prominent people they admired and wanted to be like. Those most frequently mentioned by the teens as their heroes were sports celebrities and movie stars.

Columnist Sidney J. Harris lamented the fact that every one of the thirty prominent personalities who were named was either an entertainer or an athlete. He noted that statesmen, authors, painters, musicians, architects, doctors, and astronauts failed to capture the imagination of those students. He further suggested that the heroes and heroines created by our society are people who have made it big, but not necessarily people who have done big things.

It's strange, but the world has really changed. The heroes of an earlier day were people of substance. The heroes were people who gave of themselves so others could live and enjoy life. Today all our heroes are celebrities. They rise on a wave of applause and break on the rocks of inattention. They are fantasy waiting to be exposed.

Who did you name as your hero? Was it Dave Dravecky? He pitched in World Series games and several All-Star games. Then, one day, his world was ripped apart when he was diagnosed with cancer. He fought a great fight but in the end he lost his arm, his pitching arm, to cancer. In his book, *Comeback*, Dravecky talks about the faith in Christ that helped him overcome it and to find new meaning in life. He said that baseball was important to him. It was part of who he was. Christ, on the other hand, was his life and when it was all said and done, he still had his life. Now that's a hero!

We need more spiritual heroes. When we open the book of Hebrews we see one man that stands out front and center. In chapter 11 we are introduced to Abraham. His story, beginning in Genesis chapter 12, shows us what it means to follow God faithfully. Abraham's story is one of a man who finds meaning and purpose in his life. The author of the book of Hebrews lifts Abraham up as a man who knew God. He is one of the prominent names in the faith hall of fame.

Abraham had a good life. He had a family and a place to call his own. One day he came face-to-face with God. His life would never be the same. God called him and offered him the one thing he did not have, a son. He listened to God's promises and without hesitation said, "I will be your man." Abraham didn't have it easy. He faced an uncertain future in an unknown land. He faced enemies who were ruthless and often jealous. He grew older and yet he never questioned God's promise that he would be the father of a great nation. And when he finally received the joy of bearing a son, Isaac, God asked him to trust him and give up his son. Abraham never wavered in his faith. That's why the writer of Hebrews says look to Abraham and see a hero.

True heroes are people who we can look up to and try to emulate. They are people who passionately believe in something and are even willing to die for it. Wycliffe, a very successful translating agency throughout the world, did an advertisement several years ago. It depicted a strong, athletic-looking man wading through a jungle river with a canteen on his side. The advertisement said: "Jim was voted the most likely to succeed. It's too bad Jim had it made. Personality, initiative, a college degree with honors, everything was his for the asking. Now look at him, backpacking across a jungle river, giving his life to a preliterate people barely out of the stone age, painstakingly creating a written alphabet from a previously unrecorded babble of sound. Working night and day translating the pages of the New Testament, exposing the senselessness of superstition and ignorance, relieving the pain and introducing the possibility of health, building a bridge of understanding to a neglected people. And to think, Jim could have been a success."

When they ran that ad, they had more young people sign up than at any other time. They gave kids something to live for. They gave them a bigger-than-life hero. That was Abraham. He was a man who lived out his faith and followed it all the way into the promised land. Heroes are real people. I think that is the problem with society today. Most of the people we lift up as heroes are fictional people that movie actors play. Arnold Schwarzenegger played just such a role in a movie called *The Last Action Hero*. In the movie he plays an actor who plays Jack Slater, a real action hero. In a twisted plot, a young boy gets to meet his hero and he finds that Schwarzenegger is not what he appears to be on the screen. It's a fun play on this theme of larger-than-life heroes. Although the movie does have that storybook ending, in real life they come off as mere mortals when we get up close and personal.

Contrast this with what we know about Jesus. Look closely at the picture that is painted of him in scripture. He was tested and he was tortured. He got hungry and he got tired. He sweated in the heat and cried in distress. He was real. He had a mission and didn't let anything get in his way. He loved us so much that he gave his life for us. That's what I call a hero.

The truth is that everyone has heroes — people they want to be like — but heroes are not just famous people who achieve outstanding things. They are individuals who live life with a deep and abiding faith that allows them to do great things.

Abraham's faith allowed him to follow God through the good and the bad. The only thing that separates him from us is the level of faith he demonstrated. He was an ordinary man who, through faith, became the father of the faithful. That is why the writer of Hebrews lifts him up. He is an example of what each of us can be as we live out our lives. We can be heroes to those who follow behind us.

A friend told me about John Brooks, a small church pastor he knew. He was a man acquainted with disappointments in his life. He struggled to make it through school. He faced financial hardship. His wife was stricken with an incurable disease. Yet John Brooks accepted a call into ministry because he believed God had work for him to do. He left his native Australia and traveled to America. He accepted a call to a small congregation in New England. He served that congregation faithfully. You would never know the troubles he had entertained in his young life if you saw him. He was a successful pastor, well respected by his congregation, his peers, and the community. He was a hero to the young people in his church. He told each one that God had something important for them to do and he helped them believe in themselves. They became preachers, pharmacists, teachers, moms, and dads. Every one of them also became active in their respective churches over the years as choir members, organists, Sunday school teachers, lay leaders, and board members. He became a great man, not because of anything extraordinary he had done, but because he walked with Christ and faithfully followed him — like Abraham — like you and me.

So to be a hero, you don't have to attract a lot of attention and have your name in the newspapers. You do not have to have a lot of money. You don't have to be a person in authority or wield a lot of power. You only have to live by faith and let it show.

Another Abraham, Abraham Lincoln, entered the Ford Theatre the night he was killed. The box he sat in was in the back and hard to get to. He entered it quietly and without fanfare. But someone saw him come, and one lone person stood up and began to applaud. Before long, the whole theater was standing and he received a twenty-minute standing ovation.

That was only five days after the war ended. For years, he had been the target of criticism. Yet he stayed the course and fought for what he believed was right. He lived by faith in those years and his faith was rewarded that night. Five days after the war ended he received his due and then it was done. A shot rang out and his life was snuffed out.

Abraham Lincoln was named for a hero of the faith. He lived up to his name. You and I are called Christians. We take our name from the Lord. I pray you and I may live up to our name as we seek to live a life of faithfulness. Who knows? Someone may just call us their hero someday. Amen.

Unlocking The Power Of God

What can faith do? It can part a raging sea and allow a nation to walk through. What can faith do? It can knock down the walls of a fortified city so that God can prove a point. What can faith do? It can single out a woman who follows God's lead and protect her from certain death. Today many people are into "reality" television shows where individuals are put to extreme tests. We watch them because we like to see others battle against great odds and come out victorious. When an underdog comes out on top, we garner a sense of hope that we, too, can defy the odds and win out in the challenges that come our way. The more improbable the success, the more excited we become as we watch someone triumph over all the odds.

The author of the book of Hebrews understands human nature. That is why he goes to such extremes to point out how many have succeeded and done amazing things when they relied on their faith in God. In the eleventh chapter of Hebrews beginning with verse 29, we read of the victories of the people of faith. The first few show the overwhelming power of God to do the impossible. Then the list continues with men and women who managed to carry on despite great trials and tribulations. His point is simply this: Nothing is impossible when you have faith.

Do you remember how this chapter begins? There is a definition of faith. "Faith is the assurance of things hoped for and the convictions of things not seen." In other words, faith is believing in something even if you cannot see it.

A man named Marvin Pipken believed that you really could frost a light bulb with some kind of solution that would reduce the glare. Everyone else laughed at the idea. For years it was the running gag pulled on new engineers who joined General Electric. When Marvin came along, they all stopped laughing because he believed he could do it. As a result, he managed to create a process to use an etching acid on the inside of the glass and today we are indebted to him.

You see, faith is a powerful thing in its own right. When faith is connected to the plans of God it is unstoppable. That is what the author of Hebrews is trying to tell us.

You may be sitting here today thinking that these verses do not apply to you. You may be thinking that the things we read in the Bible are more of a historical record than a statement of things we can expect today. Then look again.

There are a couple of things we need to take note of right off the bat. Each of the miracles described here leave no doubt as to who was responsible. We read about the parting of the Red Sea in Exodus 14. The people were caught in the middle. The Red Sea was on one side and a charging Egyptian army on the other. There was nowhere to go until Moses calls on God to part the waters. Moses, who is listed as one of the great heroes of faith, shows us why he is on the list. He did as God commands him without hesitation. He lifts his staff in the air and the incredible happens. Immediately, the Red Sea parts and the exodus continues as the great caravan marches through. As Pharaoh's soldiers approach in hot pursuit, we see the waters roll back and crush them underneath. The enemies are vanquished. The scriptures say, "Thus the Lord saved Israel that day from the Egyptians ... So the people feared the Lord and believed in the Lord and in his servant Moses" (Exodus 14:30-31). What made this possible? It took the faith of one man for a miracle to happen.

What about the story of Jericho? The great walled city was an impregnable fortress. It stood in the way of God's plan to hand over the promised land to his people. We read in Joshua 6 that God commands the people to march around the city seven times and to have the priests blow their horns. On the seventh day, God tells the people to shout. When they do, the walls immediately fall down and the city is taken. What made it possible? Joshua never hesitated to follow God's lead. He simply believed and did what he was told. Today he is lifted up as an example of faith.

The scriptures are filled with stories that point to the role of faith in turning impossible situations around. A boy named David stood up to a giant with only a slingshot and a few small stones. He did what the army was afraid to do. He came away victorious. A prophet named Elijah risked embarrassment and certain death. He stood up to fifty false prophets and challenged them. He came away justified. A man named Daniel would not deny his God and he faced being torn apart by lions. He entered the lion's den and escaped without a scratch.

No one would choose these trials, but each time the person put their faith in God, they came out reflecting the almighty power of God and his faithfulness to those who trust him.

Wonderful things happen when we have faith and pray, trusting God to answer. There is a story about a U.S. Marine that was separated from his unit on a Pacific island during World War II. The fighting had been intense, and in the smoke and the crossfire, he had lost touch with his comrades. Alone in the jungle, he could hear enemy soldiers coming in his direction. Scrambling for cover, he found his way up a high ridge to several small caves in the rock. Quickly, he crawled inside one of the caves. Although safe for the moment, he realized that once the enemy soldiers looking for him swept up the ridge, they would quickly search all the caves and he would be killed.

As he waited, he prayed, "Lord, if it be your will, please protect me. Whatever your will though, I love you and trust you. Amen." After praying, he lay quietly listening to the enemy begin to draw close. He thought, "Well, I guess the Lord isn't going to help me out of this one." Then he saw a spider begin to build a web over the front of his cave.

As he watched, listening to the enemy searching for him all the while, the spider layered strand after strand of web across the opening of the cave. "Hah," he thought, "What I need is a brick wall and what the Lord has sent me is a spider web. God does have a sense of humor."

As the enemy drew closer, he watched from the darkness of his hideout and could see them searching one cave after another. As they came to his, he got ready to make his last stand. To his amazement, however, after glancing in the direction of his cave, they moved on. Suddenly, he realized that with the spider web over the entrance, his cave looked as if no one had entered for quite a while. "Lord, forgive me," prayed the young man. "I had forgotten that, in you, a spider's web is stronger than a brick wall."

Time after time, we have been in similar situations and God has acted to protect, shield, and strengthen us. You do not go very far in life without facing some type of trouble. We need to remember that God can work miracles. He's the one who delivered manna from heaven to a hungry people. He's the one who helped Gideon and 300 men overcome an army of Midianites. He was the one who stilled the storm and calmed the sea as the disciples looked on.

The author of Hebrews reminds those who will listen that faith is the key to unlocking the power of God. In the closing verses of our scripture reading, he points to the great cloud of witnesses who can testify to what God has done in their lives. He then encourages us to boldly move forward in faith and confidence.

What is holding you back today? Is job uncertainty paralyzing you and robbing you from making plans for the future? Are you being tempted to do something you know is wrong and finding justification in the fact that you feel trapped in your marriage or your relationship to certain friends? Are financial pressures forcing you to sacrifice your principles and pushing you to entertain unethical practices? Then you need to turn to God and have faith that he can help you overcome these circumstances. Our text tells us that God can do anything. We are reminded in Romans 8:28 "... that all things work together for good for those who love God, who are called according to his purpose." Call on him and wait to see what he will do.

Our greatest joy is knowing that God believes in us. Before we rush out to do whatever we think has to be done right now, we need to pause and pray and be still before God, for he is able to work in the most difficult, the most impossible, circumstances of your life and bring about a miracle. Have faith in God and you will unlock his power in your life. Amen.

God Is Rock Solid

The phone rang in the pastor's office. On the other end of the line, a still, small voice was asking for help. The unidentified woman didn't say much. She simply said that her world had been turned upside down and she didn't know where else to turn. Many of us can identify with that woman. We have lived it at times. One day your husband comes home and announces he wants a divorce. You get a phone call that your son has been in a car accident. Your daughter tells you she is moving in with her boyfriend and not planning on getting married any time soon. Your boss comes into your office and tells you that your position has been eliminated due to cost constraints.

Someone once said the only constant in this life is change. Change often comes in, sweeps us away, and knocks the breath out of us. So it is only natural that we look for something that we can cling to, something that we can stand on as we face the future. The writer of the book of Hebrews addresses this in our passage this morning.

He acknowledges that we live in an unstable world and even echoes Peter's words in 2 Peter 3:10 that reminds us, "But the day of the Lord will come like a thief, and then the heavens will pass away with a loud noise, and the elements will be dissolved with fire, and the earth and everything that is done on it will be disclosed." When you witness a series of natural disasters like we have over the last few years and have come face-to-face with the devastation of terrorist acts, you might lose all hope for any stability in the future. At that moment, our writer here says, "At that time his voice shook the earth; but now he has promised, 'Yet once more I will shake not only the earth but also the heaven.' The phrase 'Yet once more' indicates the removal of what is shaken — that is, created things — so that what cannot be shaken may remain" (Hebrews 12:26-27).

In other words, after everything has been shaken up and turned upside down, we will see the things that we can cling to, the things which are rock solid and cannot be moved. Every once in a while, we catch a glimpse of them when we are suffering through some difficulty. The author of Hebrews points them out to us in this passage so we will know they are there even before the first storm clouds gather overhead.

This morning I want to talk about four of these rocks that cannot be shaken. The first is the throne of God. No matter what happens on the earth, no matter what happens in our lives, there is one thing that is secure. God's place of authority will never crumble and fall. We read in Psalm 45:6: "Your throne, O God, endures for ever and ever ..." and in Lamentations 5:19: "But you, O Lord, reign for ever; your throne endures to all generations."

When the Bible talks about God's throne, it is talking about something much bigger than a piece of furniture. It refers to God's kingship and rule on the earth. It speaks of God and his place as the supreme sovereign over creation. In essence, the writer of Hebrews is saying, "No matter what happens in your life, you can rest assured that God will not be overturned. He will remain strong and in control."

The nature of politics is that leaders change. In our country, it takes place in an orderly fashion. I always marveled that every time a new administration comes into the White House, a lot of people are out on the street looking for a job. The new leader brings in his own people. If you were on the inside before, you would now be on the outside looking in. It reminds me of the line in Exodus 1:8 where the author says, "Now a new king arose over Egypt, who did not know Joseph." Everything changed. Before long, Joseph's descendants were turned from friends to slaves.

In other countries today, change often takes place swiftly and unexpectedly. You can wake up to a new regime overnight. All the

294

laws change and you are never sure where you stand. That is how it was in biblical times. The Israelites were constantly being overrun by one nation after another. They never knew who would rise to power and sweep through the land. For centuries, they lived under the rule of foreign leaders. Even in Jesus' day, the Roman Empire put puppet kings in place to serve them.

So the idea of a stable kingdom was very appealing. No matter what era you live in, God represents permanence. In Hebrews 1:10-12 we read, "And, 'In the beginning, Lord, you founded the earth, and the heavens are the work of your hands; they will perish, but you remain; they will all wear out like clothing; like a cloak you will roll them up, and like clothing they will be changed. But you are the same, and your years will never end.' " It was unlike anything they had ever known and it is often lost on us.

Nonetheless, it is important to us because God is still the source of our hope and our grace. As long as God is in control we know that we have an advocate in high places. We have someone who cares for us and will seek out our best interests. We can cling to the throne of God and find a precious hiding place when our world is falling apart.

When Augustus Toplady penned the words of the famous hymn, "Rock of Ages," he was caught up in a sudden storm. As the wind and rain came at him, he found refuge in the cleft of a large rock. He immediately thought of God and the way he protects us in the savage storms of life. God is our rock and our refuge and he will not be shaken. He will always be there to hold onto.

If God is a sure foundation, then his word will also be unshakable. In Mark 13:31 hear Jesus say, "Heaven and earth will pass away, but my words will not pass away." Peter echoes this in his epistle when he tells us that, "the word of the Lord endures forever" (1 Peter 1:25).

The Bible is living and powerful and eternal. We can read it to find strength and courage in any circumstance in any generation. It declares the truth and gives us a peek into God's plans for all creation. It reminds us of God's call to righteousness and points us to the path that will lead us to him. The writer of Hebrews reminds his audience that it was on the mountain of God that the first words were given.

When we want to know what God expects of us, we can open the scriptures. They do not change. Our understanding may grow, but the truth remains.

When we look for God, there is no better place to find him than in his word. When we turn on the television or open up the newspaper, we find a lot of messages couched in politically correct language. No one wants to offend anyone, so we water down our conversations and end up saying little of note. We do not want to turn anyone off so we do not challenge anyone.

God does not hide the truth. He puts it out there for all to see and then lets it work in open hearts and minds. If you want to know what to do to rebuild your world, turn to the Bible. Jesus tells the parable of the wise and foolish builders in Matthew 7:24-27. He suggests that building your life on the Word of God will help you stand tall during life's greatest trials. It will hold fast and cover you when you need it most.

We need to hear the truth when our marriages and families are under attack and falling apart. We need to hear the truth when consumer debt is feeding greed and pushing people into bankruptcy. We need to hear the truth when people are turning to drugs and alcohol to fill an emptiness within them. Whenever a friend of mine starts preaching on these hot topics, he always says, "Don't get mad at me for saying these things. It's all right here in the book!" The Bible is God's little instruction book on life and it is there to guide us into a deeper relationship with him. Thank God it is a rock that doesn't change.

The church is a third "rock" to which we can cling. In Matthew 16:18 we read "... I will build my church, and the gates of Hades will not prevail against it." In recent years the church has been rocked by scandals. The church has struggled over doctrinal issues. The church has been pushed aside by secular society as being irrelevant and even marginalized. Nonetheless, the church always shows up when there is a need and people are lost and suffering.

I remember reading stories that made me sick during the aftermath of Hurricane Katrina in September 2005. People were displaced and literally left without anything: no home, no job, no food. Then one night there was a story on television that mentioned over 10,000 meals had been prepared and served at one of the shelters. The churches had gotten together and made it happen. Many of the volunteers themselves had suffered from the effects of the storm, but they answered the call to reach out and help their neighbors. These people responded to the call of God and became the church triumphant.

The truth is that ministries may come and go. Church buildings will be raised up and torn down again. Pastors and deacons will serve and then move on to new callings, but the church of Jesus Christ will always be there when needed to praise, glorify, and worship God. To the author of Hebrews, the church was not a place. The mountain of God was where the people came to worship. In verse 18 he says, "You have not come to something that can be touched, a blazing fire ..." for God is not in the mountain. God is everywhere. The point being that it was the assembly of the people that made it possible for worship to happen.

That is what Jesus was affirming at Caesarea Philippi when he lifted up Simon Peter's declaration. He was saying that the church will be built on the proclamation of Jesus Christ as Lord. Whenever we gather together, the church cannot be shaken. It is the most powerful force on earth, for it is the body of Christ. It is the hands and feet, ears and eyes, heart and soul, of our Lord. Truly nothing can stop him when he goes to work. The true church, made up of those who have given their lives to Jesus, cannot and will not be turned upside down. It is secure, permanent, and abiding.

That is why the church survived the persecution in Rome, the Protestant Reformation, and the various schisms over the centuries. God continues to bless all the fragments and makes a more bountiful whole. The church is stronger today than ever before and people are still coming to saving faith.

Finally, we have the promise of eternal life. Those who trust in God have a promise of a bright future. 1 John 2:17 says, "... the world and its desire are passing away, but those who do the will of

God live for ever." In John 10:28 Jesus says, "I give them eternal life, and they will never perish. No one will snatch them out of my hand." Paul says in Romans 8:38-39, "For I am convinced that neither death, nor life, nor angels, nor rulers, nor things present, nor things to come, nor powers, nor height, nor depth, nor anything else in all creation, will be able to separate us from the love of God in Christ Jesus our Lord."

As Christians, we have eternal life and we cannot be shaken, for Christ is our strength and he cannot be shaken. He is our life. When all that can be shaken is removed, we will remain, and we shall dwell in our eternal inheritance in that city whose architect and builder is God.

That is good news. It means we will have the ultimate victory over life's greatest enemy. It means no matter what trial or tribulation we face, it will never be able to overcome us. Like Christ, who stared death in the face and came away victorious, we too shall be more than conquerors. And God's promises will not fail. They are rock solid.

I'll never forget watching Mayor Rudolph Giuliani stand tall after the terrorist attack in New York on September 11, 2001. He declared that the city would survive the disaster and would rebuild and come back stronger than ever. He gave credit to the people and their indomitable spirit. He was right. The city has come back.

When I think of the strength of the human spirit then ponder the power of God, I know the future is bright. When we stumble, there is a rock that will not fall. When we are about to fall, God picks us up and the church gives us solid ground, God's Word charts our course, and the promises drive us forward. Thank God for this faith that cannot be shaken. Amen.

The Cost Of A Priceless Gift

Sacrifice is not valued very highly by society. Those who give the most are often frowned upon as though something was wrong with them. Most people can only think about the bottom line and what is in it for them. The cost of any action, or anything for that matter, will depend upon the prize.

With that in mind, I want to talk about our relationship with God and how we can make it better. Sandi Patti sings a song that captures a beautiful vision of God watching over us from our earliest days. The words go like this:

I watch beside your cradle. Your face touched by the moon.
My heart just aches and trembles with my love for you.

This is one of the mental images that I conjure up when I think of God, the loving father, looking down in love, reaching out with hope, encouragement, strength, and salvation.

I can only imagine what the child sees when he or she looks up at the parent. You know we catch a glimpse of it in our own families. Just look at children as they look at their mom or dad or grandparents. Instinctively, children know there is love there. That love is so great that the adults would do anything for the children, even change dirty diapers. As a child looks out of his crib at his sister or brother, he sees a bright smile and knows he is not alone and never will be alone. It is the same way when we catch a glimpse of God. Our hearts are moved to respond to him.

If you believe in God, the loving Father, then you can't help but respond and do something. Offering praise to God is one of the greatest gifts we can give, because it says we believe God is worthy of our love and admiration. God is so good. We are blessed when we praise him even if we are in the midst of difficult times.

I want to take this idea of praise a little further today. I want to tell you that God is truly pleased and glad when we praise him. Hebrews says it clearly in chapter 13, verse 16, "... for such sacrifices [sharing and praise] are pleasing to God." When we put God first, praise him and offer ourselves to him, God overflows with joy. There are dozens of scriptural passages that tell us that praise pleases God. Think about the joy of the prodigal father as he hears his son tell him how much he missed him and how good a father he was.

The thought that our praise pleases God is awesome. It means that we have something to give back to God that will powerfully express our love to him. I'll never forget the first time each of my children said "Dada." To hear a child say your name, even if it is only babble as some wise guy may point out, moves us to excitement. The same is true when we speak God's name, Abba, Father, Lord, and God. God does somersaults in heaven. That is what the scriptures say. It pleases him when we offer a gift of praise. And what greater joy can we have than knowing we have pleased God?

But you know talk is cheap. Praise can be much more than words. Hebrews says it clearly, "Let mutual love continue. Do not neglect to show hospitality to strangers." The author lists several things that reflect a generous way of life. When we think of praising and honoring God, we often think of it in the context of a worship service. In this passage, we are encouraged to think of it in a broader context. Praise arises out of the way we live our lives. If we let our faith lead us to reach out to others in love, then our lives become a gift that praises God. It is witness, consolation, help, and generosity. Words and songs cannot do it alone. They are important, but not sufficient. Praise is works and deeds. Praise without action is easy. Praise with action is wholehearted worship, whole-life stewardship, and whole-gospel discipleship.

With that definition in mind, it becomes clear that sometimes praise may mean we have to make a sacrifice. Again, I have to say that sacrifice is not a popular word in our culture. In baseball there is a play called a sacrifice. The batter bunts and gives up his opportunity to get to first base so that the other runners can move ahead. That is the call of Christ. Giving yourself for the sake of the Lord. Have you ever read the Prayer of Saint Francis of Assisi? It goes like this:

> *Lord, make me an instrument of Thy peace.*
> *Where there is hatred, let us sow love;*
> *Where there is despair, hope;*
> *Where there is sadness, joy;*
> *Where there is darkness, light.*
> *O Divine Master, grant that we may not so much seek*
> *   to be consoled,*
> *as to console;*
> *Not so much to be loved, as to love.*
> *For it is in giving that we receive, it is in pardoning that*
> *   we are pardoned, it is in dying that we are born*
> *   again to eternal life.*

Could Mother Teresa have blessed the world the way she did without sacrifice? She literally gave up everything she had and lived with the poorest of poor. She had no life but their life.

Could Billy Graham have witnessed to the gospel over these many years without sacrifice? I have been reading his autobiography and I am stunned by how much he sacrificed for God. He was always on the road. He was preaching to thousands and bringing them hope and salvation. He offered himself to God and God used him. In order to do so, he had to leave Ruth and the children home most of the time.

Tim Kimmel tells the story of love. In 1921, Lewis Lawes became the warden of Sing Sing Prison. No prison was tougher than Sing Sing during that time. But when Warden Lawes retired some twenty years later, that prison had become a humanitarian institution. Those who studied the system said credit for the change belonged to Lawes. But when he was asked about the transformation, here's what he said: "I owe it all to my wonderful wife, Catherine, who is buried outside the prison walls." She knew how to live a life pleasing to God.

Catherine Lawes was a young woman with three small children when her husband became the warden. Everybody warned her from the beginning that she should never set foot inside the prison walls, but that didn't stop Catherine! When the first prison basketball game was held, she went ... walking into the gym with her three beautiful children, she sat in the stands with the inmates.

Her attitude was: "My husband and I are going to take care of these men and I believe they will take care of me! I don't have to worry."

She insisted on getting acquainted with them and their records. She discovered one convicted murderer was blind, so she paid him a visit. Holding his hand in hers she said, "Do you read Braille?" "What's Braille?" he asked. Then she taught him how to read. Years later, he would weep in love for her. Later, Catherine found a deaf-mute in prison. She went to school to learn how to use sign language. Many said that Catherine Lawes was the body of Jesus that came alive again in Sing Sing from 1921-1937.

Then she was killed in a car accident. The next morning, Lewis Lawes didn't come to work, so the acting warden took his place. It seemed almost instantly that the prison knew something was wrong. The following day, her body was resting in a casket in her home, three-quarters of a mile from the prison. As the acting warden took his early morning walk, he was shocked to see a large crowd of the toughest, meanest-looking criminals gathered like a herd of animals at the main gate. He came closer and noted tears of grief and sadness. He knew how much they loved Catherine. He turned and faced the men, "All right men, you can go. Just be sure and check in tonight." Then he opened the gate and a parade of criminals walked, without a guard, three-quarters of a mile to stand in line and pay their final respects to Catherine Lawes. And every one of them checked back in that night. Every one.

When you live a life of praise before God, it doesn't seem like a sacrifice — it seems like a blessing. Ask Billy or Mother Teresa or Catherine Lawes, and they will tell you it wasn't a sacrifice at all. In fact, they were blessed by their choice. Think about your own relationship with your children or grandchildren. You make sacrifices for them, and you do it out of love. It is as though you were offering your life to God.

Have you thought about this as a way to worship and praise God? It is a special way to make an offering to him. The words, "Let us offer," in scripture are giving-talk. The words, "fruit of lips," recall the Old Testament teaching of firstfruits. "Sacrifice" and "sharing with others" also clearly refer to giving. This praise passage about offerings in Hebrews 13 connects the importance of spiritual giving and tangible praise. Praise and offering come together as gifts we give to God.

Firstfruits describe giving God the very best of our time, talent, energy, thoughts, witness, and money. Today, we have an opportunity to make a statement and to praise God by offering him our very best, the firstfruits of our labor. There is a cost involved but before you begin questioning that, I ask you, "What is the cost of the priceless gift God gave us?" We give not because we have to, but because we want to respond to what God has already given us.

You know we need to praise God.

As I think about God's best gift to us, I think of Jesus Christ. God so loved us that he gave us his only begotten Son. Every year during Advent, we sing carols that tell of his lowly birth. We picture that tiny babe of Bethlehem and remake how cute he is. We feel good, because babies always make us feel good. But we need to remember that with Advent comes a foreshadowing of Good Friday, a reminder that his purpose was all about sacrifice.

I want you to think about your relationship with Jesus Christ. How has he blessed you? Has he been there in your trials and in those moments when you have needed a rock to hold onto? Think about the story of Calvary. He told you that his body was given for you, broken for your sin as an offering to God. He told you his blood was poured out as an offering to seal the new covenant of eternal life. Jesus gave us his best gift and then he promised that it was just the beginning.

How are you going to respond to that? How will you offer your first gift of praise? Will you declare that you will come to worship him at church regularly for the next year? Will you declare that you will find a ministry that you can get involved with and take a lead so that your offering can bless others? Will you pick up your Bible and choose to read it regularly and even consider joining a Bible study so you can learn more about all of God's promises? Will you offer yourself to God and let him use you to bless your family, by promising to spend more time at home and with your children? Many of us have dedicated our homes to Christ and godly life. Will you find a way, a unique way that only you can find, to praise God in the coming months? Each of us was created in the image of God and yet we are each a unique individual with gifts given by God. Use your gifts to honor and praise God. Amen.

We Are One In Christ

Someone once said that action speaks louder than words and that is true. When someone reaches out to help a person in need, they have done more than give a sermon. When a person spends time at the soup kitchen feeding the hungry or hammering nails on a Habitat For Humanity house, they are telling the world what they believe is important.

Jesus instructed his disciples to be like salt, flavoring and preserving the world so that it would bring glory to God. He sent them out and told them to let the light of God shine through them so that everyone would see their good works and give praise to God. It is wonderful to see people living out their Christian calling. There is no greater joy than to witness a person's face when they have received a Thanksgiving basket or been the beneficiary of a clothing drive after a fire has destroyed the family home. When you have given yourself to Christian service, you not only glorify God, you also receive a blessing.

Unfortunately, there are too many people in the church today *talking* about faith and not enough *living* their faith. I was truly saddened several years ago, when I heard the Supreme Court decision regarding prayer at graduation exercises. It struck me again as to just how ineffective the church is being in society. There was a day when the church was the power in society, looking out for the welfare of its citizens. It was people like Roger Williams, the father of the Baptist movement in the country, who sought to protect people from religious persecution. It was he who gained the charter in Rhode Island that allowed differing faiths to co-exist in peace. The rights of each church were protected as well as the individual.

It was people like Thomas Jefferson who put a clause in the constitution to reflect our faith in God, yet to allow for our diversity. Yet, over the last 200 years, the world has moved on. The church has splintered and fragmented. It has been more interested in debating sociological ideologies and theological positions than in reaching out to the world with good news. While the church has been talking about keeping its buildings heated and preserved for the future, the government has been taking care of the poor and the disenfranchised. While the church has been talking about sin and pointing fingers at those who live in the shadows of society, AA groups and mental health agencies have been providing counseling and support groups to provide a lifeline to those who might otherwise be lost.

It is no wonder society looks upon the church as something frivolous today. The church is a place to have your wedding or a place to go to when someone you know dies. Real life takes place somewhere else. So what happened? What went wrong between the time that Jesus sent his disciples out to be salt and light and today?

Somewhere along the way we started talking about being Christians instead of living as them. After all, Jesus sent us out to feed the hungry, clothe the naked, heal the sick, and visit those in prison. He told us that we were to preach good news to those who were oppressed and overwhelmed.

The truth is that there is nothing else in life that has the potential to change the world for the better than a decision by some Christians to follow Christ and reach out to the world around them. Millions of people are dying of starvation on the other side of the world. War is raging in town after town. Disease stemming from basic unsanitary conditions is crippling and ruining able societies.

An example of what can happen is what is taking place in Korea today. In the '50s Korea was a dying nation, but several missionaries entered and brought hope in various ways. Today, it is the home of some of the largest churches in the world and their ministries are worldwide. The church has pervaded the whole society and has changed people's lives.

Now that's exactly the kind of thing that Paul was promoting in his letter to Philemon. While he was in prison, Paul came into contact with a runaway slave named Onesimus. In the course of their time together, Paul shared the gospel with him and Onesimus accepted Christ. Onesimus, who was once a lazy and spiteful slave was changed. He was a new man in Christ and now he couldn't do enough to show his appreciation. He stood by Paul and ministered to others while they were in that prison. He became an example of a changed life.

The problem was that Onesimus was still a slave, even though he now belonged to Christ. Slavery was a part of life and sewn into the fabric of society. Even as Jesus was obedient to the civil authorities, he called his disciples to follow the rules as long as they didn't impede the laws of God. So in due time, Paul sent Onesimus back to his master.

You know, I hear so much talk about oppression these days. I can't imagine anything as bad as slavery. Yet Paul talks about what it means to be a Christian in the context of the social structure. In another of his letters he says that we all have a role to play and we should do our best to serve the Lord in whatever state we find ourselves. In Ephesians 6 he says, "Slaves, obey your earthly masters with fear and trembling, in singleness of heart, as you obey Christ.... Render service with enthusiasm, as to the Lord ..." (vv. 5, 7). And he concludes with a word to the masters. He says, "and masters, do the same to them, for you know that both of you have the same Master in heaven, and with him there is no partiality ..." (v. 9).

In due time, Paul sends Onesimus back to Philemon with this letter. In it he encourages Philemon to live his faith. He gives him the opportunity to go beyond talking about what it means to follow Christ and to actually do it in the context of a slave owner and fellow Christian. Paul doesn't suggest to Philemon that he free Onesimus. He simply asks him to be who he claims to be, a disciple of Christ and a Christian brother.

It must have been hard for Paul to look in Onesimus' eyes and tell him he had to go back to his former owner. He had run away from there and was seeking his freedom. He was a different man now and ready to live life in a new estate. The last thing he wanted was to return to the past and the old life. Paul knew that the only way Onesimus could really claim his new life was to face his past and go from there. He sent him back and told him to treat his master with respect and love. It would be a challenge for both men. But in Christ, all things are possible.

Paul could do this because he believed that when one is in Christ at least three things happen. I heard it quoted once that, "Christianity is the power that makes men good." Paul claimed that our faith can make the useless person useful.

It changes lives and gives people a reason for living and loving. It is often said that a person is so heavenly minded that they were of no earthly use. But Paul declared that true Christianity makes a heavenly minded person active and working for Christ.

As a matter of fact, legend has it that Onesimus was later freed by Philemon and became the Bishop of Ephesus. When the first council was gathering to look at sacred writings, Onesimus asked to have this letter preserved to show what Christ could do to someone.

Paul also believed that Christianity gives us power for living triumphantly. It is not an escape from problems. Paul sent Onesimus back to face Philemon. He didn't dismiss the pending confrontation. He used it to help both Christians grow. Christianity forces us to face our trials, as well as our sin, head on. In doing so, he believed Christ guides, strengthens, and empowers our witness. We grow stronger because we stand in Christ. Christianity is not just another idea. It is not a philosophy. It is a way of life, and as we live with Christ, we can begin to change the world one relationship at a time.

Finally, Paul looked at what it means to be a Christian from the other side when he calls on Philemon to forgive. It's awfully easy to be a Christian when somebody else is doing all the work. Being in Christ means accepting people with all their faults and welcoming them in. It means working together to serve Christ more faithfully.

Paul's letter draws in the expression of being one in Christ and making it real. He says in Romans, that with Christ there is no Greek nor Jew, male nor female, free nor slave. He gives us a solid example of what that might look like in this epistle.

It is our job to live that out. Imagine what the world would say if we came together to feed the hungry and visit the prisons. Imagine the difference we could make if we joined hand-in-hand to build shelters for the homeless and care for the widows and orphans. The world would have to take us seriously because our words and deeds would be the same. The love of Christ would shine through us and they would know we were one in Christ. Amen.

Thank God We Can Change

Someone once said that the only constant in life is change. No matter who you are, one of the greatest challenges you will face is managing the changes that take place in life. We have limited control over some of the changes we face. Our hair changes color and sometimes falls out. We gain weight as we become less active and our metabolism slows. Our children grow up and move out of the house. The shifting economy may lead to lay-offs and relocation. The death of a spouse or the breakdown of a marriage may result in radical changes in our living arrangements. And if that isn't enough, grandchildren come along to make us humble again.

Most of us try to control the tempo of our lives. We do all we can to maintain the status quo. We might move to a larger home as our family grows. We relocate to get a better job it if seems appropriate. We make new friends as our kids get involved in various activities. We get involved in a church and attend worship regularly.

Of course, most of us would rather nothing changed and we try to keep these events at a minimum. We like doing the same old thing with the same old friends. We don't enjoy looking at new ideas. We don't want to have our attitudes challenged. I read somewhere that by the time we reach age thirty, we are pretty much set in a pattern of behavior that will last the rest of our lives.

The exception to the rule comes in one of three ways. The first exception follows a life-changing event. Major changes often occur as the result of a wedding or the birth of a first child. A new job may also spark some big changes in an older worker. These events force everyone to look at life differently but the changes are often more pronounced the older you are when the event occurs.

The second exception comes after the experience of a tragedy, like a sudden death, loss of bodily function, or as the result of some catastrophic event. Just think of the people who lost everything in Hurricane Katrina. Families were uprooted and moved halfway across the country to start over. After the events of September 11, numerous stories arose about drastic changes that people made in the way they lived life. It is only natural to take a survey of what you are doing under these extreme circumstances.

The final exception is one that many of us are familiar with. When a person has a religious encounter after age thirty, there is bound to be a radical shift in their thinking about life. That was the case with the Apostle Paul. He tells his story at least three times in the book of Acts and again shares parts of it in several of his epistles, including the letter to Timothy we are reading today. As he shares his testimony, he comes away very thankful for the experience. I have to be honest with you, Paul does the exact opposite from what you would expect. Instead of seeing it as a negative, he embraces his new life and looks at it as an opportunity.

Maybe we need to take Paul's approach and find something to be thankful for. It is obvious that he is counting his blessings over the changes that occurred in his life. In our text he gives thanks to God for his new life.

Many of us have our stories of life before Christ. Some day we ought to sit around and tell our stories. Some may even be as dramatic as Paul's story. He tells how his life was turned upside down on the Damascus Road. Before meeting Christ, he thought of himself as a paragon of virtue, a crusader for God. After the event, he sees himself as nothing more than a blasphemer, a persecutor, and a man of violence.

A friend of mine told me about a man in his congregation who was a real saint. He was generous and loving. He was a real prayer warrior. One day he and my friend were chatting and sharing some of their past experiences. My friend said he was shocked to hear the man's testimony. It included alcoholism and abusive behavior. It was a story of a family torn apart and marital infidelity. Then one day everything changed. The man met Christ at a revival meeting and he quit drinking, got a handle on his temper and his tongue, and started rebuilding his life. Every day now, the man says, "Thank God I'm not the man I used to be."

That man had the same sense of humility and honesty that Paul shares in this letter to Timothy. Paul knew what it was to be under the banner of God's grace and mercy. Time after time, he declared that it was only by the grace of God that he was able to stand before the crowds and speak to them.

You see, God had done two things. First, he forgave Paul's past, allowing him to start over. This time, Paul was going to get it right. He was no longer bound by the errors of his ways. He was, as he so eloquently put it in an earlier letter, a new creation. His past had no claim on him. Yet, he used his story to encourage others and help them understand that people could change. We don't have to be the same old person. He tells Timothy that God could now use him as an example of what God wanted for all of us.

This brings us to a second point: God gave him the ability to change. The new man was able to emerge with God's help. As the Holy Spirit entered him, Paul was now able to do far more than he ever dreamed possible. Paul wants us to know that. That is why he says in another letter, "All things are possible with God."

A funny thing happens when we begin to look at life this way. It reminds us that change can be good. It points out the fact that we don't have to remain the way we are. We can look ahead with thanksgiving and praise God that we aren't yet what we are going to be.

If you have even been to a Weight Watchers' meeting, you will know that part of their philosophy involves imagining what you will feel like, look like, and be doing in the future. Weight loss always involves making changes in your life. When you begin to imagine what the future will look like, you are half way there. You are no longer bound by the past.

Paul knew this well. He lived life with an eye to the future. He knew that he still had a way to grow in grace. He understood that he was going to change some more. He also knew that God was molding and shaping him through various experiences that would allow him to be a better servant.

We are growing and changing, too. Our faith will be stronger and we will be able to be more effective in our witness. If you are worried that you cannot quote the Bible like you want, or that you are too timid to get up and share your story, then just wait a while. As your faith develops, so will your confidence. Paul uses the illustration of being like little children in one of his letters. He suggests that maturity in the faith takes time. We will grow into it.

And, here is more good news. If you have some thorn in the flesh like Paul, that is holding you back and getting you down, it too shall pass. For in the end we shall all be transformed and ushered into the kingdom. When we suffer from disease and distress, it will not last forever. If we are being held back by some psychological baggage from our past or some physical problem, we will be delivered from them.

We all know people who suffer from Alzheimer's disease or those who have been ravaged by a stroke and lay in bed paralyzed. Our faith tells us that they, too, will be changed. They shall be made whole again. Paul says in his letter to the Corinthians, "Listen, I will tell you a mystery! We will not all die, but we will all be changed, in a moment, in the twinkling of an eye, at the last trumpet. For the trumpet will sound, and the dead will be raised imperishable, and we will be changed" (1 Corinthians 15:51-52).

Thank God that in the last days I will be changed. I wouldn't want to go around in eternity with this old body. I want to be able to move and play and dance again. Now that is something exciting to look forward to.

That brings me right back to today. Knowing that our past is forgiven and that we have been changed is good news. We can thank God for today as we recognize that no matter what shape we find ourselves, we have been promised a bright future. We can live life as it was meant to be lived.

Too many people are either preoccupied with the past or worrying about the future. They never get to rejoice in the present. Paul's message here points out this important truth. He begins the passage by thanking God for his calling. He loves the ministry and knows that God has prepared him to do just what he is doing. He is now fully engaged in the present moment.

Something changed in the make up of the organization when the Boston Red Sox came from behind to win the American League Championship Series in 2004. They were trailing the New York Yankees three games to none. The Yankees needed only one more win to clinch the series and send the Red Sox home with another disappointing finish. For 86 years, they lived with "the curse of the Bambino." Every time they got close to winning a big game or series, something extraordinary came along to prevent it from happening.

Over the years, the players changed but the curse remained. They just could not win the big game. Then, with their backs up against the "Green Monster," the Red Sox won four straight games against the Yankees in one of the most dramatic series in baseball history. It made a powerful impact on the franchise. They went on to dispatch the National League Champion St. Louis Cardinals in four games to win the World Series for the first time since 1918.

The most incredible change occurred much later. As the team took the field in the spring of 2005, they were much more relaxed. They could enjoy life now. The curse was gone and they could play ball. So it is with us. Christ came to lift the curse and we can now enjoy life and live it to the glory of God. Thank God we can change! Amen.

It All Begins With Prayer

Imagine you only have a short time to prepare your successor in ministry. In that time you can only share a few of your insights. What would you tell him or her? There is a story told about a group of seminary students that went to visit an old historic church they had heard a lot about. When they entered the huge building, they were met by a gray-bearded gentleman they thought was the janitor. He offered to lead them on a tour through the facilities and answer any questions they had.

They walked through the sanctuary, stood in the pulpit, and looked down from the balcony. When they had seen just about everything and asked every conceivable question they could come up with, the old gentleman asked a strange question, "Would you like to see what fires up this church?" They weren't really interested in touring the basement and seeing the boiler, but just to humor their host, they followed. They went down a narrow stairway to an area beneath the pulpit. As the gentleman opened the door, he said, "Behind this door is the secret of this great church. Everything that happens upstairs starts down here. This is where the fire in the pulpit begins."

The old man, actually C. H. Spurgeon, the great preacher himself, opened the door to reveal several dozen people on their knees in fervent prayer. Spurgeon would always insist that the secret of any church, big or small, was the prayers of the people. It was Spurgeon who said, "I would rather teach one man to pray than ten men to preach."

The Apostle Paul would agree wholeheartedly. In his letter to his young associate, Timothy, Paul points to prayer as being essential to his future ministry and lays out some instructions on the matter. Think about this: In Acts 6, the church is still in its infancy stages and we read that the apostles chose seven deacons to tend to the ministerial duties so they could focus on "prayer" and preaching. That is how important it is to the overall ministry.

We spend a lot of time, energy, and money on programs at church. We want to attract newcomers. We want to excite the membership. We hope to deepen discipleship. We are always on the lookout for new and innovative approaches to the gospel that will catch the attention of our people. As a result, we often overlook the powerful gift we have that is our prayer ministries.

This is true for young pastors just starting off, but we all need to be reminded sometimes. I read about one young pastor who had this impressed upon him by the preacher at his installation service. The preacher told a story about taking a drive in the country one night and running out of gas. He looked ahead and saw a church. The lights were on and he remembered it was Wednesday. Thank goodness for the prayer meeting. He stopped in and received the help he needed. The preacher then pointed out that there are an awful lot of people running low on fuel who need to be filled up by the Holy Spirit. When we are a praying people, the world can see that the lights are on in our houses of worship and they will come to us for help. He commented on how sad it would have been if there was no prayer meeting that night. He would have been lost.

Paul would agree wholeheartedly. That is why he says here, "First of all," before giving any other encouragement or instruction. He wants Timothy to realize that prayer should be at the foundational level of his ministry. He can build upward from there.

I have heard a lot of people protest when it comes to prayer. They say, "When are we going to stop praying about it and actually do something?" Sadly enough, there are some churches that use prayer as an excuse for inaction. There are far more churches, powerful and life-changing congregations, that understand that any action they take needs to begin with prayer in order to be successful.

Paul begins his tutorial to Timothy with the call to pray for everyone. He doesn't mean to pray generically. He calls on Timothy to pray for individuals. He says to pray for government officials, for teachers, for friends, and for the people who run the markets. He wants Timothy to be praying for everyone he runs into during his day. This goes right along with Paul's encouragement to pray without ceasing.

Paul sees every encounter as an opportunity to invite God into the situation. What a wonderful way to live. The truth is that everyone we know is either struggling to remain faithful to Christ or hasn't been introduced to him yet. Everyone we know is facing trials, and tests, looking for a route to happiness and meaning in life.

It is so easy to judge other people. We look at someone and make all kinds of suppositions about their background and what they believe. Instead of making these judgments, Paul would encourage us to turn that around and focus on praying a blessing for that person.

Several years ago, I heard Aidsand Wright-Riggins, the Executive Director Of National Ministries for the American Baptists, speak about growing up in the projects in Los Angeles. The end result of his testimony was that he declared he was standing before us that day because his grandmother had prayed for him. Many of his friends died along the way. They had been caught up in gangs and the like. Somehow, through no real choice of his own, he was steered away from that. He was telling us that the prayers of this righteous woman saved his life. So you do not know whose life you may be saving when you begin praying for the people you meet.

Paul makes specific mention to pray for kings and those in authority. In his day, the emperor was accusing Christians of acts of sedition and ordering them killed. Nonetheless, Paul told Timothy to pray for them. It makes a lot of sense, doesn't it? Jesus told us to pray for our enemies and to do good to them. Many of us would just as soon forget about government officials with whom we disagree. With the rising tide of anti-Christian legislation, many of us would be more comfortable praying against them. But Paul sees the government as agents of order in society. They have a role to play. In an orderly society, they can provide for peace and prosperity. Paul tells Timothy it is always in our best interest to be praying for these leaders, that they might have wisdom and vision.

Paul continues on and suggests that the peace that comes as a response to our prayer will afford us the opportunity to spread the gospel so everyone can be saved. We can be free to live lives that will reflect God's glory.

I know a man who quietly lived out his faith in his office at work. He had a calendar on his desk that had the "Bible verse of the day." On several occasions, people would stop by to look at the verse and question him about it. Even those who didn't practice any religion got caught up in it. One day, he accidentally spilled his coffee on the calendar and had to throw it away. He said he couldn't believe the disappointment that his coworkers expressed. He never realized what an impact he was making by simply sharing his faith in this quiet way. That weekend he went out and found another one to replace it.

Do you know what an intercessor is? It is a person who stands in the gap between the world and God. Paul says that is our role. We are to be praying for the deliverance and salvation of the people all around us. We have no idea how our prayers impact our workplaces, our city, our state, our country, or our world.

A friend of mine belonged to a prayer group that received permission to meet in city hall to pray for the city. They prayed for the mayor, the city council, the police and fire departments, the school board, teachers, and social workers. Not many of those people knew they were being prayed for but my friend said he saw things begin to happen in the city. He claims prayer made all the difference. Be assured that God uses them and opens doors for us to share our witness.

One other group Paul mentions that we should pray for, is the proclaimers of the gospel. Timothy might not think of himself in prayer, but Paul reminds him that he will need prayer if he is to do the work that needs to be done if all people are to come to knowledge of the truth. God desires that all hearts should turn to him. The preachers and teachers need to be prayed for so they will have the words to share. That brings us right back to the idea of praying for everyone. Here we are called to pray for those who are doing the work of the kingdom and sharing the news of Jesus' redeeming work in particular. We need to pray for the anointing of the Holy Spirit so they will be effective in all their efforts.

When we are done praying for the preachers, it is time to pray for the hearers. The gospel message tells us that people are lost. Paul writes in verse 4 that God desires "... everyone to be saved and to come to the knowledge of the truth." So our job is to pray that their ears might be open and their hearts receptive to the preaching of the word. There is one thing more powerful than prayer when it comes to changing hearts. I like the story Bill Hybils tells of a baptism service he presided over at Willow Creek Community Church several years ago. He had preached the sermon and it was time for the service of believer's baptism. Several people had been prepared beforehand and were coming down front now to enter the waters. When he came to one middle-aged woman, he noticed a man standing with her. He smiled at the man and as he approached them the man asked Bill, "Is there anything to prevent me from being baptized with my wife tonight?" He was the woman's husband and he revealed that he had made a decision for Christ that night and wanted to make his profession in baptism. Bill invited him into the water and baptized him along with his wife. They were greeting the congregation after the service, and a woman came up to Bill in tears. She told him that the man he baptized was her brother. For years, she had been praying for his salvation and he had always put her off. But that night, her prayers had been answered and she thanked him.

We may think our prayers are going unanswered, but God honors our prayers. We need to keep praying for those who do not know the Lord. At the right time, God will open their eyes to the truth.

I want to conclude by giving you this to think about. Jesus declared, "You are the light of the world. And a city set on a hill cannot be hidden." So, don't hide your light. Let it shine. We can't sit around and wait for something to happen. We can't look to the president or some good-will organization or some religious organization to save the world. That is our job. We were called to transform the world through the power of the gospel. It is an overwhelming task. We need to pray for boldness. Paul had this task. He says, "For this purpose I was appointed a herald and an apostle — I am telling the truth — and a teacher of the true faith to the Gentiles." That was who Paul was called to be. And so it is with us, as well. Unleash the power of prayer in your life and watch what God can do with it. Amen.

Proper 21
Pentecost 19
Ordinary Time 26
1 Timothy 6:6-19

Developing A Glad Attitude

It always amazes me when I read about a sports figure who decides to hold out for more money. With salaries that are often in the millions, they feel underpaid unless they are at the next level. I heard one player say to a reporter on *Sports Center*, "It's not about the money. It is about respect." A few moments later, the host of the show made the comment, "When they say it isn't about the money, it's always about the money."

This attitude of grabbing all you can get is not limited to the world of sports. It is part of the fabric of our society. Every one of us wants more. We want a better car. We look for a bigger house. We strive for a larger salary. It never ends. It seems as if our contentment can only come through the acquisition of more and more material things. If you think this is something new, then you need to look back to Paul's second letter to Timothy.

As Paul is giving his final instructions to his young friend, he talks about developing an attitude that will open the door to happiness. Paul has experienced it all in his life and he speaks from personal example. He begins by saying that contentment begins with an attitude.

We all know people who have so many blessings in their lives and yet they seem to be miserable. They are unhappy with their spouses, their jobs, their homes, and even their status in life. Living the charmed life is not a guarantee of bliss. Look at the number of Hollywood celebrities whose lives are in shambles. Divorce, alcohol, and drugs are rampant. We idolize them and think they lead the charmed life. Just the opposite is often true. They soon find that they have the same insecurities and problems as before and that the money has only added to their problems. That emptiness inside them only seems to grow with the more they have.

Paul tells us in his letter to the Philippians that he has found the secret to contentment. He says, "I have learned to be content whatever the circumstances. I know what it is to be in need, and I know what it is to have plenty. I have learned the secret of being content in any and every situation, whether well fed or hungry, whether living in plenty or in want. I can do everything through him who gives me strength." His happiness comes from knowing and serving Jesus. Paul can be happy in prison because he knows God is with him. He can be happy even though he has been thrown overboard and has lost every material thing he owns, because he still has a purpose for his life. If he ties his future to Christ, then he knows he will come out the victor.

It reminds me of Jesus' words about our treasures in Matthew 6:19. He says, "Do not store up for yourselves treasures on earth, where moth and rust consume and where thieves break in and steal...." That is what many of us do and we are disappointed. When our treasure is lost, we are lost as well. But Jesus said to store up your treasure in heaven then you will find your heart and your hope.

Paul's eyes were on heaven so a lot of the normal problems in life did not rattle him. He didn't worry about things. He decided that he was going to make the most of things and be happy with the "adventures" God brought his way. He didn't have to wait until he got out of prison to be happy. He adjusted his attitude and found a reason to be happy in that situation. And so it was all along the way.

You and I can learn from Paul. This is what he was telling Timothy. You don't have to wait until everything in your life is perfect to begin praising God and tasting joy. We can find it now by simply looking at things a little differently. The truth is that if you have been saying, "I'll be happy when...." then you will never be happy. There will always be something that gets in the way.

But if we look to God, we will be happier. Jesus says in Matthew 6:33, "But strive first for the kingdom of God and his righteousness, and all these things will be given to you as well." It's kind of like having a best friend. When you share your problems with that person, you feel better. They help you see things in a new light. The friendship itself brings you joy. So it is with God. It is our relationship with God, which is the source of contentment, and nothing else can take his place.

A second point Paul makes in his letter is that thankful people are happy people. I know another minister who makes a list of things he wants to thank God for every day and includes it in his prayers. He starts every day this way. The list is often the same. He never misses a day. He is one of the people I like to be around because he is filled with joy. I asked him about it and he said that the list reminds him of his blessings and he can't help but feel good about life when he remembers them at the start of the day.

Contrast this with another colleague who was always sharing all the "woes" he had in his life. Whenever he walked into the room, it felt like the air was being let out of a balloon. It is no fun being with him.

I know a lot of people will suggest that we are born as either an optimist or a pessimist and there is nothing we can do about it. I disagree. It is learned and comes from the environment in which we grow up. We need to learn to look for the blessings and give thanks.

That is what Thanksgiving is all about. In the midst of a Civil War, Abraham Lincoln called on the nation to pause for a day of national "thanks giving." Many would say this was the worst time to give thanks. Everything was falling apart around him. Yet he knew instinctively that this was a way to begin healing old wounds. It was a way to turn the focus off what was wrong with this country and onto what was good about it.

Even today, in a society that is more secular than religious, Thanksgiving reminds us of what we have and who gave it to us. It helps us to focus on our blessings. We need to do that because we can easily get swept away by a flood of advertising reminding us of what we don't have.

Patrick Morley talks about the effects of advertising in his book, *The Man in The Mirror*. He relays the fact that the first television programs arose as a way for advertisers to push their products on us. They have been doing that ever since. Now they encourage us to purchase the new and improved version or the latest model. Their products will give us sex appeal or make us more capable. As a result, we never seem to be happy with what we have.

My car is running perfectly fine and I have no desire to give it up until I see an ad for the new Toyota. I do not even think about buying a new suit until I walk by the window at Gentleman's Warehouse and see the sign advertising the sale. The family home is perfect for us until our neighbor moves into a larger home in an upscale neighborhood.

It must have something to do with our human nature. We can't seem to be thankful for what we have. Our eyes are always on what someone else has.

Paul reminds us that we need to keep looking up. We need to recognize where everything comes from. James tells us, "Every good and perfect gift is from above, coming down from the Father of the heavenly lights." That is why we can say with the psalmist, "This is the day the Lord has made; let us rejoice and be glad in it." We are content and actually happy because we have a God who cares. He has made us, and he has made our world. He has blessed us beyond our wildest dreams, and out of the gratitude we feel toward God for all his faithful goodness, we want to share the blessings.

That brings me to my third point. Paul suggests to Timothy that we need to have an attitude of generosity if we are to live a blessed life. There was an article in *Reader's Digest* a couple of years ago, titled "What Good Is a Tree?" It was noted in the story that a certain kind of fungus grows in the ground that allows the roots of the trees, even different kinds of trees, to come together. If one tree has access to water, another to nutrients, and a third to sunlight, the trees have a way to share with one another.

So it is with us. We are stronger individually if we are willing to share what we have with others. Too often, people have the idea that if they cling to what they have, they will be able to take care of their own needs and if they give it away, they will run out and leave themselves in a predicament.

I like the story told of Elijah and his visit to the widow of Zarephath. When he came upon her, she had very little to eat in her house, yet she fed Elijah. She was a little reluctant but she shared it anyway. Miraculously, there was enough food for them all for many days. She learned to trust God. Her trust was rewarded. God kept providing for her as long as she shared what she had with Elijah. Then the story takes a twist. Her son gets sick and dies. She is overcome by grief. Elijah goes to the boy and brings him back from the dead. The boy is alive and the woman sings God's praise. I'll bet that woman never doubted God again.

God works in mysterious ways. When you share what you have with others it always comes back to you in a blessing. It may not be monetary. It may not be a tit for a tat. In God's wisdom, the blessing comes in a form that makes your heart glad. I don't think I've ever seen a generous person lost in despair. They are often the happiest people I know. God keeps blessing them as fast as they can share what they have with others.

A friend told me about a man in his congregation who accepted Christ and decided he was going to start tithing. He figured out ten percent of his income and wrote out a check to the church. That first week his check bounced. He was a little embarrassed but he made it good. He continued writing out checks for ten percent of his income and there were a few more mishaps. In time he began contributing the tithe and then made out checks for some special offerings. He also noticed that a few of his stocks started gaining rapidly. So he gave away even more. He started funneling some of his newfound wealth into the youth ministry at church. One day, he told his pastor that the scriptures were true when they said you cannot outgive God. He tried and God kept blessing him, not only with added wealth but also in the joy he had in seeing a ministry grow. He said he had never been happier in his life.

Happiness has never been about money and possessions. It has to do with finding your place in life and living it. When you walk in the light of God's Word, you will always find peace and joy. You'll develop a glad attitude. Amen.

The Promise That Won't Be Broken

Paul was sitting in prison with every reason to be discouraged. He was just days away from his execution at the hands of Emperor Nero. He was isolated and treated like a man to be scorned, unlike his earlier stints in jail. The Emperor Nero had blamed the Christians for the great fire that destroyed the city of Rome. For the first time they were subjected to terrible persecution and citizens from every corner of the empire turned against them. Christians were burned as living torches to light the emperor's social gatherings. They were thrown to lions and killed by gladiators. They were despised throughout the empire as being cannibals. Their talk about eating the body and blood of Christ was given as testimony against them. They were considered atheists because they did not worship the official idols of the Empire. They were said to be revolutionaries because they denied the ultimate authority of Caesar and said that Jesus was Lord. It was a world that had turned ugly and brutal for the Christian community. Paul became the symbol of the upstart religious movement and Nero was looking to make an example of him.

The atmosphere of the letter reflects these circumstances. Paul is lonely. He says, "I long night and day to see you." He is feeling abandoned and he writes, "All those in Asia have turned against me ... Only Luke is with me ... Demas has forsaken me and gone to Thessalonica." The ground he sleeps on is cold and hard so he asks Timothy to bring the cloak, which he left in Troas. He is bored because time passes slowly and he has little to keep him occupied. He asks for the books and the parchments, which he left behind in

329

Troas. He is certain that the end of his life is at hand. So in typical poet fashion, Paul writes, "The time of my departure has come ... I have finished the course, I have kept the faith." There is that word of clear anticipation that he had reached the end of his life.

Yet, despite the dark days, the letter opens with Paul's usual calm and confident expression of faith and grace. Putting his own circumstances out of his mind, he reminds Timothy who it was who called him and named him an apostle of Jesus Christ. Despite the fact that Paul outwardly looked like a beaten, forgotten man, Paul knew that he belonged to Jesus. That was enough to keep him going despite the hard times.

Paul knew that Jesus had made promises that would not be broken. It didn't matter to him what was going on all around him. He looked beyond what was apparent to all and decided to live by faith and not by sight. As he sat there, he thought about Timothy and those who he would leave behind. He wondered about their faith and whether or not they could stand up to the persecution. He tried to find the right words to encourage them to keep their eyes on Christ.

In these first few verses, Paul reminds Timothy of the gospel and he calls it "the promise of life in Christ Jesus." Paul lived by the message that he proclaimed. In Romans he wrote, "I am not ashamed of the gospel because it is the power of God let loose among men, the power of God unto salvation. The gospel changes people; it delivers them; it frees them; it heals them. The gospel brings people into the fullness of their life; it sets them free to be what God intends them to be."

If you have ever watched a young child at play, you get a sense of what it means to be fully alive. Just go to the playground and you will see boys and girls filled with a desire to see, touch, and taste everything that life puts in their paths. They look at life as something to be experienced. As we get older, we try to become more sophisticated about things, but many of us are still looking to get the most out of life.

As a result we are often vulnerable to the appeals of the world. Just turn on the television or open up a magazine and you will bombarded with advertisements telling us that "we only go around once." We have to grab it while we can. "Live with gusto," we are told. We are encouraged to buy this make of car, or that whitening toothpaste, and capture the good life and all that goes with it. It is amazing how much that idea takes hold of us. We want to have it all.

Unfortunately, the images the world shows of what it takes to have the good life are fallacious. We keep grabbing for material things and end up discovering that they do not make us happy. We reach for them and come away feeling empty. There is something missing.

A few years ago, Maury Povich invited some teenagers onto his afternoon talk show to talk about their experience growing up in the suburbs. The kids were dressed in black. Their faces were painted pale white and they took on the pallor of death. Their hair was unkempt and they looked lost. Maury kept asking them, "Why do you dress in this bizarre way? What is behind this look?" They responded, in all honesty, "What else is there?"

Their answer was a silent protest against the emptiness of life, against the sense of being cheated by life, by the world, and by society. The truth is that the world doesn't have anything meaningful to offer us. Will money bring satisfaction? We read of Martha Stewart and other corporate executives who served or are now serving time in prison because, despite their millions, they could not find contentment. The rich are more prone to divorce and nervous breakdowns. For all their wealth, they cannot buy what it takes to give life meaning and purpose.

Some would say that power and the ability to control one's destiny can bring happiness. Yet, how many stories have we heard about people who have sacrificed to get to that position only to find out that they have lost all their friends and even their family to get there? Whoever it was that declared it to be lonely at the top, was speaking from personal experience. To get to the top in this world, you are expected to destroy all competition. Unfortunately there is often a lot of "friendly fire" on the way up the ladder.

Some look at love and sexual pleasure as being the ultimate of satisfaction. The world is filled with erotic images that paint sex as an end in itself. What we soon learn is that without a deep and

331

abiding love, it becomes passionless and filled with emptiness. It becomes nothing more than something to do.

It is of little wonder that the young people on Maury's program looked the way they did. They were at an age when life should have been exciting and filled with endless opportunities. These were kids who ought to be hungry for life, looking forward to it. But the world had shown them an image of what the good life was all about and it left them disillusioned and despairing. What they had already tasted in life had left them feeling hopeless, empty, and abandoned.

Which brings us back to Paul. At the end of his career, he writes to remind Timothy that the hope of the world can only be found in the gospel. As he is sitting there in prison, with every reason to be discouraged, he tells his young friend that Jesus Christ offers every one of us a promise of meaningful and productive life. The circumstances of life are inconsequential. You can be sailing along with every blessing falling into place or you can be stuck in prison with a limited future, and the promise is still good and ready to be claimed.

I am sure that Timothy was worried about Paul. I am sure he was worried about the future. To this introverted, sensitive, sometimes fearful young man in Ephesus, Paul describes again the ingredients of the promise of life in Jesus Christ. He says to Timothy, "Remember the words of your mother and grandmother and let them be rekindled again." When things are going well, faith is easy. When the fire is burning bright, we forget how hard it was to start. We need to remember that it started somewhere. Paul encouraged Timothy to look back and let the sparks be rekindled. He reminded him that God has given him a treasure to share and it includes the promises of God.

What is this treasure and what are these promises that Paul speaks about to Timothy? The first promise is that we will receive grace. Grace is getting something we don't deserve. You cannot earn it. It is given simply because God loves us. It shows itself in terms of forgiveness. God sees us in our sinful state and decides to offer us a complete pardon. So many people try to earn God's favor and end up feeling frustrated. The good news is that God has abundant grace for all who are open to receive it.

A second promise is that God wants to walk with us. His incarnation is proof enough of his desire to enter into our lives. He doesn't want to watch from afar. He wants to come into our world. He wants to welcome us into his loving arms. That is the point of his grace. His forgiveness is not a simple exercise of his power and ability to do so. He does it for a purpose. He wants us to know him and love him as much as he knows and loves us.

A third promise is that we will receive power from above. In our human condition we are weak and subject to temptation and the wiles of the devil. God promises that when we come to him we will receive the power to stand up to the devil, to obey God's Word and to walk with God.

In Christ, we find we are able to do what we could not do before. Jesus now stands with us and we have the power of the Holy Spirit within us. This is what makes it possible for the alcoholic to leave their drinking, for those struggling with infidelity to remain faithful to their spouses, for the gambler to turn away from the games of chance. We cannot do it on our own, but we have been promised power from above so that we might do extraordinary things.

A fourth promise is that we will gain new understanding and grow in wisdom. God promises that if we follow him, he will open our eyes to truths that we never knew before. He will lift the veil and we will see things that we never saw. He will turn us around so that we can begin to walk by faith not by sight. It will be as if we have been lifted up and can see things from a new vantage point. We will be made aware of the bigger picture. The new understanding will strengthen our faith and equip us to serve even more faithfully.

A fifth promise is that we will receive mercy. The difference between mercy and grace is that grace gives us what we do not deserve, while mercy withholds what we do deserve. It is God's mercy, which tempers the difficulties of our lives and adjusts them to our weakness of faith. We take God's mercy for granted. We think that life ought to be easier. This is especially true of new Christians. We do not think it is fair that we should have to suffer.

333

In a fallen world the exact opposite is true. Every day ought to be nothing but disaster and sheer chaos. Every day, every moment ought to be filled with malice, hatred, viciousness, and betrayal. The fact that those things only come rather infrequently into our lives is due to the mercies of God. We ought to expect nothing but the direst hardships, but actually we are given hours and days — sometimes weeks and months — of joy, blessing, peace, excitement, and adventure. That is due to the mercies of God. That is what allowed Paul to sing God's praises even when he was stuck in prison with little hope of a future. He saw God's mercy and realized how blessed he was in spite of his circumstances. Wow!

A sixth promise is that we will have God's peace, the peace that passes all understanding. Peace is that inner sense of well-being. It is knowing that God is in control and that you are in his hands. It is the peace that a man named Les Main knew when the doctor told him he had terminal cancer. A parishioner of a fellow pastor, Les was only 62 years old when he learned of his diagnosis. He wasn't happy about the cancer. His faith was strong and in the following months he learned just how deep that faith was. As he shared his testimony, he was always quick to point out that he and Jesus were going through this together. He would say, "As long as Jesus holds my hand I knew everything, absolutely everything, will be all right." That is the same sentiment that Paul shares in Philippians 1:21 when he says, "For to me, living is Christ and dying is gain." It is that kind of inner peace that allows you to sing hymns and offer prayers when your world is turning upside down.

This is what the world is looking for as it strives to find joy and happiness. These treasures are what will make a teenager sit up and smile. These are the gifts that God offers and we are called to share with the world.

These are the promises that cannot be broken or stopped as long as there are witnesses to tell the story. So let's take up the challenge and share these promises with the world. Amen.

Sermons On The Second Readings

For Sundays
After Pentecost
(Last Third)

Whose Inheritance Is It?

Donna Schaper

To my first pastor,
Pastor Witte

Proper 23
Pentecost 21
Ordinary Time 28
2 Timothy 2:8-15

The Gospel Is Unchained ...

I went to the store to buy a new pair of blue jeans. The clerk asked if I wanted slim fit, easy fit, or relaxed fit, regular or faded, stone washed or acid washed, button fly or regular fly ... and that's when I started to sputter. Can't I just have a pair of blue jeans, size fourteen? Then I went to the grocery store and found 85 varieties of crackers, 285 kinds of cookies, and thirteen different kinds of raspberry jelly. Can't I just get a cookie and a cracker and a bottle of jelly any more?

I am in chains by the number of choices that I have! They keep me too busy to pray and too busy to praise and too busy to focus. How can I break my chains on behalf of the unchained gospel? By letting less meet more and fewer meet finer.

According to Barry Schwartz in *The Paradox Of Choice: Why More Is Less*, there are two kinds of people: the satisficers and the maximizers. A satisficer is the one who is willing to live with the good enough rather than insisting on the best. Nobel Laureate Herbert Simon developed "satisficers" as a realistic alternative to the notion of the utility maximization presupposed by classical economists. Schwartz argues strong for the satisficers being the ones who have the best lives.

For example, if a supermarket chain attempted to calculate the very best alternative before deciding where to place a new store, the research costs would bankrupt it while more intrepid competitors would move in. Even in the terms of maximum utilization of everything and everybody, satisficers can declare a site good enough and not complete their research. One way to break the chains that keep the unchained gospel from blessing us is to become a satisfied one, not a maximized one.

The organization today that can make decisions the most quickly will win. That is true of personal choices, too. I remember having cancer and my sister-in-law, who is a physician assistant, saying that I had to take control of the treatment and the choices about treatment. I remember saying, "Oh, my. How can I possibly do that?"

Happiness as opposed to profitability is the goal of life, according to Schwartz. In his article in the April issue of *Scientific American*, "The Tyranny of Choice," he develops a scale by means of which subjects rate their relative maximizer/satisficer proclivities. It is a seven-point scale which has statements like, "When shopping, I have a hard time finding clothing I love" or "Whenever I watch television, I channel surf."

Maximizers feel worse about a given unit of loss than about a corresponding unit of gain. Forgoing alternatives or "Opportunity costs" in economist's terms means that people program themselves to be acutely aware of what we are not getting. "Satisficers" instead program themselves to see how full our glass is rather than how empty it is.

When the writer of second Timothy tells us that the gospel is unchained, he is telling us that it is satisfied. That it is rich because it has few needs. It only needs to be. Jesus did not rush from appointment to appointment or shop to shop to find the best things. He was fully present to where he was, when he was there. He was deeply satisfied by God. He had no chains in blue jeans or jelly, decision trees, or need for more. He didn't take the chains off worldly things so much as he refused to put them on in the first place.

A minister giving a sermon at a wedding, shocked the congregation by saying that the grass is *always* greener on the other side. There will always be someone prettier, funnier, and smarter ... but marriage is not a matter of comparison-shopping. Considering your decision irrevocable allows you to pour your energy into making things better.

This focused decision-making is how Jesus felt about the one he called Father. He didn't need another Father or a better Father or a different Father. He loved with depth the one had.

In the gospel way of living, more becomes less and most of us are well aware of it.

"Fewer finer" is the slogan every good decorator will tell you. Pruning a bush makes it grow beautifully. Letting it overtake your yard has nothing to do with beauty.

This agricultural parable means only one thing: focus your attention on the gate, on the right way in to life. Stand guard against the invaders. Who are the invaders? They are like advertisers; they are voices that are only using you. Be welcome in the main gate of the house as opposed to some kind of slave who has to use the slave quarters or service entrance. Walk through the finest gate.

The practical way to focus attention on important things is first to understand the matter of attention itself. Biologically, attention consists of four processes that take place in about 1/200 of a second.

- Arousal — the brain's alertness
- Orientation — the brain's motor center focuses
- Detection — is this normal, safe, new, edible...?
- Execution — the frontal lobe connects everything with memory, irrelevant stimuli are blocked and the motor center begins working toward the goals

Inattention is also a necessary function of a healthy brain. The brain chooses to execute certain messages and to ignore others. The reign of the yawn in daily life should not surprise us at all. Let's be honest. Most of us aren't paying attention to most things most of the time.

That's why my favorite phrase is TMI — too much information. It's a phrase which I'm sure you have heard. Biologically, the brain directs attention. Spiritually, there is a TMI, too. We get chained by TMI — and to hear and know the gospel, we have to break free.

Spiritually, I want to suggest a sheep dog. They may be my favorite kind of dog. They act like Jesus. They bark when needed! They keep the sheep safe from intruders. If you are a person who worries about the way life is too full, too overstimulated — and yet you want abundance, consider being like a sheep dog. You will unchain yourself from things that harm you on behalf of things that satisfy you.

We might call this conclusion "canine theology," in Jim Forbes' great term. Jesus wants us to focus our attention on the main gate to the main community of love and abundance and happiness. He is warning us here that there are many competitions for our attention. If the house is on fire, with too much information, bark! Bark. If the country is on fire with too much greed, bark. If the country is hurting other countries because of greed for oil or whatever, bark louder. If that doesn't work, put your nose right in their faces. If that doesn't work, pull the covers off. Nothing can happen unless you and the nation wake up! So wake up to the firestorm and oppression and chains of too many choices. Don't bark at rampant capitalism if you have not tamed your own heart of desire. Don't bark at others until you have focused your attention yourself.

You are not a slave. You are people who go in through the main door of life. You are satisfied by the unchained gospel. It has set you free. The only thing you are willing to maximize is your freedom from "stuff" for the gospel.

Itchy Ears

As usual, the epistle is a little more graphic than we can quite grasp. Itchy ears: what a concept just in physical terms. Experience it for a minute. You itch, you scratch, you sort of know you shouldn't scratch because it will only make the itch worse. But still you scratch, while wondering how the itch ever got started in the first place. What a concept: itchy ears as a vehicle for spiritual truth.

When we itch, we scratch. We awaken. We know we are not comfortable. We want to be comfortable. This epistle tells us about the itchy ears of the would-be saints. We don't want evil. We want good ... but something itches us. We know things are not as they should be. To get the message of our itch, we need to scratch below the surface of both evil and good and see what is happening down there. We use a negative strategy: We find out what evil is so that we may see good. We let our spiritual itches guide us.

Way too many people tell me they have been "wounded." Priests and pastors complain of the tedium of complaints. Women speak of insensitive husbands. Mothers talk of insensitive daughters. We get angry a lot. Even political candidates are judged by how they measure their own madness. Indeed, many have been hurt and not just those who can articulate the hurt. Mothers long on welfare who stand in abusive lines with hurt feet are also angry. They can't get out of line because that is how they feed their children. They, therefore, "eat" their anger.

What causes all this itching, bothersome hurt? I fear the word is big. It is evil. Evil, estrangement from God, causes hurt.

341

The Bible doesn't even bother sitting around asking questions about evil. Evil is assumed — in the creation story, in Jesus' encounter with a speaking devil in the wilderness, in the Lord's Prayer, "deliver us from evil," and in countless other places. Saint Paul doesn't even think about doubting the existence of evil! He presumes it. In fact, he speaks from a chained woundedness as "an ambassador in chains." His words come from deep within a confession of his own, "Pray that in proclaiming it I may speak as fearlessly as I ought to." In the letter to Timothy, we are reminded how much our ears itch. Paul knows he should be without fear or itch. He is not without fear. Still he speaks.

To think about evil in a twenty-first-century context, in the United States of America, I fear we have to start earlier than the author of Timothy does. We have to go back to go forward. It is not a simple itch, this perennial mosquito-bite-level harassment itch. It is much more basic and ancient than that. Evil, this itchy estrangement from God, has a long history — and not just in Christianity.

Some of you know about Procrustus, the Greek God who guarded the gates to Athens. Athens was the center of culture and power and beauty in these days but to get there you had to pass by Procrustus and his bed. Whatever part of you didn't fit on his one-size-fits-all bed, he chopped off. If you were too tall, your legs went. If you were too short, you were stretched. Procrustus is a form of evil called conformity. We are all to be one size and one shape. As we approach this notion of evil, I ask you what part of you was cut off? What did you have to leave behind to fit in this world? What has Athens done to you?

When you itch, are you itching for the part of you that has been amputated? Was it something important, like your hope or your faith or your capacity to love? If so, scratch and scratch hard!

Or let me tell you about Persephone. You know her as the maiden who had nothing to do but pick flowers. She spent life in a meadow just figuring out which ones were most beautiful. All of a sudden one day, on her way to pick a flower way across the field, the earth opens up and she is consumed. She is abducted into the underworld. Many people speak of the lives of adolescent girls this way: They figure out around age twelve that they can no longer be

342

either smart or athletic and still fit the bed of marriage and femininity. So they go underground. Many therapists call underground the place where you can't act on what you know, so you stop knowing it. This underground is not just about girls. Many Vietnam veterans went crazy because they couldn't believe what they saw. Their only solution was to go crazy. This abduction of Persephone is any major betrayal that abducts you and takes you to places you never wanted to go. I think of unexpected poverty. Like the man sitting on the beach with his wife, reading the paper, "Maud we are no longer on vacation, the company folded." Abductions into the underground happen to lots and lots of people. The people themselves are not evil. But our responses can be evil. We can let disappointment kill us or we can find our way through. We can deny that we itch. We can turn off. We can shut down. This strategy will hurt us long term even if it protects us short term. Going underground is not a good place to find God.

Indeed, the god of the underground is Pluto, whose name also means "great riches." This is the complaint that is really a request. The anger that is really a begging for relationship. The siege that is really the invitation to salvation. Ah, breakthrough. Evil: when you can't act on what you know so you stop knowing it. Indeed, I think of mothers ... who surely know that something has happened to their child when the child is abused by a teacher or a Boy Scout leader or a priest. But why don't they let themselves know what they know? Because they are curving in on their own power, which is miniscule, and refusing God's power which would let them not only know what they know but act on what they know. Is it really true that the Roman Catholic church did not know what the priests were doing to their children? No, instead, it is knowing something but then denying it because you can't act on it.

Why don't we know evil? Why do we itch painfully but not scratch? Because we can't figure out a way to act our way out of the conformity of not knowing it.

Our souls have been cut off in our own particular Athens. Evil is our cooperation with evil. Good is our knowledge of evil. We are the problem and we are the only solution to the problem. We itch and we are our own bug spray against the mosquitos that "bug" us.

Before we even bother with strategies against evil, we'd have to believe that we needed it. Let me tell you about Inana, a Sumerian goddess. She has precisely the opposite of Athenian's experience with evil. She is asked to take things off. Inana has a sister who is in trouble in the underworld and Inana thinks it will be a cinch to go down and save her. Because she is so much a somebody in the upper world, she thinks the lower world will also obey her will. On the first level on the way down, Inana is asked to surrender her headdress. At the second gate, she is asked for her necklace. At the third, her breast plate, at the fourth her girdle, and at the last gate she is asked to take off her very gown. Naked and bowed low, she enters the underworld.

This reminds us so much of going to the hospital. We give up our role, our identity, our jewelry. In county hospitals, they put these belongings in a paper bag. We are disabused of any specialness about ourselves at all.

Or, is it actually Christ's path to the cross which Inana is following? He, too, is stripped of everything only to come out victorious. How does he have the victory? Not by his earthly roles or upperworld distinctions, but by the power and grace of God.

I hope these various characters are beginning to show you something about us. You see, in Peru, to be a shaman is to expect to be dismembered on your way. Here, many of us think we can get out clean and whole. Ancient myths and Saint Paul join forces to say that isn't so. Our itchy ears are also warnings: They tell us what we already know but don't want to realize.

By the way, don't be too hard on those mothers and fathers who didn't see that their child was abused. Or the wives who didn't tell anybody that they were getting beat up and, therefore, got drunk every night along with their abusive husbands. Often silence is a way of protecting from violence. This kind of silence is evil — because there is an alternative. The alternative is truth, but we have to help each other speak the truth.

Itchy ears open us to the Word of God, for good, against evil. They deserve our best attention.

The antidote to evil lies in our choice to go or not to go into the underworld. Whatever we repress comes back and is accessible and alive. Indeed, Persephone comes through her trial and emerges stronger and better. Inana is a much better queen because of her time in the underworld, and I do believe we will be better people if we let ourselves go through what we know, yet fear. Remember Saint Paul in another letter to the Ephesians, wrote: "Pray that I speak as fearlessly as I ought."

Walter Lippman, the great journalist, defines procrustean behavior as a determination to make the evidence fit the theory. Isn't that what we do when we deny evil in our lives? Don't we become procrustean, and chop off part of what we know on behalf of what we hoped would be true?

Instead, we might pray with Paul that we become as fearless as we ought to be. That we enter the underworld aware that it brings riches. That we go to the cross aware of resurrection. That we follow Jesus with the vigor that Paul tried to follow him. When we make this decision, this turn, it is like what happens to Persephone at the crossroads. There she meets Hecate who tells her she can turn toward life or death. She "unrepresses." She opens herself to truth. In Paul's words, she puts on the belt of truth and puts in her hands the sword of the Word of God. She itches for the truth of her soul and the truth of the gospel.

If you can't act on what you believe, you stop hearing it. Act on the cross. We are a people of the cross. We have an underworld of which we are not afraid. We go there to rise. We follow Jesus.

The EPA recently announced that the National Security Council misled the public on September 11 when it said that there were no or little adverse health effects for workers cleaning up the mess of the twin towers. Why? For "National Security Concerns." Fascinating. An assault on the facts and the truth, procrustean, because there was nothing we could do about it. Before we become too judgmental about our government, note that the personal security system is often hiding beneath something like personal security concerns. The government didn't do this without help.

Twelve thousand people died in Europe last summer from warming. Not just from a heat wave but also global warming. Fascinating. Breathe now, avoid the rush later. An assault on the facts and the truth, procrustean, because we think there is nothing we can do about it.

Utility plants have just been released from anti-pollution upgrades. Why? Because those of us who care about air think there is nothing we can do to save it.

Many candidates are going to be forced by a mean media to be "positive"! Anger and screaming will not be allowed.

Some intimate advice, in the words of Noelle Oxenhandler, helps. "As soon as we let our partner off the hook for the way we feel, he or she is able to respond in ways that we need." Ah. I was feeling particularly blue this week about something. Then I read a story about a gardener. She said that whenever someone came over to see her garden, she took him or her on a tour of it. They were always less enthusiastic than she thought they should be. I saw my funk in this disappointment. People seemed to like my garden less than they should or might. I was hurt but only by my own evil.

The gardener realized that to have a garden does not require others' enthusiasm for it so much as an enthusiasm of her own. Her enthusiasm about her garden is what mattered. Not the procrustean bed of what other people liked or didn't like.

In this little truth about enthusiasm for our own garden, we can see the whole big business about evil. We are not to let other people tell us what is true or valuable. If air is valuable, then air is valuable. If we get crucified trying to save it, so what? We have gone to the underworld and emerged with truth as our belt. We don't need to make believe any more. Because of the grace and power of Jesus Christ expressed in Paul's itchy ears and fearless and fearful speech, we can speak the truth we know, in vital ways. Other people don't have to agree with us. As long as we agree with God and practice that presence, all will be fine. The armor of Christ is not a bulletproof vest! It is a form of great vulnerability that yields even greater strength. Our ears begin to itch and we realize that we are all in this together, not just the good and not just the bad. All and each have fallen short of the glory of God. We know we are in the middle and the muddle of disappointing our maker quite frequently. We don't distort the evidence to make it fit our self-perceptions. We let our ears itch and find our way back to God.

Proper 25
Pentecost 23
Ordinary Time 30
2 Timothy 4:6-8, 16-18

Flying Coach To Nirvana

A good friend of mine, Bob Frederickson, is writing a travel book called *Flying Coach To Nirvana.* I stole his title for this sermon because I want to do simply what he took 400 pages to accomplish. His book is a collection of essays about visits he has made to Gabon in Africa, the West Indies, and on and on. He thinks of his trips as simple, populist, and personal; his point is that anyone can travel. Traveling is an art that doesn't take big bucks as much as it takes big dreams.

His tone is the same way I think about the lament in today's letter to Timothy. The writer says he has been poured, spent, done, and still God stuck with him. We travel through life and we are all poured and spent. Just think about how you feel when you return home after a long trip: you are both filled and empty. When the writer of Timothy talks about being poured and spent, we are in a similar situation. We have ended one piece of our journey and are on our way to another part. We have exited to enter. We know we have nothing left for one stage of our journey, and yet we know another one is about to begin.

We are both empty and full. Buddhists love to speak of pitchers as needing to empty before they can fill. When Timothy talks about how poured out he is on behalf of the gospel, it is because he knows something good is on its way to fill in.

The great Chinese writer describes good travelers as people who "have no fixed plans and are not intent on arriving." Timothy was *intent* on arriving: He gave it his all. He let all go on behalf of Christ. He wanted, and wants, all of us to get there, too.

Some of us just get afraid when we are spent. Others know that to empty is to fill. We know that life's trip to heaven and eternal life involves a lot of coach-class flying. We approach the airport "hoping for an upgrade" but know that we could get stuck in a middle seat. We are not always comfortable. Sometimes we are downright exhausted. But still we empty and risk emptying by an array of commitments that amaze all of us. We make commitments, we try to love each other — and love is always an emptying act — and find ourselves strangely filled along the way.

A *New Yorker* cartoon watches a family separate at a big, well-decorated-for-the-season shopping mall. The father says good-bye to the rest of the family, "Okay, we'll meet back here in about $500." Unfortunately, many of us think of the road to Nirvana in these ways. It is long, expensive, and not something you want to do in coach. You want to go to Nirvana first-class — and then you find yourself broke, in credit card debt, filled with an emptiness and an indebtedness that can be downright scary.

Today, I want to tell you that you can go first-class to Nirvana or the end of your lives by having first-class dreams. Dreams help us when we are empty and emptied — because they remind us that we will be filled. We live through what the Buddhists call the fertile void, unafraid of the way our energy is poured out along the way. We know this fertile void as a necessary act of living. We empty. We fill. We empty again and we fill again.

We can fly coach to Nirvana. It doesn't take big money to get all the way to Nirvana so much as it takes big dreams. If you can dream, you can travel to Nirvana. You don't have to guard your energy so much as protect your dreams. You can say a hefty and sincere "Yes," without fear of being devoured by the world.

I keep running into the phrase, "cocooning," to describe Americans in the wake of 9/11. We are cocooning, as a way to stay safe from others. We, and them, is the premier division of the world; our cocoon and their cocoon. We are so afraid that the "strangers" may take from us what we don't have, so afraid that we will empty and not fill again, that we avoid each other. This very avoidance keeps our wells from refilling again to overflow.

Writer William Miller in his new book, *The Mystery Of Courage*, understands the very way we live as a deepening cocoon. Miller argues that a new kind of courage is needed. It is the courage to come out of our cocoons. It is the courage to risk being emptied by a friendship or a relationship. It is willing to let disrupting things and people into our lives. People who take in foster children are crazy, right? People who teach Sunday school are spending more than they have, right? No. We empty to fill. By emptying we fill. We can have what we give away, not what we cling to, not the security which then imprisons us.

Consider a normal evening. We come home from work, frazzled and spent. We walk into our kitchens and are not surprised that our partner and kids are not home. We take what we like most out of our refrigerators and put it in the microwave and stare at the paper on the kitchen table. Let's say it is Wednesday and our favorite television show is on, followed by a game with the home team. Our pulse quickens a little. The show is good, our partner comes home, we exchange a few words, we find the game boring, and so we move to the den to do an overdue memo on our computer. First we check our email and the latest news, then we play a computer game and say good night to our spouse. Then we go to bed. Is this, asks Miller, an unChristian evening? We have not coveted our neighbor's spouse, stolen anything, or ordered anyone around. We enjoyed moments of a pleasant, well-fed evening, eating what we liked and watching what we liked and doing what we liked. Miller calls this a retreat to a cocoon of autonomy and excessive self-determination. He argues that indeed this is what most people around the world want also, a safe, quiet cocoon. It is the marvelous first-world freedom to do next-to-nothing while getting three squares a day.

I personally crave nothing more than a quiet evening at home. I want not to be at church meetings or community meetings or watching kids perform. I surely do not mean that there is something wrong with "down time." Instead, there is something right with going from good down time to good "on time." There is something important about engagement with each other and it must be protected. Miller concludes his book by arguing that we are still (and nonetheless) surrounded by the possibility of engagement, both inside and from these cocoons. Here on the shelf is the poetry we could read to each other. There in the corner are the flute and the guitar we could play together. Right next to the kitchen is an underused dining room table. Not far from our home are the playing fields where we could teach our sons and daughters tennis or rejoin a softball league with our beloved. Within easy reach are the museums where local painters show their work and the concert hall where the citizen's symphony plays. There are also meetings where activists struggle to find the patriotic way to peace.

Will we be spent by engagement? Absolutely. We will be refilled by engagement? Absolutely.

Many radicals argue that devotion to family and communal celebration seems a bland and retrograde goal. It is better than consumption and shopping but not exactly the stuff of bold designs and revolutionary politics. But, if I tell you big dreams are the fare you need to get to Nirvana, not big money, I ask you where are your big dreams? Of course, they include peace. They include rice for Afghani children. They want women at the table. And all these dreams may require something from you. Not $500 bills so much as ways to find the courage to cross the threshold from the television room to the dining room, from the home to the community. There are other thresholds to cross. We need to move out of the room of unencumbered self-determination, all personal freedom all the time into a world that has a lineage, a legacy, a past, and therefore a future. We may, and must, engage each other, by the grace and hope of God for human community.

Every act of engagement will be costly. It will raise the price of our coach tickets. We will experience some of these costs of community building as emptying. We will fear that we will run dry. The promise of God, however, is that Nirvana, heaven, wonderful, eternal life is at the end of the tunnel. We will be filled again. So stop worrying about being poured, spent, or "done." You ain't finished yet. Nor is God finished with you nor is your journey finished. God will stick with you, whether you spread yourself thinly or thickly in life. God will pour you out — and fill you up again and again. Amen.

Proper 26
Pentecost 24
Ordinary Time 31
2 Thessalonians 1:1-4, 11-12

Boasting And Praying For You

Recently, I was asked to give a prayer at the area chamber of commerce meeting, with these instructions: "Make it brief, and don't mention God too much."

How am I supposed to do that? I can't stop boasting about God. God's work is so impressive to me that snowflakes don't even describe it. Nor do hummingbird's nests. Nor fireworks. Nor breakfast. God is so grand to me that I have to boast.

What I most like to boast about is theology. Nature is second only to theology. Most of us understand how to boast about the sunrise or the ocean, the mountains or the fall leaves. We know about beauty and the incredible amazement in God's creation. We discover and rediscover awe by watching a bird outside of our windows. But fewer of us know how to enjoy our theology.

By theology I mean the invitation and commandment to enter every human difficulty with God's hope. I mean being dominated by God talk, God walk, God think, and God activity. I mean being held by God and no one else. I mean the sure victory of transforming love over suffering. We are to get up every day and participate in the new age, the new common wealth, the transformed time of God. We are to get our hands dirty. We are to live as though God's time is already here. We are to live joyfully with a sense of great possibility. We don't need to rely on force or violence. We may act but we need not force or control. We don't have to save the world so much as love it. We count on God's work to win out in the end. We are people who live as though God is here, active, and victorious.

What is theologically right about Jesus? About what dare we boast? Jesus suffered well. We will all suffer, but very few of us will suffer well. Jesus loved well. He forgave his enemies. There is a kind of jujitsu to Jesus. He throws the negative forces back at these enemies. Theology is the turn toward God-living that reverses the pattern of the world and releases the forces of God and good in every human encounter. Jujitsu is an ancient form of sumo wrestling from the sixteenth century. It relies on balance. The issue is not to dominate your opponent but to improve yourself. We do not operate through physical strength but the skillful use of balance. The element of surprise is key. In the jujitsu of Jesus, effective nonviolence exposes the limitations of adversaries so thoroughly that oppressors are caught off balance and stumble over their own shortcomings. We live by God's energy and power, not by the powers of the world.

How can we not boast about these wonderful agile moves that any of us can do? How can we not boast about the God who shows us the way? How dare we take a "Pilate" on this level of good news? Many of us will, when confronted with life's difficulties, get out the water and wash our hands. Instead, once we know the power and love of God expressed in theology, we find a time for spiritual fire, the shiver of grace. We become free not to be afraid of any great interpretive fight. We tell the chamber of commerce that we can't stop talking about God. We become aware of how important the arts of interpretation are. Theology bests nature as a matter for awe and wonder because it is the art of interpretation. It is knowing that God is in charge, while others are suggesting we downplay that news.

When we have "Yes" or "No" conversations and do what we are told, we lose, prematurely, the war of interpretation or theology. Theology is nothing more nor less than the knowing of God. Once we know God, we can't stop boasting about God.

Remember also that war starts in interpretation. Cruelty starts in interpretation. Your joy starts in interpretation. When we know God, we can't help but sing and speak and come out of our hiding places.

I think of a boy who loved to play hide-and-seek. He found the perfect hiding place. The only problem was that his perfect hiding place was so good that the other children couldn't find him! They went on to another game. He was alone and hidden. He cried and cried. Instead, he could have found himself and begun boasting. We are people who come out from hiding to boast. This is no time for people of faith to hide. It is very much time for us to speak.

I heard a rumor in jujitsu class. In that class we turn the force that is coming against us back on itself. There, with Jesus, we imagine the triumph that can come out of trouble, the good news in the bad news. There we see what the poet said about the broken vessel. It crashed on the floor, leaving itself wide open for something new.

Anyway, the rumor I heard was about the Mel Gibson Christian foundation. Instead of enriching Hollywood, the great movie, *The Passion Of The Christ*, caught the jujitsu of theology and enriched others. The foundation helped people who were hurt by violence in the name of Christ. I heard that the foundation gave away all the profits that the movie made. And then I heard everyone saying, "This is what it is to know Jesus in the power of the transformed now."

If God had made the movie about Jesus, and God did, all the money would have been given away, just as all of Jesus' power was given away to the world. This is the kind of God about whom we may dare boast. In fact, how dare we not boast?

Now no one really likes a boaster or even a booster. We find such people self-serving and not really good vehicles for carrying the gospel. When we boast, we need to find a way to boast with humility about ourselves and pride in our God. The litmus test, the way we know whether we are boasting as people of faith or as people of pride, is whether we personally gain or not. Like the Mel Gibson Christian foundation, the best proof of the gospel is when it is given away. It is spread around. It is not about us. It is about God. We relinquish and release when we boast. We point, like a good steeple, to the heavens, not to our position or résumé on earth. Indeed who we are and what we have as a reputation is important in the service of God.

Getting invited to the chamber of commerce meeting to speak is important — it matters. It matters that we prepare well and speak well and that we have good pointer fingers in our PowerPoint presentations. What matters more, though, is the ledger at the end of the day. Does the ledger show God with more points, more money, more adherents? Or is it we who grow in these ways? Both can happen simultaneously, but boasting about God is boasting about God. It is not sneaky self-promotion. There is a difference.

That's why the jujitsu is so important. It is important to be agile in the service of the gospel. It is important to know how to turn the light on the right subject at the right time. Surely we must practice our wrestling. We must get good and deft at it. We must train. Then we must wrestle with the constant temptation to have the light shining on ourselves. When the light comes toward us, it is our job to reflect it back, twice the size, to the God who made us good wrestlers in the first place.

Proper 27
Pentecost 25
Ordinary Time 32
2 Thessalonians 2:1-5, 13-17

Do Not Be Quickly Shaken

Several years ago, Lyle Schaller made the observation that ministry, once a "high status, low stress" vocation was now just the opposite: "high stress and low status." Why? Clergy have a double calling, both to secure and to shake people up. They need to be prophetic and pastoral at the same time. Most people want ministers to stabilize their lives, to keep them from being shaken. The goal many parishioners come to church to achieve is stability. They don't want to be shaken. They want to be secured. Unfortunately, ministers also shake people up.

Saint Paul enters this remarkably interesting double bind to tell us that we are not to be easily or quickly shaken. In other words, we are to have a wild equilibrium in the middle of great disequilibria. We are to be peaceful in the midst of conflict. We are "all shook up" for Jesus. Christians are wildly happy, luxuriously free, and always in trouble, according to one old folk saying.

"Ministers appear dangerous to people," observes social critic, David Heifetz, "When you question their values, beliefs, and habits of a lifetime, you place yourself on the line. You tell people what they *need* to hear, rather than what they *want* to hear. Although you may see with clarity and passion a promising future of progress and gain, people will see with equal passion the losses you ask them to sustain." We must learn to be stable in destabilization. We must learn to be not shaken when we are all shook up. We want God to both stabilize us and challenge us. We don't want to put God in the cage we call our own security — nor can we withstand too much shaking. The task of the minister is to secure people for danger, to stabilize people for spiritual adventure, and to do both at the same time.

One of the things I learned in seminary was to *never* act surprised. If someone tells you that he is sleeping with his daughter, say, "Tell me more." Don't say, "You are doing what?" The person who makes such a confession is trying to trust you. You will not be trusted if you freak out.

Likewise, ministers can't be trusted if they are only telling people what they want to hear. If a person makes you uncomfortable — and still seems to love you — you have begun to understand what the letter to Timothy is talking about. We are all shook up, and we are not shaken. It is a "both/and." As clergy and congregations, we are called to the daily resistance of death. Death is the great passivity. Death is the great harmony. Death is the time when we have no more stress and no more unanswered questions. Life is the great activity. Life is the great chaos of harmony and disharmony weaving in and out of each other. Life is a time of stress. By the gospel, we are secured for, and from, stress.

Most of us live under the commandment to get bigger and better. All this rushing for more shakes us up. There is inevitable tension in our ministries and beyond. The way we handle that tension is what makes or breaks us. When we are glad for the arrival of conflict, we show that we know how to be "not quickly shaken." We expect conflict. We know its cross-yielding capacities. We welcome conflict and stress. We do not whore after stability. It is a false God for ministers, congregations, and in life.

I took my new dog on a walk. He had come to us in Massachusetts from Miami and had never seen snow, never seen stairs, and never felt cold. In each experience, he resisted, as in sitting at the bottom of the stairs and refusing to climb, in first feeling the snow on his feet and trying to jump up in the air, in putting a dumb look on his face when he climbed out of the airplane carrier in the north after leaving the tropics only three hours earlier. What impressed me was that he was only afraid once. After he managed each cold and fear, he went on. He didn't repeat the fears over and over. He just had to do them once. I have declared him brilliant, another companion on the road to glory, where we don't have time for repeat fears of the cold. He reminds me of materially poor people whose inner spirit lets them sing in refugee camps at night. There they are free of the poverty of the rich; many of whom have forgotten how to sing. He reminds me of people who learn how to be scared and still be happy. He reminds me of people who tolerate great difficulties with serenity and gladness. He just got badly shaken up once.

Don't be afraid if every now and then you get shaken up. Life does that to people. Do be afraid if your goal in life becomes not to ever be shaken up. You will climb no stairs. You will become afraid of love. You will consent to fear. When we are not "quickly shaken," we hitch our wagons to a higher star than stability. We hitch it to peace, the one that passes all understanding.

Many lay people have similar professions to that of the securing and dangerous ministry. Teachers have to help students let go of earlier securities in order to prepare for larger ones. We have to leave kindergarten to go to first grade — and each step is dangerous. Each new learning replaces some previous learning. College professors know exactly what it is to teach critical theory and biblical literature: Students who come from strong church backgrounds often get mightily scared at the application of critical theory to sacred texts.

Physical trainers have similar issues. They must use enough weight in weight training that it hurts so that the muscles can grow. In fact, trainers will assure you that the more you hurt after a training, the stronger you are becoming. There is a direct relationship between stress and security in physical training.

Financiers who do well place increasingly larger bets on increasingly large amounts of money. They do so in order to reap larger gains and to secure themselves from a future of constant betting. Letting go of security creates adventure, which then recreates new levels of security — which must be reinvested or "re-bet."

Knowing these things about the strong relationship between stress and security, we are able to better understand the words to Timothy about not being too easily shaken. We may dare to be glad at the arrival of conflict because we know it is going to help us as much as stress us. We know how growth happens. It happens by the grace of stress, managed by the stability of hope and faith.

Not only may we be glad at the arrival of conflict, we can also keep a smile on our face when we are in difficult situations. Clergy are advised to have a non-anxious presence when faced with great human difficulty. We are all advised to have an inner calm when faced with outer storms. It, more than anything else, will help us. Inner calm is our insurance policy in times of trouble. Inner calm comes from faith — and it also comes from understanding that being shaken is not the end of the world.

We may be people who are not quickly shaken if we keep ourselves free from conflict, free from fear, and continue living in grace. Inner calm is not only when the tension in our neck subsides; it is also the presence and power of the peace of God. It is a peace which passes understanding. We know we should be scared, but we are not. Whether the issue is personal unemployment or global terrorism, depression or loneliness, we are people who are unshaken. We may be shook, but we are unshaken. We live at a deeper level, in a place even we don't always understand. It is the place of God in us. It is the place of peace in us. It is belly deep and it is a remarkable gift from a remarkable God.

Weary In Well Doing

What makes people weary is conflict. We are torn apart, split in two, we are challenged at our core in large and small ways all day long. We say wryly, "No good deed goes unpunished," running right into the conflict of getting weary in well doing.

Biologists tell us we have two choices in most situations: We can fight or take flight or tend and befriend. The fight and flight response is most often articulated in funny hand motions — where we both beckon the person close and push them away at the same time. The animal part of most humans knows exactly what this means. We are standing at a party with a beverage in our hand — we are smiling, but inside we are wishing we could run away. Human contact can be quite scary! Because it is also so wonderful, none of us, including the writer of the book of Thessalonians, is surprised that there is conflict around contact.

The other biological response, being given more evolutionary attention now, is to tend and befriend. Biologists tell us that this response to nurture, care, lick, cuddle, and touch is also a natural one. We who have been hurt by conflict also know about its healing power. We know what it means to be touched on the shoulder and allowed back into the meeting our anger just removed us from. We know what it is like to care so much for someone or something that we can't bear its hurt. We stand close to the one who is hurt. We tend and befriend. We tend and befriend in very small ways — the handwritten note, the flowers or jar of jelly, the invite to our son's soccer game. We get close after conflict — as well as fighting and flighting. When we get close again, after conflict, weariness ends. Joy sometimes begins.

The epistle advocates a style of conflict management that is more than biological. It is fundamentally spiritual. It is the strategy of humility. Humility is not so much a strategy as a bent, not even so much a bent as a posture, not even so much a posture as a habit. Christians try to be humble people. Even when someone we love is hurt, we maintain humility. Even when we are scared to death, we maintain humility. This spiritual habit will take us a long way toward positive conflict preparation and resolution.

Many ecologists are teaching us how to think small again. It is a way we have lost. They say that the main reversal in our thinking is to understand just how beautiful small is. Humble is one aspect of small as beautiful. Small interventions make us less weary than grandiose ones. Humility does not tire in the way that pride does.

Many of us find the world trivializing and demeaning. We have tried really hard and we have still been hurt by life. We may act like we know what to do next but we really don't. We may put one foot in front of the other but not know why or how. We all but pant for great direction and guidance.

Many say, "I'm feeling pretty burned out." More truth could be said by those who have never been lit. What Thessalonians describes is the experience of being lit. Of receiving the great light and knowing how to follow it to paths of meaning and purpose instead of life as a real game of trivial pursuits.

How would we look and be different if we refused weariness in well doing? We would be free of worry and fear. We would have no time for despair. We would avoid the gossipy games of putting others down so that we could feel momentarily lifted up. We would not need such crutches. We would get out of bed in the morning eager to love someone and touch something of purpose and value. We would not go to bed at night until we had participated in God's plan to lift up the poor and troubled, blind and lame. We would not say, "I don't know how to help" so much as "How can I help?"

We may need practice. We may have just the flickering of light within us and on our path. We may need help. We may need to find out whether we are spiritually depressed. We may need to get over something that is taking up all the space, like a virus, on our hard drive. We may need to rest. We may be too tired to be lit. We may need to just say out loud, "I am weary."

The destination is what matters. It is the panting, the urgency, the truly wanting to be spiritually alive and awake that matters. If we can't practice, and if we don't want to walk around in the dark anymore, perhaps what we need to do is work on our sense of urgency. Like a great ball player, we may have to learn to want to win the game again. We may have to yield the shields that protect us from hope — and hope again. Let them go! Being lit is magnificent. It is the antidote to weariness.

Getting beyond weariness in well doing is often a matter of catching the right bug and eliminating the wrong ones. At both the conscious and the unconscious level, these days, many of us are worried about contagion. The threat of biological and chemical warfare remains in our minds if not also on our globe. The threat of the SARS virus remains alive. (One editor friend of mine hates the word we have given this virus — "Severe" and "Acute": both don't need to be in the same sentence.) We are newly aware that one small piece of foam probably took down a mighty space ship. Small, invisible things are more than carrying their weight. It is almost as if we have all become homeopaths — that version of medicine that inoculates with the smallest of substances in order to produce the largest of healing.

Indeed, there are many negative forms of contagion. You can "catch something" and suffer with it for weeks. Simultaneously there are positive forms of contagion, like in homeopathic medicine or in being around contagious people or in understanding just how this gospel of ours works.

Jesus inoculates the world with his suffering and his love — and next thing we know we, too, are contagious with hope. We are immune from fear. We are able to spread a love that we didn't know we had. We are wise in ways we did not think were possible. We are the ones who sense that life is sweet.

The small has power both positive and negative. If a piece of foam can bring down a plane, a piece of love can lift it up again.

361

How do we appear when we are no longer weary? When others are sour, we are sweet. When others are complaining, we are probing for the positive solutions to whatever mess we are in. When others are afraid and mongering fear, we find ways to comfort and calm. When life is too large for us and questions too complex, we stay still. We are not ones who think everything has to be answered now or done today or finished in our lifetime. We know how to wait. We have patience. While we are waiting, we know the joy of a garden walk, a bird at the feeder, and a good piece of chocolate cake. We are waiting for the day when all people have good cake, sweet lives, and great joy. We know it is coming — and that's why we aren't afraid. We know God is in charge — and that sweetness is what God has in mind for all.

Also, we know that we are not alone. Imagine God trusting the salvation of the world to a dozen disciples. Imagine the confidence that was placed in something so very small. Clearly, the strategy is a kind of chemical, not physical, warfare. It is an inoculation. It is a contagion. It counts on Jesus being infected by God and Jesus infecting others and those others infecting others. And guess what? It worked. There was no public relations budget — no forcing of the issue by armies or advertising. One believed, then another believed, and then a third. Today we find Christianity more than a vibrant world religion, just now growing with vigor in Africa and Asia and South America that makes the northern continents look small. Positive contagion is the gospel strategy God used to save the world.

Many people would like to tell you that Christianity is a great world religion that fell into the wrong hands. I beg to differ. Indeed, Christianity is a great world religion. And indeed, some of its spirit did fall into the wrong hands. People have hit each other over the head with Jesus on more than one occasion. I remain consoled that so much of its spirit is in your hands and in the hands of people as ordinary as gardeners and fishermen and single women without a portfolio. That spirit is as strong as any virus — and it will infect the world, if not sooner then later. The writer of Thessalonians was clearly one of the carriers of the gospel. Today, remarkably, we are reading his tale.

What does it mean to be inoculated by faith? It means that we trust the small. We become like gardeners who know that the smallest of seeds make the grandest of flowers. I think of the great lupine seeds, which are so small you have to scatter them with a mix of sand in your hand. Lupines easily can be a foot tall with an inlay of flowers in several colors that defies the tiling on the great temples in Morocco. We become like a bit of yogurt culture, which can firm up a whole pot of warm milk. Of course, there are negative viruses as well. I think of the way we used to make vinegar, under the sink in a glass jar. The substance used is "mother of vinegar" and I am sure it has a spiritual, as well as a physical, meaning.

Can you remember how that works? A cloud of chemicals is taken from vinegar gone old. It is placed in a combination of water or apple juice or cider or wine, left over from the table after the guests have all gone. As these leftovers become available, we put them in the hidden jar. It all becomes vinegar in contact with the mother.

Congregations and families can be infected that way, too. The smallest amount of vinegar, if allowed to contaminate the sweet, can sour the whole barrel. The folk saying is absolutely right: One bad apple can spoil the bunch. Likewise, infection can be positive. One good apple can improve the whole bunch. My point is that God uses small powerful virus-like seeds to get Jesus launched into the world. We become inoculated positively, with faith and hope and love by Jesus' entry into the world. From there, we become contagious — and spread the news. We try to stop the vinegar — and start the wine.

Some of us try to inoculate a whole confirmation class for their confirmation of their baptism. We have so little time to tell them the whole Christian story, but we can't worry about curriculum overload so much as worry about what they see when they come to church. You are their main teachers.

This elevation of the small to the powerful is a very hard lesson for people raised in the bigger-is-better world. I watched two men at the hospital the other day. They knew each other only slightly. One said, "I just had three parts of my heart done." The other said, "That's nothing, I had five." I thought, "Oh, boy. Isn't it great just to have one part done, if it is blocking blood to the heart? Why is it better to have more?" But I know that our world is inoculated with the large — and I know how lethal that largeness is. Bigger says it's better, but it's not. The mightiest nation in the world is at war with several of the smallest, right now.

Weariness in well doing comes from trying to do too much, too big. Forget that. Stick with the small interventions.

Another reversal in our thinking is that of prevention. Old ways of thinking have to do with programmatic moppings up of what has gone wrong. I think of the department of children and family services — or of most medicine. New ways of thinking have to do with creating the bodies and world and children that we want *now*. One is preventive and long term and focuses on wellness; the other is palliative and short term and focuses on sickness. The very strategy that God uses in the resurrection of Jesus is a preventive, long-term, wellness-focused strategy. It inoculates the world with hope.

Good leadership understands this strategy very well. Good leadership makes people's strengths effective and their weaknesses irrelevant. We create teams that balance each other's strengths. If some member of our team or family is detail crazed and fussy, and another is so large pictured that she never met a detail she understood, that is a good team. We just have to render their strengths effective and their weaknesses irrelevant. We can inoculate each other with this kind of thinking as easily as we can inoculate with the old ways. We must be perfect or we have to be gotten off of the team or out of the family. We must be fixed and improved. Yech! Who wants to be fixed or improved? Indeed who can be fixed and improved? Most of us have fairly permanent warts to which we are very attached. In God's world, these warts are accepted.

Humility joins God in understanding the wart part — and then ignoring it. We may have warts. We may have made messes in conflicts. We may be exhausted and not just in well doing but also in wrong doing. We are not perfect. Instead we are lifted up by God who sees it all, knows it all, and loves us all.

Falling Short
(Of The Glory Of God)

Sam Goldwyn, the great picture maker, said of one of his movies, "I don't care if the picture makes money. I just want every man, woman, and child in America to see it."

Goldwyn has the same relationship to small and large, short and tall, that many of us have. We want both. We don't want the money — we just want what goes with the money, which is the freedom. We don't want to win the argument; we just don't want to lose it, either. We don't want the kids to be just like us, to be clones of their parents, but we don't want the apple to fall too far from the tree either. As long as everybody sees *our* picture, we don't need the money, either.

Both Jesus and the writer of Romans join us on the trapeze that suspends us over matters of scale, size, large, and small. Paul knows he has fallen short. He knows we have all fallen short. How can I stand tall in the gospel when my desk is littered with contradictory demands? When several different supervisors are asking me for several different things simultaneously? When the pink slips come out in my business, how do I stay cheery if I am a survivor? With whom do I identify, the boss or the remaining custodian? How can I sing after the terrorist bombings and before the sounds of war fill my living room? How can we sing the Lord's song in a strange land? How can we keep from falling short? There is too much to do and too little time in which to do it.

Jesus offers the mustard seed as a way through the quagmire of conflicting demands and shortness. He says that a little faith goes a long way. He actually seems to be telling the disciples that they don't need a lot of faith so much as they need a little faith. Let the congregation say, "*Phew!*" I think that is spelled P-H-E-W. Phew.

Instead of faith being the same kind of matter that most things are — heroic action, gobs of courage, trusting the untrustworthy, long meetings, thousands of phone calls, renegotiated positions on top of renegotiated positions, locating the lost emails that renegotiated the renegotiated positions ... instead of faith being that kind of complexity, it is a simplicity. It is inching toward the positive, not leaping toward the positive. It is leaning toward hope, rather than dwelling in hope. It is the assumption that God is in charge, not the certainty that God is in charge. Faith is inching, leaning, assuming, and hoping ... it is looking out the window toward the future more than it is staring fixed at the tangles of the present. It is grass waving toward God in clear wind, on that clear day when you can see forever. It is not a swamp where the grasses are stamped down on top of each other, tortuously tangled. Faith is a clearing in a great woods. Faith is small. If you have faith like a mustard seed, Jesus says that you can move mountains. We are all spiritual midgets. We are all small. We are all not enough. But still, if we have the faith that Paul wants for the Romans, we can move mountains.

This matter of getting small and large right reminds me of two things that comedian Dave Barry said. One is "No matter what happens, somebody will find a way to take it too seriously." Just because something has happened in our lives, it can't be taken too seriously — something impossible to even account, as accountants look for a place to put three trillion dollars of loss on a ledger that can't be found — just because a big thing has happened doesn't mean that all the rest of the folderol is equally big. This is no time to sweat the small stuff. Although my perception is that more and more people seem to be trying, this is not a time to sweat the small stuff. All have sinned and fallen into small stuff.

Barry also said, "When trouble arises and things look bad, there is always one individual who perceives a solution and is willing to take command. Very often, that individual is crazy." The Nigerians have a word for times like these, which is *wazu-wazu*, things gone nuts and layered, scattered and messed up, the way a house looks after a large dinner party or weekend of guests. It is a good word, meaning the swampy tangle of our strange land, where it is pretty hard to sing the Lord's song. Thus we pick up one piece of the house at a time, room by room, slowly.

We sing a short song, not the big song of victory over our enemies, but a simple song. We may even hum, instead of sing. Albert Camus, the French existentialist, won the Nobel Prize for Literature in 1957. He said, "If human beings cannot always make history have a meaning, they can always act so that their own lives have one." He sounds a lot like Haw in *Who Moved My Cheese?* Haw found simple steps forward; he didn't let fear govern him. Those who let fear silence their song end up lost — not so much by the circumstances of their time as by their own fear of those circumstances. Oddly, it is not the unaccountable horror that silences our song so much as the accountable fear that we develop in response to it. When we think we are short, we behave short. We short out. Faith allows us to opt in, small as we are.

Jesus' antidote to fear is faith. Faith that is small, not large. If you can't find a big answer to the big question raised by 9/11 — "Why do they hate us so much?" — try a small one. Unpack they: "Who is *they?*" Unpack us: "Who is us?" Don't let big questions govern. Make it your size. Why do some hate some so much? There is even a little answer to that question. It is that we don't know their names and they have to know ours. They have to know our currency and we don't even know how to pronounce theirs.

Consider more hints of the power of the small over the large. A great nation finds itself at war with a small nation. It sends food to that nation's borders; it feeds the refugees. It helps the innocent. This small act makes the nation great in a way that not sending the food would only make it small. We have reason to love our country every week: It is a generous place with generous people.

Smaller pictures follow. A student got to the end of his final exam in college and found this question on the test, "What is the first name of the woman who cleans the classroom?" With that question, to which he did not know the answer, his commencement began. There is a small hint to these big times there: Those who were already small will be even more threatened than those who were not.

Another picture. Long ago, a ten-year-old boy entered a hotel coffee shop and sat at a table. "How much is an ice cream sundae?" he asked. "Fifty cents," replied the waitress. The boy studied his change. "How much is a bowl of plain ice cream?" "Thirty five cents." He got the plain ice cream and left a fifteen cent tip, and the waitress never forgot the kid. He did the right thing, the small thing. Many of us could be reallocating our own budgets in this way right now. We can learn from the small.

A final picture is one I also wish every man, woman, and child in America would see. A boy gave his sister a much-needed blood transfusion. When the sister was restored to health, the boy summoned the doctor and asked, "Will I start to die right away?" He thought his gift was much larger than it was. He, too, confused the large with the small.

On Reformation Day it is very important to notice that there are a lot of magnificent small churches all across the world. These small churches have fallen no more "short" than large ones. *All* is the key word for Paul. All do small pieces of the gospel well, and all, even the big guys, fall short. When the Reformation began in Europe, it began as a seed of religious freedom. It began small. It probably never assumed it would be large. Each and every large historical movement has followed this seed-like pattern. Like children, great ideas are short and small before they are large and tall. In a local ministry, it can't matter how many souls are calmed. It can only matter that one or two find God. God is not an accountant. We don't have to do more to be loved more by God. Reformed churches continue to plant small seeds that guard religious freedom. They don't plant large trees so much as small seeds.

Sometimes little sacrifices can go a long way. They can show more love than we even need to deliver. They can turn the tide of history in a way that the large cannot. Trust the small. Trust the first step more than any other step. Trust the seed. Trust the short. The rest will follow.

All Saints
Ephesians 1:11-23

Whose Inheritance Is It?

The Holy Spirit gives us our inheritance. It does not come from our parents or grandparents, our nation or our race. Our inheritance is a gift from God. We have it as a dominion and domination. Domination — when we get first things absolutely first — is not a bad thing! Once we know the source of our inheritance, no other gods can rule us. Saints are the people who know this. Saints know who gave them what they have — and they don't imagine that they are like the used car dealer who, having inherited the car dealership from his father, declares himself a self-made man. Saints are God-made men and women, not self-made men and women. In fact, that "self-made" theory is one of the most dangerous of all. It broaches a dangerous idolatry that somehow creation didn't happen in us, just in others.

Surely we do make parts of ourselves. Life is what we "make" of it — and the Creator God, living now in us as Holy Spirit made this very clear. We were created and then left to make something of ourselves. We were given all the raw material and set free to be co-creators with a divine God. Had God wanted to have us as puppets, God would have "over made" us. Instead God "under made" us, leaving the finishing work to us. It is like we are a toy that comes in a large box at Christmas: some assembly is required.

While acknowledging the debt we owe to our Creator God, and giving it the nuance of our personal assembly, our personal "get up and go," we then return to the extraordinary dependency we have on God. Some of us get good chemistry in our brains; others get a propensity for depression. Some of us get good genes;

369

others get early cancer. There are degrees and layers of awesome chance in the very physical make up that we have. Each is created and developed, made and given, determined and wildly open and free.

There is an old saying that every oak tree started out as a couple of nuts that stood their ground. Often we interpret a quote like this as saying that we make ourselves by our decisions. It could be that the real trick to being human — much less being a saint — is that we stand in our created ground and light. We know God makes us. We know that it is God who has made us and not we ourselves. Saints align themselves as spiritual inheritors: we know of whom and who makes us. Does that imply that we can all be saints? Indeed it does. We can all be people who know to whom they belong.

Similarly, there is an old saying, "The apple never falls far from the tree." Many have said this to me about my children, intending it to be a compliment. I know too many really fine parents whose kids turned up far from the tree, let's say on drugs, to accept the compliment. What I know is there is some awesome chance and even more amazing grace at the heart of parenting. We do not make our children, either. They participate with us and with God as gifts of grace. They do require some assembly. We can rejoice in trees and apples, particularly if they don't fall from the tree. But taking credit is a crime. We do not take credit for what God has wrought by grace. In fact, the surest way to un-saint or de-saint or non-saint ourselves is to start taking credit for the gifts that God has given us by the grace of the Holy Spirit.

Saints are different from normal people in that they understand this. By the power of the Holy Spirit, they remember God's creation in each moment. They stay alive to it.

We will not always be on the right path. A truly happy person is one who can enjoy the scenery on a detour. We will forget the source of our inheritance and take wrong turns. What the Holy Spirit gives to saints is like a map. We are shown the way to be people who know who they are. One of the great markers of our being on the right path is that we live more by grace than boasting. When the boasting comes out, watch out. You are probably on the detour. Enjoy the scenery, understand that you can be forgiven, don't get upset, but do get back on the right road.

Saints are not just known by their humility and thanksgiving and inheritance. They are also known for not being lukewarm. This message is found throughout scripture. A heart that is on fire, even if it bewilders us at times, is equipped to serve. God freely chooses his saints from among the great sinners, but never from among those who are lukewarm — from those who do not risk anything. Indeed, some of the greatest saints are people who know the scenery on the detours: They know they have spent a lot of time on the wrong path and are thrilled to have a chance to get back on the straight and wide, which some erroneously call the narrow path. I think of people who have become regulars at Alcoholics Anonymous, or people who have served time in jail. These people know what it means to be lost — and are excited about what it means to be found.

Excitement about God may be something that you have given up on. You may think you are too old for it or too bruised for it or too used up for it. You may think, therefore, that you cannot be a saint. You can. Saints have seasons, too, just like vines. In our lives, we must learn that we cannot always live in the springtime of the rising new sap, or the summer of growth and formation; we cannot always live in the autumn of rich fruit bearing, or in the winter of rest and seeming deadness. Each of these seasons has its place, and all are interdependent and necessary. God's inheritance is for young and old alike, rich and poor alike, strong and weak alike, gifted and ordinary alike. No matter who we are, we can be saints by the simple act of recognizing God as the source of our power and life. We trust the sap of vitality and purpose when we get off our path and purpose — and then we rise again from the dead. Indeed, as William Stringfellow once said, life is all about conquering death and deadness every day. We are to resist death, particularly the death of the Spirit, on behalf of life.

People who refuse the art of sainthood are handicapped. The physical eye easily spots physical deformity and blemishes in others and in oneself. It is not so easy for the eye of the spirit to spot a spiritual dwarf, hunchback, or cripple. Yes, it is always easier to

371

see these spiritual deformities in others than in oneself. The spiritual eye knows how to be grateful for what God has given and avoids both detours and handicaps. The spiritual eye knows that when we are not in a state of grace and gratitude, that we are probably off the path and letting our handicap overcome us.

Such spiritual X-ray work is sometimes called the "naked truth," or the "unvarnished truth." In literature and art it is called realism, but to spot ingratitude in one's would-be saintly self is not only difficult but also painful, and no one wants to take the descending path to that naked, unvarnished truth, with all its unacceptable humiliations. It is much more comfortable to stay on the level of the plain and ordinary, to go on being just plain and ordinary. Plain and ordinary people are out to get something. They forget that they already have something. We all have spiritual money in the bank. We have a divine inheritance. We don't talk about the unsaintly marks of the ungrateful, but all of us have them from time to time. We have private jealousies, resentments, fantasies, and greeds. We want something that we already have!

The great Sojourner Truth, who is a saint by most people's standards, when told that she was less than a mosquito, responded, "But I sure can make you itch." She knew her inheritance. She knew to whom she belonged. Nobody was going to make her feel small.

We need to be very careful to assure that our gratitude for our inheritance is authentic. Some of us fake gratitude and live in an underground world where we are actually deeply greedy for more. Dietrich Bonhoeffer often spoke of cheap grace as meaning grace at bargain-basement prices, cut-rate forgiveness, cut-rate comfort, and cut-rate sacraments. He also spoke of grace as the church's inexhaustible pantry, from which it is doled out by careless hands without hesitation or limit. It is grace without a price, without costs. Costly grace is the gospel that must be sought again and again, the gift, which has to be asked for, the door at which we must knock. It is costly because it calls to discipleship; it is grace, because it calls us to follow Jesus Christ. It is costly, because it costs people their lives; it is grace, because it thereby makes them live. It is costly because we have to give up the fantasy that we are self-made people.

It is costly ... above all, because it was costly to God. "We were bought with a price" (1 Corinthians 6:20). Nothing can be cheap to us, which is costly to God.

If you find yourself oddly judged by the absence of gratitude for your inheritance in your life, find a way to slow down and remember who you are. We must develop a "path of more resistance" to the shouts from culture that tell us we need more, from the whispers from culture that say we are nobodies and must become better and more. The beginning place for sainthood is the knowledge that we are the people to whom God has given a great inheritance. When we start there, we have nowhere else we must go.

I like to think as a gardener when it comes to this question of being made by God or owing success to self. There is little risk in becoming overly proud of one's garden, because gardening, by its very nature, is humbling. It has a way of keeping you on your knees. A similar posture is due the God who grows humanity. We are best served by using our knees when it comes to our inheritance.

Like Cole Porter's famous dictum that every one of his songs should have a "lemon line," so that the other lines look better, saints are advised to double their portions of humility. Catholics whose priests have "gone bad" can take heart: the sacraments withstand the sinner. Protestants whose preachers are boring can take heart: The Word of God survives most clergy. Saints are often confused with clergy, and this is a significant mistake. Clergy are not any better than anyone else — they can be, by understanding by whom they are made and whose word they carry.

When we ping the saint for the saint's crystal, when we try to discern if "this" is the Holy Spirit speaking, we often travel through the following matters. We remember our baptism — we have a visit from our humility — we acknowledge our lemon side — we give thanks to God that we might be able to be a saint and not be either holy, perfect, or superior to others. The shiver of grace in the saint begins right here: God might use us! We know this use may be a mistake, that God may have placed a bet on the wrong horse. Many clergy and many saints shiver. We shiver — and then break the bread and pour the wine. Like Moses, we see the trace of God in our life. We allow that shimmering thread of an experience, whatever it is, to carry us to altars and beyond. We dedicate our fragile vessel to the Word and sacrament of God. We carry the Word. We spill the wine. We break the bread. We lead the church, the body of Christ, as part of the body with special responsibilities, whether we are lay or clergy, saints or people on a long detour. Still we try to get back to the main road, for our main chance.

When we shiver as saints with grace and thanksgiving for our inheritance, everything changes. We are no longer people who hold up their own weight. We float with the Spirit. Steven Wright, the famous physicist, swears he woke up one morning and "all of my stuff had been stolen and replaced by exact duplicates." When we tip toward sainthood, when we receive our inheritance, we experience this kind of change. Not only do we change, everything around us changes!

The appreciation deficit is gone. The gratitude famine is gone. The empty cup is gone. We fill up and spill over like an endless waterfall of appreciation for what God has done to and through us. Amen.

When Christ Is King ...

Many people don't like the theological language of Christ as king. They say it is too old-fashioned: democracies don't have kings. They say it is too masculine: we all believe in gender equality. What they don't say is what it means. When we declare that Christ is king, we mean that Christ is the most important matter, the one with the most power for us, personally. On Christ the King Sunday this is a great day to see what this means — whether we like the language of king or not.

When we know that Christ is king, we live by grace and not by law. We live by grace and not by the power of our own works. We live what author, Amy Tan, calls "The Opposite of Fate." It is grace. It is engagement. It is, for better or worse, our western religion's activism at work. In contrast to the acceptance of fate and chance and what the road offers to us, there is an activism in Christianity. We live with a full house in our hand. We make our luck. We act with mercy — and make a difference in the road. We are led forth by Christ and live so as to imitate him. In that imitation is our power, our core, our urgency, our life.

Living by Christ means mobilizing mercy. We become merciful toward our own stupidity. We experience grace. We become merciful toward those who rob us, like the Good Samaritan did. We mobilize mercy by giving more than we have — and we find that what returns is double the payment. Over and over we hear people say, when we thank them for extraordinary acts, "I received so much more than I gave." Christ showed us the way to multiply by subtraction: We follow that lead.

I often think of life as one long potluck supper; you never know who is coming or what they are bringing. The feast survives in this very uncertainty. When we try to get to the "dim sum of all things" or to understand why things happen the way they do, we are always better bringing our best dish to the feast, in the hope that our surplus will secure the generations. When mercy is mobilized, personal responsibility — a truly wonderful thing — engages a community. When both social and personal responsibility is in full-tilt conversation with fate, truly great nations and people emerge. When we follow Jesus as king, we maximize our personal responsibility for the world by mobilizing mercy and compassion. We also maximize the strength of communities so that we are not alone.

Those who know Christ is king mobilize mercy and compassion. We are eager for personal and communal responsibility. We know we have the help we need to love the way we want to love. We are *cored* to Christ.

I saw a bumper sticker on a truck once that read, "If you were on trial for being a Christian, would there be enough evidence to convict?" This is a very good question. How do we know that our core is attached to Christ? By how much mercy is in motion around us. By how many enemies are loved. By how many risks we are taking. That's how.

We take these risks because Christ holds us in an "inner net." We are people who know we are not alone, who know that Jesus is with us. We take risks as secure and secured people. We do things that we really can't do on our own, like be good to those who hurt us. We do it because Christ is king, not because we are great or strong people. We are wildly secure, even when the trouble is our own.

Jim Crawford, the senior pastor at Old South Church in Boston for three decades, was visiting a man in the hospital. The man was very angry that he had cancer and was not being healed of it. Very angry. "Why me?" he kept asking. Crawford is said to have responded to the man, "Why not you?" There is a turn in the process of accepting Christ. We tip. Some combination of the sacred and the ordinary congeals into a certainty. This coalescence, this shiver, is like a mountaintop experience even though we may have it over our morning coffee. In other words, don't feel that you need to have "lights, camera, action" to receive the power of Christ. They may come, but then again, they may not.

People who have Christ as their king mobilize mercy. We take risks, we have a magnificent security, and we also have a joyful vibrancy. Nothing can really shake us up. We live on the creative and holy edge on which Jesus lived. Being a Christian is not a leisure-time activity but a high-adventure pursuit. Christians have accepted the challenge. Each day is brimming with possibilities, and these people want to seize those possibilities. They are excited about more opportunities to put more mercy into more motion. They revel in the challenge. Yet, along with this excitement is a quiet peace, a trust that God walks with them. That is the security.

Christians are risk takers — self-starters — and they live George Bernard Shaw's words, "and dream things that never were." In the pursuit of Christ the king, excellent Christians are not afraid of being uncomfortable. They ask the tough questions about themselves. (Who are we? What sort of image are we presenting to the world? What would Jesus do in this situation? Are we doing enough?) They are not afraid to walk into city hall, or over to the next desk in their office, or to reach across the back fence if they know that is where they need to be. In essence, they have denied themselves a comfort zone for now so that they see themselves as a new (while certainly imperfect) creation; those old taboos are gone, polite convention no longer rules. While they are not belligerent or righteous, they have a new power to go places they would never have dreamed of going, to let words come from their mouths they might once have kept secret in their hearts. Christ is king in them.

People who crown Christ with mercy, security, and risk-taking are often thought to be a little weird. They are often being tested to see if they are the real things. Some people make a lot of noise about Christ-centeredness and are not the real thing. I like what I heard the Benedictine theologian, Joan Chittister, say, on the subject of "spirituality": "If it's the real thing (and *sometimes* it is), it does not turn the mind off; it turns it on." The question that always has to be asked about experiential religion is: What does it lead to in terms of both thinking and acting? *What* "spirit," precisely, is

377

being invoked here? The world is full of spirits, and as the first epistle of Saint John reminds us, "Not every spirit is of God." Probably the most "spiritualistic" events of our epoch — if we discount Woodstock and the rock concerts for a moment — were the famous Nuremberg rallies of Adolf Hitler and company. "Test the spirits!" (1 John). Christ-centered, Christ-cored people are more than willing to be tested.

Paul Tillich used an interesting phrase to speak of people who were centered in God and Spirit. Here we are using the word Christ, aware that the Trinity is also being invoked. Tillich said that people filled with the Spirit are people who have been grasped by God. When people are grasped by God in such a way as to say that they are centered in Christ, they point to that which transcended themselves: They pointed to the Christ, whom the Spirit made present to them in a new and deeply meaningful way. If a person is pointing to himself or herself, they are probably a phony. Christ-centered people must pass Jesus' test as expressed so fully and frequently by Saint Paul. By their fruits you shall know them.

Christ-centered people, Christ-kinged people, are secure enough for risks and full enough to spend big on mercy. They are also ready to engage the deepest, and therefore the most vulnerable, kind of involvement in the realities of our world in depths of participation that most of us, likely, had not bargained for. Christians are free because Christ is their king. We are free for the wise foolishness, the foolish wisdom, of the crucified God, and are blest by it. It is a freedom that can be enjoyed only by people who are ready to admit their own utter incapacity to achieve it on their own. We have to stop being our own king and our own ruler. It is not the freedom of the rich who "have" everything. It is instead the freedom, according to Douglas John Hall, "of those who are conscious enough of their emptiness and lack to realize that they must 'ever ask anew' for intimations of a truth that, in its fullness, forever eludes and transcends them; a truth, however, that is willing and more than willing to impart itself in its sufficiency for the here and now, and to those who ask for it humbly and in solidarity with all who hunger and thirst."

The king Christ starts out humbly enough for us to grasp. He starts out as a child. This strange royalty has to be acknowledged. A boy who grew up in Los Angeles as a Mexican immigrant speaks this way of Jesus:

> *As a young child I always wondered why Santa didn't deliver gifts to us the way he did the well to do Anglo kids ... Maybe he was afraid to come into the Barrio ... Maybe he just didn't like Mexicans or poor people. Larry Gilliland, a poor white friend, didn't ever seem to get much more than us ... so maybe Santa just forgot us poor folks. At least we had the homemade tortillas and tamales which Larry liked and we shared with him. When you went back to grade school after the holidays, the class would have to participate in a show and tell, where students would talk about their Christmas ... and show off some of their toys ... one year it came to be my turn and I had nothing to offer ... It had been a difficult year and my parents were not able to buy us much that Christmas ... and so I told them that I had Christ, pure and simple, for Christmas. And they all didn't believe me.*

Christ, pure and simple, is not always the poignant absence of material goods that a child experiences. Christ is also a presence and a present. There really is a lot at stake in Christ as king, isn't there? It is not just some night long, long ago in a galaxy far, far away when Wise Men spotted one star that was acting funny and traveled afar. No, it is about whether in the midst of these "dark streets shining with everlasting light" there is an energy that puts the ever-ready bunny to shame. So let us go over to Bethlehem, soon, and see this thing which has come to pass.

Christians go back to Christmas to understand the humility and humanity of their king. We then go forward to mobilize mercy and to take risks because we are so deeply grasped and secured.

Think On These Things

In the letter to the people at Philippi, Paul wanted us to think on things that are beautiful, pure, and excellent. He wanted to teach us asset-based thinking. He wanted to teach us the art of appreciative inquiry. He wanted to limit criticism and the culture of complaint. Paul wanted us to be thankful.

Oddly, being thankful does not come naturally to us.

We stayed at our best friend's house while taking our daughter on a college visit. We forgot to send a thank-you note. We had a wonderful time — good food, clean sheets, great talk. But still we forgot to send a thank-you note. How we forgot that this particular friend stands on formality I'll never know! We had spent dozens of thanksgivings together when our group of six maintained a regular practice with each other. Her note always showed up two days after the feast. Regularly. Nice vellum stationery. Sometimes monogrammed, sometimes not. She was the kind of person who spent time buying her stationery and never forgot a thank-you note.

I had become the kind of person who got too busy to send thank-you notes. I had also become the kind of person who forgot who my friends really are. I had forgotten to think on the good things. I'll blame email. I am so programmed by its speed that sometimes I go home and enter my password in the microwave. I have a list of fifteen phone numbers to contact my family of five. My reason for not staying in touch with certain friends is that they don't have email addresses. When I make calls from home, sometimes I add a nine to get the outside line. Sometimes, when I like a poem or joke someone sends me, I send it to my so-called friends.

Well, this particular very real friend did me a great favor. She lambasted me for not sending her a thank-you note, by email of course. She felt unappreciated. She felt like I had forgotten who she was — and I had. In the process of forgetting her, I had forgotten a piece of me. I had forgotten to think on the excellent things, the things that matter.

The story of the lepers comes to mind to team with the epistle to the Philippians. There are two points about this story of the lepers that really matter. One is that only one remembers to send the thank-you note. The rest, to their own great peril, forget. Secondly, the one who remembers is the leper of the lepers. He is a Samaritan. The nine are Jews. He was in all likelihood part of the great pack of lepers who stood at the city gate. No one wanted them because they were contagious. If the lepers stood outside the gate, this leper stood outside the group that stood at the gate.

His return to Jesus is amazing, then, on two counts: He is the outsider of the outsiders and yet is the only one who knows what his healing means. The rest are cured; he is healed. What Jesus says to him is that this faith he finds, deep within himself, has made him well. Jesus might also say that his capacity to be grateful has made him spiritually well. His capacity to think on the fine things is the source of his healing.

What I covet for us today is that we find out how to become the one who turns back to how we can remember our thank-you notes — how we can have the kind of faith that makes us well.

Gratitude is not a should. It is not a will. It is not a willpower. Gratitude is a grace. When we become the one who turned back, we experience the gratitude we are always trying to experience.

I know what it's like. "I have everything, why don't I feel good?" "I have so much more than others, why don't I act grateful?" Something happens to the nine that keep them from turning back to give thanks. Please don't blame them. Have you ever wanted to just get rid of a sore in your mouth? On the day it leaves, do you give thanks? I doubt it. You just go on. Have you ever just wanted to be over the flu, over the cancer, over the chemo, over the *it* that you are experiencing today? Over it so you could go on ... and get back to regular maintenance of the email.

Be careful here. Whatever it is we are trying to get over is our life. Life is interruptions. Life is the thing we're trying to get over. It is this grand haste toward a life that will come that prohibits gratitude. Where in the world do we think we are going? So many of us bop about like the sandpiper, edging the waves, looking for more food, fast, fast, fast. We forget the thank-you notes in more ways than the merely social.

In the grand rush to a better life, we forget the life we have. We forget what the great and difficult French woman, Collette, said, surely with a twinkle in her eye, "All we can control is what we hold in our arms, while we hold it." Did not the tenth leper follow her advice? He held his healing in his arms. He held it tight. He took it back to Jesus. He experienced gratitude. He experienced the great holding on to life. Did the people at Philippi take Paul's advice seriously? Did they bother to focus on the fine things?

The gratitude that comes by grace, again, is not willed. "I should be more grateful." It is not a should. The gratitude that comes by grace, is not a matter of willpower. By the power of God, I will send more thank-you notes. Instead, the gratitude that comes by grace is one that comes from looking up, looking out, and looking around.

One Friday night, our church was a beehive of activity. A dinner of rice and beans was being prepared in the kitchen for a youth group that was staying over night. Anthony and Mark and Mary were putting a rehearsal dinner together in the courtyard. At about 3:30, I looked up from my desk and its piles of unanswered/unanswerables and saw the cold, brown tables on which so much of our life here is lived. I saw that the winter light was on its way, too. Next time I looked up, I saw white tablecloths. Then the candles came out. Then the magenta and white orchids, followed by the burnt orange and red miniature calla lilies. The light continued to envelop the activity and the courtyard. I walked down the hall. The rest of the staff was noticing the same thing I was noticing. A few joined me with tears in their eyes.

Something very beautiful was happening. People were making a feast for a friend. People were making a feast for strangers.

People were making a feast. People were making these feasts inside a kind of burnt yellow light that could not have come from any one but God. Really, who can do twilight the way God does twilight? Especially the November kind that both starts early and ends late, that lets us live inside its radiance as though we were glowing, too. The light and the people and the feast were enchanting the courtyard. Now I don't want to get sappy, but to be given the grace to experience joy outside my window, in our church's courtyard, is a form of returning that happens in the story of the healed and lonely leper. We return to joy. We return to gratitude. We no longer know how to be indifferent. Indeed, we wonder how we could ever look at life indifferently again. There it is, the feast, the life, the light, and the people. Friends remembering friends. It's right outside all of our windows, not just mine. The fine things are always there, hoping that we will have the sense to notice them.

They will be at your table on Thursday, too.

There is a great little book called *30 Things Everyone Should Know How To Do Before Turning 30* by Siobhan Adcock. These skills include how to wrap a present, use a full place setting properly, hold your liquor, whistle with your fingers, fold a fitted sheet, and write superior thank-you notes. Ah. If you want to understand what happens in the story of the ten lepers, learn this skill. Learn how to write superb thank-you notes, not just to your friends but also to God.

Let's go now to God. God, in Jesus, in this story, was ignored. Nine forgot. One did not. Jesus has one of his rare moments of pique. "Were there not nine who were healed?" Why did only one return? When we refuse the grace that gives us gratitude, we do offend Jesus' generosity.

I daresay we offend that generosity in more ways than one.

Consider how we do health care in our land. Let me try to approach the matter of prescription drugs lightly. There is absolutely no truth to the rumor that we have put the entire church's endowment in health care stocks. The fact that they may have risen by thirty percent in the last few weeks has no affect on us here. We wouldn't think of making a profit off the healing of leprosy. Why are some people making profit off of other people's leprosy? Because we have refused the grace for gratitude: We think that our healing depends on us and our economies and our profits and our machinations. We have not looked out our window to see the light, the feast, and the friends. We have not been overcome enough with gratitude and run to our God and praised with a loud voice. With all you have given us, mighty God, how dare we let greed prevail?

In greed, we seek for more. In gratitude, we know there is enough to go around. There is enough for everyone. In this grace, we move toward each other. In a life based on greed, we think there is not enough. We think we know best. We think we must protect ourselves and not the lepers at the gate. The outsiders — even though sometimes the outsiders are extraordinarily grateful people — are to be kept outside. When gratitude and praise overtake you, you forget to be afraid. You become able to trust. You have time for the finer things and for the thank-you notes because you are overflowing with joy and gladness.

We are graced with gratitude when we look outside our window and find friends making feasts for friends — which will happen all week long.

We can be the one who comes back. We can be the one who returns. We can be the one who thinks on the finer things.

Lectionary Preaching After Pentecost

The following index will aid the user of this book in matching the correct Sunday with the appropriate text during Pentecost. All texts in this book are from the series for the Second Readings, Revised Common Lectionary. (Note that the ELCA division of Lutheranism is now following the Revised Common Lectionary.) The Lutheran designations indicate days comparable to Sundays on which Revised Common Lectionary Propers or Ordinary Time designations are used.

(Fixed dates do not pertain to Lutheran Lectionary)

Fixed Date Lectionaries *Revised Common (including ELCA)* *and Roman Catholic*	**Lutheran Lectionary** *Lutheran*
The Day Of Pentecost	The Day Of Pentecost
The Holy Trinity	The Holy Trinity
May 29-June 4 — Proper 4, Ordinary Time 9	Pentecost 2
June 5-11 — Proper 5, Ordinary Time 10	Pentecost 3
June 12-18 — Proper 6, Ordinary Time 11	Pentecost 4
June 19-25 — Proper 7, Ordinary Time 12	Pentecost 5
June 26-July 2 — Proper 8, Ordinary Time 13	Pentecost 6
July 3-9 — Proper 9, Ordinary Time 14	Pentecost 7
July 10-16 — Proper 10, Ordinary Time 15	Pentecost 8
July 17-23 — Proper 11, Ordinary Time 16	Pentecost 9
July 24-30 — Proper 12, Ordinary Time 17	Pentecost 10
July 31-Aug. 6 — Proper 13, Ordinary Time 18	Pentecost 11
Aug. 7-13 — Proper 14, Ordinary Time 19	Pentecost 12
Aug. 14-20 — Proper 15, Ordinary Time 20	Pentecost 13
Aug. 21-27 — Proper 16, Ordinary Time 21	Pentecost 14
Aug. 28-Sept. 3 — Proper 17, Ordinary Time 22	Pentecost 15
Sept. 4-10 — Proper 18, Ordinary Time 23	Pentecost 16
Sept. 11-17 — Proper 19, Ordinary Time 24	Pentecost 17
Sept. 18-24 — Proper 20, Ordinary Time 25	Pentecost 18

Sept. 25-Oct. 1 — Proper 21, Ordinary Time 26	Pentecost 19
Oct. 2-8 — Proper 22, Ordinary Time 27	Pentecost 20
Oct. 9-15 — Proper 23, Ordinary Time 28	Pentecost 21
Oct. 16-22 — Proper 24, Ordinary Time 29	Pentecost 22
Oct. 23-29 — Proper 25, Ordinary Time 30	Pentecost 23
Oct. 30-Nov. 5 — Proper 26, Ordinary Time 31	Pentecost 24
Nov. 6-12 — Proper 27, Ordinary Time 32	Pentecost 25
Nov. 13-19 — Proper 28, Ordinary Time 33	Pentecost 26
	Pentecost 27
Nov. 20-26 — Christ The King	Christ The King

Reformation Day (or last Sunday in October) is October 31 (Revised Common, Lutheran)

All Saints (or first Sunday in November) is November 1 (Revised Common, Lutheran, Roman Catholic)

U.S./Canadian Lectionary Comparison

The following index shows the correlation between the Sundays and special days of the church year as they are titled or labeled in the Revised Common Lectionary published by the Consultation On Common Texts and used in the United States (the reference used for this book) and the Sundays and special days of the church year as they are titled or labeled in the Revised Common Lectionary used in Canada.

Revised Common Lectionary	Canadian Revised Common Lectionary
Advent 1	Advent 1
Advent 2	Advent 2
Advent 3	Advent 3
Advent 4	Advent 4
Christmas Eve	Christmas Eve
The Nativity Of Our Lord/ Christmas Day	The Nativity Of Our Lord
Christmas 1	Christmas 1
January 1/Holy Name Of Jesus	January 1/The Name Of Jesus
Christmas 2	Christmas 2
The Epiphany Of Our Lord	The Epiphany Of Our Lord
The Baptism Of Our Lord/ Epiphany 1	The Baptism Of Our Lord/ Proper 1
Epiphany 2/Ordinary Time 2	Epiphany 2/Proper 2
Epiphany 3/Ordinary Time 3	Epiphany 3/Proper 3
Epiphany 4/Ordinary Time 4	Epiphany 4/Proper 4
Epiphany 5/Ordinary Time 5	Epiphany 5/Proper 5
Epiphany 6/Ordinary Time 6	Epiphany 6/Proper 6
Epiphany 7/Ordinary Time 7	Epiphany 7/Proper 7
Epiphany 8/Ordinary Time 8	Epiphany 8/Proper 8
The Transfiguration Of Our Lord/ Last Sunday After Epiphany	The Transfiguration Of Our Lord/ Last Sunday After Epiphany
Ash Wednesday	Ash Wednesday
Lent 1	Lent 1
Lent 2	Lent 2
Lent 3	Lent 3
Lent 4	Lent 4
Lent 5	Lent 5
Sunday Of The Passion/Palm Sunday	Passion/Palm Sunday
Maundy Thursday	Holy/Maundy Thursday
Good Friday	Good Friday

The Resurrection Of Our Lord/ Easter Day	The Resurrection Of Our Lord
Easter 2	Easter 2
Easter 3	Easter 3
Easter 4	Easter 4
Easter 5	Easter 5
Easter 6	Easter 6
The Ascension Of Our Lord	The Ascension Of Our Lord
Easter 7	Easter 7
The Day Of Pentecost	The Day Of Pentecost
The Holy Trinity	The Holy Trinity
Proper 4/Pentecost 2/O T 9*	Proper 9
Proper 5/Pent 3/O T 10	Proper 10
Proper 6/Pent 4/O T 11	Proper 11
Proper 7/Pent 5/O T 12	Proper 12
Proper 8/Pent 6/O T 13	Proper 13
Proper 9/Pent 7/O T 14	Proper 14
Proper 10/Pent 8/O T 15	Proper 15
Proper 11/Pent 9/O T 16	Proper 16
Proper 12/Pent 10/O T 17	Proper 17
Proper 13/Pent 11/O T 18	Proper 18
Proper 14/Pent 12/O T 19	Proper 19
Proper 15/Pent 13/O T 20	Proper 20
Proper 16/Pent 14/O T 21	Proper 21
Proper 17/Pent 15/O T 22	Proper 22
Proper 18/Pent 16/O T 23	Proper 23
Proper 19/Pent 17/O T 24	Proper 24
Proper 20/Pent 18/O T 25	Proper 25
Proper 21/Pent 19/O T 26	Proper 26
Proper 22/Pent 20/O T 27	Proper 27
Proper 23/Pent 21/O T 28	Proper 28
Proper 24/Pent 22/O T 29	Proper 29
Proper 25/Pent 23/O T 30	Proper 30
Proper 26/Pent 24/O T 31	Proper 31
Proper 27/Pent 25/O T 32	Proper 32
Proper 28/Pent 26/O T 33	Proper 33
Christ The King (Proper 29/O T 34)	Proper 34/Christ The King/ Reign Of Christ
Reformation Day (October 31)	Reformation Day (October 31)
All Saints (November 1 or 1st Sunday in November)	All Saints' Day (November 1)

Thanksgiving Day
  (4th Thursday of November)
	Thanksgiving Day
	  (2nd Monday of October)

*O T = Ordinary Time

About The Authors

John T. Ball has served numerous United Methodist congregations throughout western Ohio. A graduate of Ohio State University and Boston University School of Theology, he has had articles published in *Circuit Rider*, *Christian Ministry*, and *Emphasis*. Ball is the author of *Barefoot In The Palace* (CSS).

Richard E. Gribble, CSC, is an associate professor in the department of religious studies at Stonehill College in North Easton, Massachusetts. The author of more than a dozen books and over 175 articles, Father Gribble is the former rector/superior of Moreau Seminary at the University of Notre Dame. He is a graduate of the United States Naval Academy and served for five years on nuclear submarines before entering the priesthood. Gribble earned his Ph.D. from The Catholic University of America, and has also earned degrees from the University of Southern California and the Jesuit School of Theology at Berkeley. Among Gribble's previous CSS publications is a three-volume series on *The Parables Of Jesus*.

John B. Jamison spent more than two decades as a full-time pastor of United Methodist congregations in Illinois. He has a deep interest in how technology and the new culture of "digital learners" is changing our lives, reflected in his current role as director of the Center for Innovation in Teaching and Learning at Colorado Mountain College in Glenwood Springs, Colorado. Jamison maintains his connection to the church by serving as an interim pastor for Presbyterian congregations. The author of *Time's Up!* (CSS), Jamison has participated in the United Methodist Academy for Preaching, and he has created a variety of print, television, and radio material.

Clayton A. Lord, Jr., recently celebrated his twentieth anniversary as the pastor of First Baptist Church in Norwich, Connecticut. A graduate of the University of Connecticut and Andover Newton Theological School, Lord is very active in both denominational work and community ministry. He is the author of *The Church Newsletter Handbook* (Judson Press).

Donna Schaper has had a varied career as a writer, pastor, denominational executive, college chaplain, and community organizer. She is currently the senior minister of historic Judson Memorial Church in New York City. Prior to that, she served as senior pastor of Coral Gables Congregational Church in Coral Gables, Florida. Schaper is the author of numerous books, including *When a Parent Dies* and *The Art of Spiritual Rock Gardening*, and her articles and meditations frequently appear in a variety of publications, including the *New York Times*. She is a graduate of Gettysburg College, Gettysburg Seminary, and the University of Chicago. To learn more, visit her website at www.donnaschaper.org.

Title: Sermons On The Second Readings, Series II, Cycle C

ISBN: 0-7880-2398-5

INSTRUCTIONS TO ACCESS PASSWORD FOR ELECTRONIC COPY OF THIS TITLE:

The password appears on the reverse side of this page. Carefully cut the card from the page to retrieve the password.

Once you have the password, go to

http:/www.csspub.com/passwords/

and locate this title on that web page. By clicking on the title, you will be guided to a page to enter your password, name, and email address. From there you will be sent to a page to download your electronic version of this book.

For further information, or if you don't have access to the internet, please contact CSS Publishing Company at 1-800-241-4056 in the United States (or 419-227-1818 from outside the United States) between 8 a.m. and 5 p.m., Eastern Standard Time, Monday through Friday.